Fifty Lectures for Mathcounts Competitions

Volume 2

Solution Manual

http://www.mymathcounts.com/index.php

ACKNOWLEDGEMENTS

We would like to thank the following math contests:

The Mathcounts Competitions, the nation's premier middle school math enrichment, coaching, and competition program.

The AMC 8, an examination in middle school mathematics designed to promote the development and enhancement of problem solving skills.

The AIME (American Invitational Mathematics Examination).

The China Middle School Math Competition.

Contributors

Yongcheng Chen, Ph.D., Author
Guiling Chen, Owner, mymathcounts.com, Typesetter, Editor

Copyright © 2016 by mymathcounts.com. All rights reserved. Printed in the United States of America. Reproduction of any portion of this book without the written permission of the authors is strictly prohibited, except as may be expressly permitted by the U.S. Copyright Act.

ISBN-13: 978-1530805709
ISBN-10: 1530805708

Please contact mymathcounts@gmail.com for suggestions, corrections, or clarifications.

Table of Contents

19. Evaluating Algebraic Expressions — 1
20. Divisibility — 7
21. Solving Equations — 15
22. Solving Inequalities — 22
23. Venn diagrams — 27
24. Combinatorics — 33
25. Angles and triangles — 44
26. Classification of triangles — 48
27. Similar triangles — 54
28. Pythagorean Theorem — 63
29. Quadrilaterals — 68
30. Trapezoids — 73
31. Parallelograms — 78
32. Angle bisectors and medians — 85
33. Triangular inequality — 90
34. Area Method — 94
35. Polygons — 101
36. Circles — 111
Index — 119

This page is intentionally left blank.

50 Lectures for Mathcounts Competitions   (19) Evaluating Algebraic Expressions

SOLUTIONS

Problem 1. 1.

$12xy - 1 = 12 \times \dfrac{1}{2} \times \dfrac{1}{3} - 1 = 2 - 1 = 1.$

Problem 2. $6\dfrac{1}{2}$.

$(\dfrac{1}{x} + \dfrac{1}{y}) + \dfrac{x}{y} = (2+3) + \dfrac{3}{2} = 6\dfrac{1}{2}.$

Problem 3. $\dfrac{3}{16}$.

$\sqrt{ab} = \sqrt{\dfrac{3}{32} \times \dfrac{3}{8}} = \sqrt{\dfrac{3^2}{2^8}} = \dfrac{3}{2^4} = \dfrac{3}{16}.$

Problem 4. $1\dfrac{4}{11}$.

$\dfrac{1}{x+y} = \dfrac{1}{\dfrac{2}{5} + \dfrac{1}{3}} = \dfrac{1}{\dfrac{2 \times 3 + 1 \times 5}{15}} = \dfrac{15}{11} = 1\dfrac{4}{11}.$

Problem 5. $1\dfrac{7}{27}$.

$(x+y)(\dfrac{x}{y}) = (\dfrac{2}{3} + \dfrac{3}{4})(\dfrac{\frac{2}{3}}{\frac{3}{4}}) = (\dfrac{17}{12})(\dfrac{8}{9}) = \dfrac{34}{27} = 1\dfrac{7}{27}.$

Problem 6. 9900.

$\dfrac{x!}{(x-2)!} = \dfrac{x(x-1)(x-2)!}{(x-2)!} = x(x-1) = 100 \times 99 = 9900.$

50 Lectures for Mathcounts Competitions   (19) Evaluating Algebraic Expressions

Problem 7. $\dfrac{3}{8}$.

$$\dfrac{\dfrac{1}{x}}{\dfrac{x}{y}} = \dfrac{y}{x} = \dfrac{\dfrac{1}{4}}{\dfrac{2}{3}} = \dfrac{3}{8}.$$

Problem 8. $\dfrac{2}{25}$.

$$\dfrac{xy}{5x+3y} = \dfrac{\dfrac{3}{5} \times \dfrac{2}{3}}{5 \times \dfrac{3}{5} + 3 \times \dfrac{2}{3}} = \dfrac{\dfrac{2}{5}}{3+2} = \dfrac{2}{25}.$$

Problem 9. 10,100.

$$\dfrac{(n+1)!}{(n-1)!} = \dfrac{(n+1)n(n-1)!}{(n-1)!} = (n+1)n = 101 \times 100 = 10,100.$$

Problem 10. $\dfrac{189}{2}$.

$$\dfrac{6x+7y}{xy} = \dfrac{6 \times \dfrac{2}{3} + 7 \times \dfrac{1}{14}}{\dfrac{2}{3} \times \dfrac{1}{14}} = \dfrac{4 + \dfrac{1}{2}}{\dfrac{1}{21}} = \dfrac{\dfrac{9}{2}}{\dfrac{1}{21}} = \dfrac{189}{2}.$$

Problem 11. $\dfrac{2}{3}$.

$$\dfrac{\dfrac{1}{y}}{\dfrac{1}{x}} = \dfrac{x}{y} = \dfrac{2}{3}.$$

Problem 12. $\dfrac{9}{7}$.

50 Lectures for Mathcounts Competitions   (19) Evaluating Algebraic Expressions

$$\frac{1+\frac{1}{x}}{1+\frac{1}{y}} = \frac{\frac{x+1}{x}}{\frac{y+1}{y}} = \frac{(x+1)y}{(y+1)x} = \frac{(\frac{1}{2}+1)\times\frac{3}{4}}{(\frac{3}{4}+1)\times\frac{1}{2}} = \frac{\frac{3}{2}\times\frac{3}{4}}{\frac{7}{4}\times\frac{1}{2}} = \frac{9}{7}.$$

Problem 13. $\frac{2}{3}$.

$$\frac{1}{2}x^6 y^7 = \frac{1}{2}\times(\frac{3}{4})^6(\frac{4}{3})^7 = \frac{1}{2}\times\frac{3^6}{4^6}\frac{4^7}{3^7} = \frac{1}{2}\times\frac{4}{3} = \frac{2}{3}.$$

Problem 14. 1.

$2^{x+4} = 32^{2x-1}$ $\Rightarrow$ $2^{x+4} = 2^{5(2x-1)}$.

Thus we have $x+4 = 5(2x-1)$ $\Rightarrow$ $x+4 = 10x-5$ $\Rightarrow$ $9 = 9x$ $\Rightarrow$ $x = 1$.

Problem 15. 54.

$$\frac{36}{x} = \frac{36}{\frac{2}{3}} = 54.$$

Problem 16. $2\frac{2}{3}$.

$$\frac{n+5}{n} = \frac{3+5}{3} = \frac{8}{3} = 2\frac{2}{3}.$$

Problem 173. $\frac{25}{36}$.

$$(a+b)^2 = (\frac{1}{2}+\frac{1}{3})^2 = (\frac{5}{6})^2 = \frac{25}{36}.$$

Problem 18. 100.

$$x^2 + 2xy + y^2 = (x+y)^2 = (7\frac{4}{5} + 2\frac{1}{5})^2 = (\frac{39}{5} + \frac{11}{5})^2 = 10^2 = 100.$$

Problem 19. 10,100.

3

50 Lectures for Mathcounts Competitions   (19) Evaluating Algebraic Expressions

$$\frac{(n+1)!}{(n-1)!} = \frac{(n+1)n(n-1)!}{(n-1)!} = (n+1)n = 101 \times 100 = 10,100.$$

Problem 20. $\frac{4}{41}$.

$$\frac{\frac{1}{x}}{\frac{1}{4}} = \frac{4}{x} = \frac{4}{2+3+5+7+11+13} = \frac{4}{41}.$$

Problem 21. 896.

$(a+b)(a-b) = a^2 - b^2 = 30^2 - 2^2 = 900 - 4 = 896$.

Problem 22. $\frac{2}{5}$.

$$(x+\frac{1}{x})^{-1} = (\frac{x^2+1}{x})^{-1} = \frac{x}{x^2+1} = \frac{2}{5}.$$

Problem 23. 11.

$$\frac{x^2 - 2xy + y^2}{x-y} = \frac{(x-y)^2}{x-y} = x - y = 28 - 17 = 11.$$

Problem 24. $\frac{175}{16}$.

$$\frac{(2v)^2}{3u^2} \cdot \frac{3(u-2)^2 + 6v}{u+(u-2)^2} = \frac{(2v)^2}{3u^2} \cdot \frac{3[(u^2-4u+4)+2v]}{u+u^2-4u+4} = \frac{(2v)^2}{u^2} \cdot \frac{(u^2-4u+4)+2v}{u^2-3u+4}$$

$$= \frac{(10)^2}{4^2} \cdot \frac{(4^2-4\times 4+4)+2\times 5}{4^2-3\times 4+4} = \frac{(5)^2}{2^2} \cdot \frac{14}{8} = \frac{25}{2} \cdot \frac{7}{8} = \frac{175}{16}.$$

Problem 25. 12.
Method 1:
$3y^3 + 3y^2 + 3y + 3 = 3+3+3+3 = 12$.

4

50 Lectures for Mathcounts Competitions   (19) Evaluating Algebraic Expressions

Method 2:
$$3y^3 + 3y^2 + 3y + 3 = 2y^3 + (y^3 + 3y^2 + 3y + 1) + 2 = 4 + (y+1)^3 = 12.$$

Problem 26. 29.6.
$x^y = 2187 \Rightarrow 3^7 = 2187$
$y^x = 343 \Rightarrow 7^3 = 343$
So $x = 3$ and $y = 7$.
$$(\frac{x}{y})^{x-y} = (\frac{3}{7})^{3-7} = (\frac{3}{7})^{-4} = \frac{7^4}{3^4} = 29.6.$$

Problem 27. $\frac{83}{4641}$.

$x = \frac{3}{7} - \frac{6}{13} = \frac{3 \times 13 - 6 \times 7}{7 \times 13} = -\frac{3}{7 \times 13}$; $y = \frac{4}{17} - \frac{7}{9} = \frac{4 \times 9 - 7 \times 17}{17 \times 9} = -\frac{83}{17 \times 9}$.

$xy = -\frac{3}{7 \times 13} \times (-\frac{83}{17 \times 9}) = \frac{83}{7 \times 13 \times 17 \times 3} = \frac{83}{4641}.$

Problem 28. 9.
$2^a = 32 \Rightarrow 2^a = 2^5$. So $a = 5$.
$a^b = 625 \Rightarrow a^b = 5^4$ So $b = 4$.
$a + b = 5 + 4 = 9$.

Problem 29. 3.
We know that $a = 3b \Rightarrow b = \frac{a}{3}$

$$\frac{a+b+c}{a+b-c} = \frac{a + \frac{a}{3} + \frac{2a}{3}}{a + \frac{a}{3} - \frac{2a}{3}} = \frac{1 + \frac{1}{3} + \frac{2}{3}}{1 + \frac{1}{3} - \frac{2}{3}} = \frac{1+1}{1-\frac{1}{3}} = \frac{2}{\frac{2}{3}} = \frac{6}{2} = 3.$$

Problem 30. 1.

$a + \frac{1}{b} = 1 \Rightarrow a = 1 - \frac{1}{b} = \frac{b-1}{b} \Rightarrow \frac{1}{a} = \frac{b}{b-1}$ \hfill (1)

50 Lectures for Mathcounts Competitions   (19) Evaluating Algebraic Expressions

$$b + \frac{1}{c} = 1 \quad \Rightarrow \quad \frac{1}{c} = 1 - b \quad \Rightarrow \quad c = \frac{1}{1-b} \qquad (2)$$

$$c + \frac{1}{a} = \frac{1}{1-b} + \frac{b}{b-1} = \frac{1}{1-b} - \frac{b}{1-b} = \frac{1-b}{1-b} = 1.$$

Problem 31. 1/24.

$$\frac{a}{a^2 + a + 1} = \frac{1}{6} \quad \Rightarrow \quad a^2 + a + 1 = 6a \quad \Rightarrow \quad a + \frac{1}{a} = 5$$

$$\frac{a^2}{a^4 + a^2 + 1} = \frac{1}{\frac{a^4 + a^2 + 1}{a^2}} = \frac{1}{a^2 + \frac{1}{a^2} + 1} = \frac{1}{(a + \frac{1}{a})^2 - 1} = \frac{1}{5^2 - 1} = 1/24.$$

50 Lectures for Mathcounts Competitions   (20) Divisibility

SOLUTIONS

Problem 1. 942.
We need to look at the last two digits of each number. We see that only 42 is not divisible by 4. So the answer is 942.

Problem 2. 8.
The number is divisible by 4 and 9. For $\overline{a74a}$ to be divisible by 4, a could be 4 or 8. For $\overline{a74a}$ to be divisible by 9, $2a + 7 + 4 = 2a + 11$ should be divisible by 9. The only possible value for a is 8.

Problem 3. 34%.
There are 50 odd numbers between 0 and 100.
There are $\left\lfloor \dfrac{100}{3} \right\rfloor = 33$ numbers between 0 and 100 that are multiples of 3 and 17 of them are odd.
The answer is $\dfrac{17}{50} = 0.34 = 34\%$.

Problem 4. 10.
The even number $\overline{4a5,b32}$ must be divisible by 3, and 11.
$2 + b + a - (3 + 5 + 4) = b + a - 10$ must be divisible by 11. So $a + b = 10$.

Problem 5. 8.
Method 1:
Since A is a digit, A could be 1 to 9.
We test each of them and we see that 1, 2, or 5 work.
The answer is $1 + 2 + 5 = 8$.

Method 2:
$\overline{A65A} = 1000A + 650 + A \equiv 0 \bmod A$ $\Rightarrow$ $650 \equiv 0 \bmod A$
$1 \times 2 \times 5 \times 13 \times 5 \equiv 0 \bmod A$
Since A is a digit, A could be 1, 2, or 5.
The answer is $1 + 2 + 5 = 8$.

Problem 6. 4.
We know that 591,3d8 is divisible by both 3 and 4.
$5 + 9 + 1 + 3 + d + 8 = 26 + d$ must be divisible by 3. So d can be 1, 4, or 7.
Only 48 is divisible by 4. So the answer is 4.

Problem 7. 5.
The positive integer must be divisible by 7×11.
There are $\left\lfloor \dfrac{400}{7 \times 11} \right\rfloor = 5$ numbers.

Problem 8. 4.
n must be even (0, 2, 4, 6, or 8) and $3 + n + 8 + 5 + n = 2n + 16$ must be divisible by 3. So n is 4.

Problem 9. 4.

The number should be divisible by 3, 5, and 4.
Since the last digit is 0, it will be divisible by 5.
The sum of the digits should be divisible by 3, so K can be 1, 4, or 7.
The last two-digit should be divisible by 4, so the only value for K is 4.

Problem 10. 6.
Since the sum of the digits is 18 that is divisible by 9, the last two digit of such 4-digit numbers must be divisible by 4.
So the last two digits must be 36, 56, or 64.
In each case, we have two such numbers: 4536, 5436, 3456, 4356, 3564, and 5364.

Problem 11. 101.
$\underline{abab} = 100a + 100b + 10a + b = 101a + 101b = 101(a + b)$.
The largest prime number is 101.

Problem 12. 5
$20 + d - 2 \times 2 = 16 + d$ must be divisible by 7. So d is 5.

Problem 13. Yes, it is.

$77778 - 2 \times 4 = 77770$ that is indeed divisible by 7.

Problem 14. 18.

$3 + 1 + d + 2 + 6 = 12 + d$ $\Rightarrow$ $d = 0, 3, 6,$ and 9.

The sum of all possible values of d is $0 + 3 + 6 + 9 = 18$.

Problem 15. 64.

Let the three-digit number be $\underline{abc}$. $c + a - b$ must be divisible by 11.

We have three cases:

Case 1: $c + a - b = 0$.

132, 143, 154, 165, 176, 187, 198

253, 264, 275, 286, 297

374, 385, 396

495

We have $16 \times 2 = 32$ such numbers.

Case 2: $c + a - b = 11$.

968, 957, 946, 935, 924, 913, 902

847, 836, 825, 814, 803

726, 735, 704

605

We have $16 \times 2 = 22$ such numbers.

The answer is $32 + 32 = 64$.

Problem 16. 6.

We have the following three cases that each number is divisible by 11 but not 5.

In each case we have two such numbers by switching the positions of 3 and 6.

$\underline{4}\,\_\,\underline{5}\,\_$

$\underline{5}\,\_\,\underline{4}\,\_$

$\_\,\underline{5}\,\_\,\underline{4}$

So the answer is 6.

Problem 17. 17.

$\$391 = 17 \times 23$.

We see that both 17 and 23 are prime numbers. Since the number of students is more than two and fewer than twenty, it must be 17.

Problem 18. 4.
The sum of the digits $907a32$ is $9 + 0 + 7 + a + 3 + 2 = 21 + a$ and it must be divisible by 3. So a could be 0, 3, 6, 9. The answer is 4.

Problem 19. 150.
Method 1:
We have 900 3-digit numbers. 450 of them are even. One third of them are divisible by 3. So the answer key is $450/3 = 150$.

Method 2:
Let the first two digits be a and b.
We have four cases for the units digit:
Case 1: the last digit is 0.

$$\underline{}\ \underline{}\ \underline{0}$$

We have $a + b + 0$ that must be divisible by 3.
$a + b$ could be 3, 6, 9, 12, 15, 18.
If $a + b = 3$, we have $(a, b) = (3, 0), (2, 1),$ and $(1, 2)$.
If $a + b = 6$, we have $(a, b) = (6, 0), (5, 1), (1, 5), (4, 2), (2, 4),$ and $(3, 3)$.
If $a + b = 9$, we have $(a, b) = (9, 0), (8, 1), (1, 8), (7, 2), (2, 7), (6, 3), (3, 6), (5, 4),$ and $(4, 5)$.
If $a + b = 12$, we have $(a, b) = (9, 3), (3, 9), (8, 4), (4, 8), (7, 5), (5, 7),$ and $(6, 6)$.
If $a + b = 15$, we have $(a, b) = (9, 6), (6, 9), (8, 7),$ and $(7, 8)$.
If $a + b = 18$, we have $(a, b) = (9, 9)$.

We get $3 + 6 + 9 + 7 + 4 + 1 = 30$ such numbers.

Case 2: the last digit is 2.

$$\underline{}\ \underline{}\ \underline{2}$$

50 Lectures for Mathcounts Competitions   **(20) Divisibility**

We have $a + b + 2$ that must be divisible by 3.
$a + b$ could be 1, 4, 7, 10, 13, 16.
If $a + b = 1$, we have $(a, b) = (1, 0)$.
If $a + b = 4$, we have $(a, b) = (4, 0), (3, 1), (1, 3)$, and $(2, 2)$.
If $a + b = 7$, we have $(a, b) = (7, 0), (6, 1), (1, 6), (5, 2), (2, 5), (4, 3)$, and $(3, 4)$.
If $a + b = 10$, we have $(a, b) = (9, 1), (1, 9), (8, 2), (2, 8), (7, 3), (3, 7), (6, 4), (4, 6)$, and $(5, 5)$.
If $a + b = 13$, we have $(a, b) = (9, 4), (4, 9), (8, 5), (5, 8), (7, 6)$, and $(6, 7)$.
If $a + b = 16$, we have $(a, b) = (9, 7), (7, 9)$, and $(8, 8)$.
We get $1 + 4 + 7 + 9 + 6 + 3 = 30$ such numbers.

Case 3: the last digit is 4.

$$\underline{}\ \underline{}\ \underline{4}$$

We have $a + b + 4$ that must be divisible by 3.
$a + b$ could be 2, 5, 8, 11, 14, 17.
If $a + b = 2$, we have $(a, b) = (2, 0)$, and $(1, 1)$.
If $a + b = 5$, we have $(a, b) = (5, 0), (4, 1), (1, 4), (3, 2)$, and $(2, 3)$.
If $a + b = 8$, we have $(a, b) = (8, 0), (7, 1), (1, 7), (6, 2), (2, 6), (5, 3), (3, 5)$, and $(4, 4)$.
If $a + b = 11$, we have $(a, b) = (9, 2), (2, 9), (8, 3), (3, 8), (7, 4), (4, 7), (6, 5)$, and $(5, 6)$.
If $a + b = 14$, we have $(a, b) = (9, 5), (5, 9), (8, 6), (6, 8)$, and $(7, 7)$.
If $a + b = 17$, we have $(a, b) = (9, 8)$, and $(8, 9)$.
We get $2 + 5 + 8 + 8 + 5 + 2 = 30$ such numbers.

Case 4: the last digit is 6.

$$\underline{}\ \underline{}\ \underline{6}$$

We have $a + b + 6$ that must be divisible by 3.
$a + b$ could be 3, 6, 9, 12, 15, 18.
If $a + b = 3$, we have $(a, b) = (3, 0), (2, 1)$, and $(1, 2)$.
If $a + b = 6$, we have $(a, b) = (6, 0), (5, 1), (1, 5), (4, 2), (2, 4)$, and $(3, 3)$.
If $a + b = 9$, we have $(a, b) = (9, 0), (8, 1), (1, 8), (7, 2), (2, 7), (6, 3), (3, 6), (5, 4)$, and $(4, 5)$.
If $a + b = 12$, we have $(a, b) = (9, 3), (3, 9), (8, 4), (4, 8), (7, 5), (5, 7)$, and $(6, 6)$.
If $a + b = 15$, we have $(a, b) = (9, 6), (6, 9), (8, 7)$, and $(7, 8)$.

If $a + b = 18$, we have $(a, b) = (9, 9)$.
We get $3 + 6 + 9 + 7 + 4 + 1 = 30$ such numbers (same as the case 1).

Case 5: the last digit is 8.

$$\underline{}\ \underline{}\ \underline{8}$$

We have $a + b + 8$ that must be divisible by 3.
$a + b$ could be 1, 4, 7, 10, 13, 16.
If $a + b = 1$, we have $(a, b) = (1, 0)$.
If $a + b = 4$, we have $(a, b) = (4, 0), (3, 1), (1, 3),$ and $(2, 2)$.
If $a + b = 7$, we have $(a, b) = (7, 0), (6, 1), (1, 6), (5, 2), (2, 5), (4, 3),$ and $(3, 4)$.
If $a + b = 10$, we have $(a, b) = (9, 1), (1, 9), (8, 2), (2, 8), (7, 3), (3, 7), (6, 4), (4, 6),$ and $(5, 5)$.
If $a + b = 13$, we have $(a, b) = (9, 4), (4, 9), (8, 5), (5, 8), (7, 6),$ and $(6, 7)$.
If $a + b = 16$, we have $(a, b) = (9, 7), (7, 9),$ and $(8, 8)$.
We get $1 + 4 + 7 + 9 + 6 + 3 = 30$ such numbers (same as the case 2).
The answer is $30 \times 5 = 150$.

Problem 20. 3.
$3000 \cdot d + 548 = (11 \times 272 + 8) \cdot d + 49 \times 11 + 9$
So $8d + 9$ needs to be divisible by 11.
We see easily that $d = 3$ works.

Problem 21. 6.
The sum of the digit of $3730n5$, $3 + 7 + 3 + 0 + n + 5 = 18 + n$ must be divisible by 3.
So n could be 0, 3, 6, or 9.
We see that none of $373 - 5 = 368$, $373 - 35 = 338$, and $373 - 95 = 278$ is divisible by 7.
So the answer is $n = 6$ and $373 - 65 = 308 = 44 \times 7$ is divisible by 7.

Problem 22. 360.
The first five composite numbers are 4, 6, 8, 9, and 10.
The least common multiple of these numbers is $2^3 \times 3^2 \times 5 = 360$.

Problem 23. 11.

Let the two-digit number be *ab*. We have $10a + b + 10b + a = 11(a + b)$. So the answer is 11.

Problem 24. 2.
$213 - 20b = 13 - b$ must be divisible by 11. Since *b* is a digit, $b = 2$.

Problem 25. 7.
Method 1:
The two-digit whole numbers must be even and divisible by 7.
There are $\left\lfloor \dfrac{99}{7} \right\rfloor = 14$ two-digit whole numbers divisible by 7. Among them, half are even.
So the answer is 7.

Method 2:
The first two-digit whole numbers divisible by 7 is 14 and the last one is 98.
$98 = 14 + (n - 1) \times 14 \Rightarrow \quad n = 7$.

Problem 26. 15.
$49C345$ must be divisible by 3. So $4 + 9 + C + 3 + 4 + 5 = 25 + C$ must be divisible by 3. *C* could be 2, 5, or 8. The sum of them is $2 + 5 + 8 = 15$.

Problem 27. 6.
There are $\left\lfloor \dfrac{99}{15} \right\rfloor = 6$ two-digit whole numbers divisible by 15. So the answer is 6.

Problem 28. 4.
The four-digit even number $5{,}7d2$ must be divisible by 9.
$5 + 7 + d + 2 = 14 + d$ must be divisible by 9. So $d = 4$.

Problem 29. 4.
The number should be even and divisible by 9. $3 + 7 + 4 + n = 14 + n$ must be divisible by 9. So $n = 4$.

Problem 30. 315.
The number needs to be divisible by $5 \times 9 = 45$.

Note that $45 \times 5 = 225$ is s square number and $45 \times 6 = 70$ is even. So $45 \times 7 = 315$ is the answer.

Problem 31. 16.

$708,a6b,8c9$ is divisible by both 9 and 11.

$7 + 0 + 8 + a + 6 + b + 8 + c + 9 = 38 + a + b + c$ must be divisible by 9. So $a + b + c$ can be 7, 16, and 25.

$9 + 8 + 6 + 8 + 7 - (a + b + c) = 38 - (a + b + c)$ must be divisible by 11. So $(a + b + c)$ can be 38, 27, 16, and 5.

So only 16 meets two conditions and is the answer.

SOLUTIONS

Problem 1. Solution: 4.

$\dfrac{n}{6} = \dfrac{6}{9} \quad \Rightarrow \quad n = \dfrac{36}{9} = 4$.

Problem 2. Solution: $\dfrac{1}{6}$.

$2 - 7n = 5n \quad \Rightarrow \quad 2 = 5n + 7n \quad \Rightarrow \quad 2 = 12n \quad \Rightarrow n = \dfrac{1}{6}$.

Problem 3. Solution: -26.

$n + (n+1) + (n+2) = -75 \quad \Rightarrow \quad 3n + 3 = -75 \quad \Rightarrow \quad 3n = -76 - 3 \quad \Rightarrow$
$3n = -78 \Rightarrow \quad n = -26$

Problem 4. Solution: 1/8.

$5 + 2(3n+1) = 8 - 2n \quad \Rightarrow \quad 5 + 6n + 2 = 8 - 2n \quad \Rightarrow \quad 6n + 2n = 8 - 2 - 5 \quad \Rightarrow$
$8n = 1 \quad \Rightarrow \quad n = \dfrac{1}{8}$.

Problem 5. Solution: 3.

$M + N = 18$ \hfill (1)
$M - N = 12$ \hfill (2)

$(1) - (2):\ 2N = 6 \quad \Rightarrow \quad N = \dfrac{6}{2} = 3$.

Problem 6. Solution: 14

Let $x - 1$ and x be the two consecutive positive integers.
$x^2 - (x-1)^2 = 27 \quad \Rightarrow \quad x^2 - (x^2 - 2x + 1) = 27 \quad \Rightarrow \quad 2x - 1 = 27 \quad \Rightarrow$
$2x = 28 \quad \Rightarrow \quad x = 14$.

Problem 7. Solution: 7.

Let x be the positive integer.
$(x^2)^2 = 2401 \quad \Rightarrow \quad x^4 = 2401 \quad \Rightarrow \quad x = 7$.

Problem 8. Solution: 90.

Let x be the original number.

$x - \frac{1}{2}x = 45 \Rightarrow \frac{1}{2}x = 45 \Rightarrow x = 45 \times 2 = 90$.

Problem 9. Solution: 92.

$\frac{4}{9} + \frac{5}{6} = \frac{d}{72} \Rightarrow d = 72(\frac{4}{9} + \frac{5}{6}) = 32 + 60 = 92$.

Problem 10. Solution: 3.

$\frac{3(6+8y)}{10} = 9 \Rightarrow 3(6+8y) = 9 \times 10 \Rightarrow 18 + 24y = 90 \Rightarrow$

$24y = 90 - 18 \Rightarrow 24y = 72 \Rightarrow y = \frac{72}{24} = 3$.

Problem 11. Solution: $\frac{1}{15625}$.

$\frac{1}{5} \times \frac{1}{5} \times \frac{1}{5} \times \frac{1}{5} = 5 \times 5 \times N \Rightarrow \frac{1}{5} \times \frac{1}{5} \times \frac{1}{5} \times \frac{1}{5} \times \frac{1}{5} \times \frac{1}{5} = N \Rightarrow N = \frac{1}{15625}$.

Problem 12. Solution: 4

$11x - 4(2x - 3) = 24 \Rightarrow 11x - 8x + 12 = 24 \Rightarrow 3x = 24 - 12 \Rightarrow$

$3x = 12 \Rightarrow x = \frac{12}{3} = 4$.

Problem 13. Solution: no solution.

Let $b = a + 1$, $c = a + 2$, and $d = a + 3$. We see that $b + c = 2a + 3 = a + d$.

$\frac{x-a}{x-b} = \frac{x-c}{x-d} \Rightarrow (x-a)(x-d) = (x-c)(x-b)$

$\Rightarrow x^2 - ax - dx + ad = x^2 - cx - bx + bc \Rightarrow cx + bx - ax - dx = ad + bc$

$\Rightarrow x(b + c - a - d) = ad + bc$.

We see that the left hand side of the equation is always – and the right hand side is always not 2. So the equation has no solution.

Problem 14. Solution: 2.25.

$$\frac{19}{x} = \frac{1^0 + 2^1 + 3^2 + 4^3}{4^0 + 3^1 + 2^2 + 1^3} \Rightarrow \frac{19}{x} = \frac{1+2+9+64}{1+3+4+1} \Rightarrow \frac{19}{x} = \frac{76}{9} \Rightarrow$$

$$x = \frac{19 \times 9}{76} = 2.25.$$

Problem 15. Solution: 30

$a \times b = 10$ \hfill (1)
$b \times c = 6$ \hfill (2)
$c \times a = 15$ \hfill (3)

(1) × (2) × (3): $(a \times b \times c)^2 = 10 \times 6 \times 15 \Rightarrow a \times b \times c = \sqrt{10 \times 6 \times 15} = 30$.

Problem 16. Solution: 24.

$$1 + \frac{n}{2 + \frac{1}{1 - \frac{1}{2}}} = 7 \Rightarrow \frac{n}{2 + \frac{1}{\frac{1}{2}}} = 6 \Rightarrow \frac{n}{4} = 6 \Rightarrow n = 6 \times 4 = 24.$$

Problem 17. Solution: − 32.

$$\frac{x-1}{3} - 1 = \frac{2x-1}{5} + 1 \Rightarrow \frac{x-1}{3} = \frac{2x-1}{5} + 2 \Rightarrow \frac{x-1}{3} = \frac{2x+9}{5}$$

$$\Rightarrow 5(x-1) = 3(2x+9) \Rightarrow 5x - 5 = 6x + 27 \Rightarrow$$

$$-27 - 5 = 6x - 5x \Rightarrow x = -32.$$

Problem 18. Solution: 1.

$3(2x+5) - 3x = 2(x+5) - 3(2x-4) \Rightarrow 6x + 15 - 3x = 2x + 10 - 6x + 12 \Rightarrow$
$3x + 15 = 22 - 4x \Rightarrow 7x = 7 \Rightarrow x = 1$.

Problem 19. Solution: $1.61

$3P + 2E = 60$ \hfill (1)
$2P + 3E = 55$ \hfill (2)

(1) + (2): $5P + 5E = 115 \Rightarrow P + E = 23 \Rightarrow 7(P+E) = 23 \times 7 = 161 = \$1.61$.

Problem 20. Solution: 33.

Let three positive integers be a, b, and c from smallest to largest.
$b - a = 12$ (1)
$c - b = 4$ (2)
$a + b + c = 79$ (3)
(1) + (2): $c - a = 16$ $\Rightarrow$ $a = c - 16$ (4)
(2) can be written as: $b = c - 4$ (5)
Substituting (4) and (5) into (3): $c - 16 + c - 4 + c = 79$ $\Rightarrow 3c = 99 \Rightarrow c = 33$.

Problem 21. Solution: 49.
Let the number be x.
$x + x^2 + \sqrt{x} = 2457$.
We see that $49^2 = 2401$ and $50^2 = 2500$. So x must be less than 40.
We try $x = 49$.
$x + x^2 + \sqrt{x} = 49 + 49^2 + \sqrt{49} = 49 + 2401 + 7 = 2457$.
So the answer is 49.

Problem 22. Solution: 5.
$\dfrac{2-x}{3-x} = 4$ $\Rightarrow$ $2 - x = 4(3 - x)$ $\Rightarrow$ $2 - x = 12 - 4x$

$\Rightarrow$ $4x - x = 12 - 2$ $\Rightarrow$ $3x = 10$ $\Rightarrow$ $x = \dfrac{10}{3}$

$\dfrac{3-y}{2-y} = 4$ $\Rightarrow$ $3 - y = 4(2 - y)$ $\Rightarrow$ $3 - y = 8 - 4y$

$\Rightarrow$ $4y - y = 8 - 3$ $\Rightarrow$ $3y = 5$ $\Rightarrow$ $y = \dfrac{5}{3}$

$x + y = \dfrac{10}{3} + \dfrac{5}{3} = \dfrac{15}{3} = 5$.

Problem 23. Solution: 0.
$\dfrac{3}{x+1} - 4 = 3 - \dfrac{4}{x+1}$ $\Rightarrow$ $\dfrac{3}{x+1} + \dfrac{4}{x+1} = 3 + 4$ $\Rightarrow$ $\dfrac{7}{x+1} = 7$

     $\Rightarrow$ $x + 1 = 1$ $\Rightarrow$ $x = 0$.

50 Lectures for Mathcounts Competitions   **(21) Solving Equations**

Problem 24. Solution: -5.

$\dfrac{3d-1}{4d-4} = \dfrac{2}{3} \Rightarrow \dfrac{3d-1}{4d-4} = \dfrac{2}{3} \Rightarrow 3(3d-1) = 2(4d-1)$

$\Rightarrow 9d-3 = 8d-8 \Rightarrow 9d-8d = -8+3 \Rightarrow d = -5$.

Problem 25. Solution: 17.

$ab = 18$ (1)
$bc = 24$ (2)
$ac = 48$ (3)

$(1) \times (2) \times (3)$: $(a \times b \times c)^2 = 18 \times 24 \times 48 \Rightarrow a \times b \times c = \sqrt{18 \times 24 \times 48} = 144$ (4)

$(4) \div (1)$: $c = 8$
$(4) \div (2)$: $a = 6$
$(4) \div (3)$: $b = 3$
$a + b + c = 6 + 3 + 8 = 17$.

Problem 26. Solution: $-\dfrac{b}{a} - 1$.

$ax^2 + bx + ax + b = 0 \Rightarrow ax^2 + (b+a)x + b = 0$.

The sum of the roots is $-\dfrac{(b+a)}{a} = -\dfrac{b}{a} - 1$.

Problem 27. Solution: 18.

$0.\overline{5}x = 10 \Rightarrow \dfrac{5}{9}x = 10 \Rightarrow \dfrac{1}{9}x = 2 \Rightarrow x = 2 \times 9 = 18$.

Problem 28. Solution: 28.

$\dfrac{1}{2} \cdot \dfrac{2}{3} \cdot \dfrac{3}{4} \cdot \dfrac{4}{5} \cdots \dfrac{55}{56} = \dfrac{1}{2x} \Rightarrow \dfrac{1}{56} = \dfrac{1}{2x} \Rightarrow \dfrac{1}{28} = \dfrac{1}{x} \Rightarrow x = 28$.

Problem 29. Solution: 0.30.

Let x and y be the cost of one pen and one pencil, respectively.

$2x = 5y$ (1)
$x + y = 1.05$ (2)
$(2) \times 2$: $2x + 2y = 2.10$ (3)

(3) – (1): $2y = 2.10 - 5y$ $\Rightarrow$ $7y = 2.10$ $\Rightarrow$ $y = \dfrac{2.10}{7} = 0.30$.

Problem 30. Solution: 200

$H = 2M$ $\Rightarrow$ $M = \dfrac{H}{2}$ \hfill (1)

$M = 2L$ $\Rightarrow$ $L = \dfrac{M}{2} = \dfrac{H}{4}$ \hfill (2)

$M + H + L = 350$ \hfill (3)

Substituting (1) and (2) into (3): $\dfrac{H}{2} + H + \dfrac{H}{4} = 350$ $\Rightarrow$ $\dfrac{7H}{4} = 350$

$\Rightarrow$ $H = 200$.

Problem 31. Solution: 25

Let the number of rows be x.

$600/x$ is the number of students in each row.

$(600/x + 5)(x - 4) = 600$

Solve for x: $x = 24$ and $x = -20$ (this one is the extraneous root).

So $x = 25$.

Problem 32. Solution: $10\dfrac{1}{3}$.

$1.5 for the first one-third mile

$5.5 – $1.5 = $4.

Let x be the number of quarter miles $4 can take.

$0.4x = 4$ $\Rightarrow$ $x = 10$. So the number of miles is $10 \times \dfrac{1}{4} = 2.5$ miles.

$10 – $5.5 = $4.5

Let y be the number of one-twelfth miles $4.5 can take.

$y = \dfrac{4.5}{0.05} = 90$. So the number of miles is $90 \times \dfrac{1}{12} = 7.5$ miles.

The answer is $\dfrac{1}{3} + 2.5 + 7.5 = 10 + \dfrac{1}{3} = 10\dfrac{1}{3}$.

50 Lectures for Mathcounts Competitions — (21) Solving Equations

Problem 33. Solution: 9ft.
Let x and y be the two lengths with $x < y$.

$x + y = 20$ \hfill (1)

$x^2 + y^2 = 202$ \hfill (2)

Squaring both sides of (1): $(x + y)^2 = 400$ $\Rightarrow$ $x^2 + 2xy + y^2 = 400$ \hfill (3)

Substituting (2) into (3): $2xy = 198$ $\Rightarrow$ $xy = 99$ \hfill (4)

So x and y are the two roots of the quadratic equation: $t^2 - 20t + 99 = 0$ $\Rightarrow$
$(t - 9)(t - 11) = 0$.
So $x = 11$.

Problem 34. Solution: 8.
Let x be the number of boys and c be the cost of the canoe.
Each person pays $\$\, c/x$.

$$\frac{c}{x-2} = \frac{c}{x} + 3 \quad\Rightarrow\quad c\left(\frac{1}{x-2} - \frac{1}{x}\right) = 3 \quad (1)$$

$$\frac{c}{x+1} = \frac{c}{x} - 1 \quad\Rightarrow\quad c\left(\frac{1}{x+1} - \frac{1}{x}\right) = -1 \quad (2)$$

(1) ÷ (2):
$$\frac{\frac{1}{x-2} - \frac{1}{x}}{\frac{1}{x+1} - \frac{1}{x}} = \frac{3}{-1} \quad\Rightarrow\quad -\left(\frac{1}{x-2} - \frac{1}{x}\right) = 3\left(\frac{1}{x+1} - \frac{1}{x}\right) \quad\Rightarrow$$

$$-\frac{1}{x-2} + \frac{1}{x} = \frac{3}{x+1} - \frac{3}{x} \quad\Rightarrow\quad \frac{4}{x} = \frac{3}{x+1} + \frac{1}{x-2} \quad\Rightarrow$$

$$\frac{3}{x+1} + \frac{1}{x-2} - \frac{4}{x} = 0 \quad\Rightarrow\quad \frac{3x(x-2) + x(x+1) - 4(x+1)(x-2)}{(x+1)(x-2)x} = 0$$

$\Rightarrow$ $3x(x-2) + x(x+1) - 4(x+1)(x-2) = 0$ $\Rightarrow$

$3x^2 - 6x + x^2 + x - 4x^2 + 4x + 8 = 0$ $\Rightarrow$ $-x + 8 = 0$ $\Rightarrow$ $x = 8$.

50 Lectures for Mathcounts Competitions   (22) Solving Inequalities

SOLUTIONS

Problem 1. $n > -5$.
$0.5(8 - 2n) > -(2n + 1) \quad \Rightarrow \quad 4 - n > -2n - 1 \quad \Rightarrow \quad 2n - n > -4 - 1$
$\quad \Rightarrow \quad n > -5$.

Problem 2. $h < 3$.
$4h - 3 < 9 \quad \Rightarrow \quad 4h < 9 + 3 \quad \Rightarrow \quad h < 3$.

Problem 3. 2.
$6x - 10 < x + 15 \quad \Rightarrow \quad 6x - x < 10 + 15 \quad \Rightarrow \quad 5x < 25 \quad \Rightarrow \quad x < 5$.
$3x - 2 > 2 + x \quad \Rightarrow \quad 3x - x > 2 + 2 \Rightarrow \quad 2x > 4 \Rightarrow \quad x > 2$.
The solution is $2 < x < 5$. We have two integer solutions: 3 and 4.

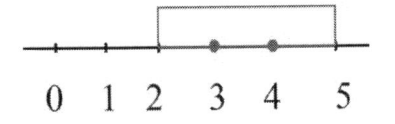

Problem 4. 7.
$n - 3 \leq 6 \quad \Rightarrow \quad n \leq 6 + 6 = 9$
$3n > 6 \quad \Rightarrow \quad n > 2$
The solution is $2 < x \leq 5$. We have seven integer solutions: 3, 4, 5, 6, 7, 8, and 9.

Problem 5. -5.
We have two cases:
$z + 2 \leq 3 \quad \Rightarrow \quad z \leq 1$
$z + 2 \geq -3 \quad \Rightarrow \quad z \geq -5$
The integer solutions are $-5, -4, -3, -2, -1, 0, 1$. The least integer solution is -5.

Problem 6. 24.
We square both sides of $5 < \sqrt{n} \leq 7$ to get: $25 < n \leq 49$.
The number of whole numbers is $49 - 26 + 1 = 24$.

Problem 7. $2a - 2b$.
$(2a - |2b|) = 2a + 2b$.
Since $b < 0$, $2a + 2b < 2a - 2b$.

Problem 8. $x < -1$.
$3x - 2 > (6x + 4) + (2x - 1)$ $\Rightarrow$ $3x - 2 > 6x + 4 + 2x - 1$
$\Rightarrow$ $3x - 6x - 2x > 4 - 1 + 2$ $\Rightarrow$ $-5x > 5$ $\Rightarrow$ $x < -1$.

Problem 9. 105.
Squaring both sides of $10 - \sqrt{7} < \sqrt{n} < 10 + \sqrt{7}$ to get: $(10 - \sqrt{7})^2 < n < (10 + \sqrt{7})^2$ $\Rightarrow$ $107 - 20\sqrt{7} < n < 107 + 20\sqrt{7}$.
The integer solutions are $55 \leq n \leq 159$.
The number of integer solutions is $159 - 54 + 1 = 105$.

Problem 10. 3.
$\frac{1}{3} < \frac{x}{5} < \frac{5}{8}$ $\Rightarrow$ $\frac{5}{3} < x < \frac{25}{8}$.
The largest integral value of x is 3.

Problem 11. 3.
When $n = 1$, we have $2^1 = 2 > 1! = 1$.
When $n = 2$, we have $2^2 = 4 > 2! = 2$.
When $n = 3$, we have $2^3 = 8 > 3! = 6$.
When $n = 4$, we have $2^4 = 16 > 4! = 24$.
So the answer is 3.

Problem 12. 7.
When $x = 1$, we have $1 + 1 = 2 < 10$.
When $x = 4$, we have $4 + 1 = 5 < 10$.
When $x = 9$, we have $9 + 3 = 12 > 10$.
So x must be the value between 5 and 8.
When $x = 7$, we have $7 + \sqrt{7} \approx 9.646 < 10$.

When $x = 8$, we have $8 + \sqrt{8} = 8 + 2\sqrt{2} > 10$.
So the answer is 7.

Problem 13. -1

Squaring both sides of $|x-2| > |2x+1|$ to get: $(x-2)^2 > (2x+1)^2$ $\Rightarrow$

$x^2 - 4x + 4 > 4x^2 + 4x + 1$ $\Rightarrow$ $0 > 3x^2 + 8x - 3$ $\Rightarrow$ $(3x-1)(x+3) < 0$.

The solutions are plotted in the figure below.

The integer solutions are $-2, -1$, and 0. The arithmetic mean is $\dfrac{-2-1+0}{3} = -1$.

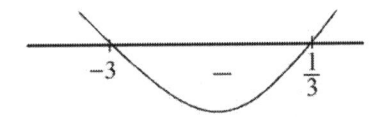

Problem 14. -11

$|2x+7| \leq 16$ is equivalent to $2x + 7 \leq 16$ and $2x + 7 \geq -16$.

The solutions are $x \leq \dfrac{12}{2}$ and $x \geq -\dfrac{23}{2} = -11.5$.

The least integer value of x is -11.

Problem 15. -18

$|x+2| < 5$? is equivalent to $x + 2 < 5$? and $x + 2 > -5$.

The solutions are $x < 3$ and $x > -7$.
The sum of the integer solutions is $-6 - 5 - 4 - 3 - 2 - 1 + 1 + 2 = -18$.

Problem 16. 17(cards).

$\dfrac{3}{4}J = \dfrac{2}{3}M$ $\Rightarrow$ $9J = 8M$

Since 8 and 9 are relatively prime, the smallest value is 8 for J and 9 for M.
The answer is $8 + 9 = 17$.

Problem 17. 6.

$$\frac{1}{n} < 0.2 \quad \Rightarrow \quad n > \frac{1}{0.2} = \frac{10}{2} = 5.$$

The least whole number value of n is 6.

Problem 18. 7.

$$(\frac{1}{2})^n < 0.01 \quad \Rightarrow \quad \frac{1}{2^n} < 0.01 \quad \Rightarrow \quad 2^n > \frac{1}{0.01} = 100.$$

$2^7 = 128$. The answer is 7.

Problem 19. 5.

Since n is positive, we have $n^2 > 16 \Rightarrow (n-4)(n+4) > 16$.
The solutions are:

The least positive integer n is 5.

Problem 20. 0 integers.

$$-n < \frac{1}{2}n + 3 \Rightarrow -3 < \frac{1}{2}n + n \Rightarrow -3 < \frac{3}{2}n \Rightarrow n > -2.$$

$$n + \frac{5}{2} \leq \frac{-n}{4} \Rightarrow n + \frac{1}{4}n \leq -\frac{5}{2} \Rightarrow \frac{5}{4}n \leq -\frac{5}{2} \Rightarrow n \leq -2.$$

There is no integer solutions.

Problem 21. 4 (values).

$|n| > 2 \quad \Rightarrow \quad n > 2$ or $n < -2$. n can be 3 or 4.
$|n| < 5 \quad \Rightarrow \quad n < 5$ or $n > -5$. n can be $-3, -4$.
The answer is 4.

Problem 22. 6(square units).

The figure is as follows. The area is $\frac{4 \times 4}{2} - \frac{2 \times 1}{2} - \frac{2 \times 1}{2} = 6$.

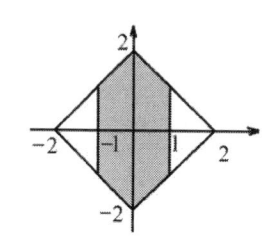

25

Problem 23. $-2 < x < 0$.

$x + x^2 < -x \quad \Rightarrow \quad x(x+2) < 0$.

The solutions are plotted as follows: $-2 < x < 0$.

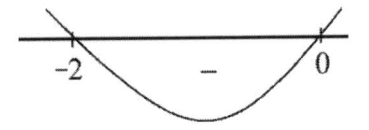

Problem 24. 162.

$a + b = 18 \quad \Rightarrow \quad (a+b)^2 = 18^2 = 324 \quad \Rightarrow \quad a^2 + b^2 = 324 - 2ab$.

Since we want the smallest value of $a^2 + b^2$, $2ab$ should be maximized. We know that ab has the maximum value if a and b are as close as possible. So we let $a = b = 9$.

The answer is then $a^2 + b^2 = 324 - 2ab = 324 - 2 \times 81 = 162$

Problem 25. 61.

$30^2 = 900 < 842$ and $31^2 = 961 > 942$. So N is 30 and M is 31. The sum is $30 + 31 = 61$.

Problem 26. 8.

$5^{96} > n^{72}$

$n^{72} < 5^{96} < (n+1)^{72} \quad \Rightarrow \quad n^9 < 5^{12} < (n+1)^9 \quad \Rightarrow \quad n^3 < 5^4 < (n+1)^3$

$\Rightarrow \quad n^3 < 625 < (n+1)^3$

We know that $8^3 = 512 < 625$ and $9^3 = 729 > 625$.

So n must be 8.

Problem 27. 12.

$a^2 + 2ab + b^2 = 144 \quad \Rightarrow \quad (a+b)^2 = 12^2$.

So $a+b = 12$ or $a+b = -12$.

The greatest possible value is 12.

Problem 28. -16.

$x^2 + 8x = x^2 + 2 \times 4x + 4^2 - 4^2 = (x+2)^2 - 16$.

The smallest possible real value is obtained by setting $x + 2 = 0$, which is -16.

SOLUTIONS:

Problem 1. Solution: 15 (students)
There are 42 – 14 = 28 students participated in the two clubs. Let S be the number of students in the Science Club.
We know that $n(A \cup B) = n(A) + n(B) - n(A \cap B)$, we have 28 = 18 + S – 5. So S = 15.

Problem 2. Solution: 13 (homes).
Let x be the number of homes needing neither.
By the formula, $n(A \cup B) = n(A) + n(B) - n(A \cap B)$, we have 23 – x = 7 + 5 – 2
$\Rightarrow \quad x = 13$.

Problem 3. Solution: 12 (% or percent).
Suppose the school has exactly 100 students.
We have the following information:
60 students are female.
100 – 60 = 40 students are male.
40 students have brown eyes.
30% × 40 = 12 male students have blue eyes.
So we know that there are 40 – 12 = 28 male students with brown eyes.
So there are 40 – 28 = 12 female students with brown eyes.
Therefore the answer is 12%.

Problem 4. Solution: 45 (percent).
Suppose the school has exactly 100 students.
We have the following information:
60 students participate in sports.
60 × 25% = 15 students in track.
So 60 – 15 = 45 students in the school participate in sports but not in track.
Therefore the answer is 45%.

Problem 5. Solution: 511 (subsets).
$n(A \cup B) = 6 + 8 - 5 = 9$. The number of sets is $2^n = 2^9 = 512$.
The number of non-empty subsets is 512 – 1 = 511.

Problem 6. Solution: 8 (members).
By the formula, $n(A \cup B) = n(A) + n(B) - n(A \cap B)$, we have $A \cup B = 5 + 7 - 4 = 8$.

Problem 7. Solution: 4 (elements)
Let x be the number of elements in A are also in B.
$n(A \cup B) = n(A) + n(B) - n(A \cap B)$, we have $10 = 6 + 8 - x$. $x = 4$.

Problem 8. Solution: 10 (men).
Method 1: Number of people who are not married: $100 - 85 = 15$.
Number of people who do not have a telephone: $100 - 70 = 30$.
Number of people who do not own a car: $100 - 75 = 25$.
Number of people who do not own their home: $100 - 80 = 20$.

At most $15 + 30 + 25 + 20 = 90$ people do not have one of the four things.
So the answer is $100 - 90 = 10$.

Method 2: **The tickets method**
Step 1: Give each man a ticket for each activity he is in. $85 + 70 + 75 + 80 = 310$ tickets are given out.
Step 2: Take away the tickets from them. People who have 3 or more tickets will give back 3 tickets. Students who have less than 3 tickets will give back all the tickets.
Step 3: Calculate the number of tickets taken back: at most $3 \times 100 = 300$ tickets were taken back.
Step 4: Calculate the number of tickets that are still in the students hands. $310 - 300 = 10$. At this moment, any man who has the ticket will have only one ticket. These men are the ones who are married, have their own telephone, own their own car, and own their own house. The answer is 10.

Problem 9. Solution: 7 (elements).
Let x be the number of elements in B.
$n(A \cup B) = n(A) + n(B) - n(A \cap B)$, we have $10 = 6 + x - 3$. $x = 7$.

Problem 10. Solution: 25 (people).
The number of people participate in talking or skating.

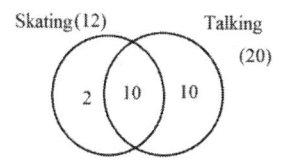

The answer is 22 + 3 = 25.

Problem 11. Solution: 8 (elements).
By the formula, $n(A \cup B) = n(A) + n(B) - n(A \cap B)$, we have $10 = A + 5 - 3 \Rightarrow A = 8$.

Problem 12. Solution: 4 (students).
From the given conditions, we draw the Venn diagram (figure 1).
Since eight of the students who spoke English did not speak Spanish, we know that $u = 2$ (figure 2)
The sentence "Of the eight students who spoke French" tells us that $v = 2$ (figure 3).
The sentence "Eight of the students who spoke Spanish did not speak English" tells us that $w = 5$ (figure 4).
So the answer is $x = 24 - 6 - 2 - 3 - 3 - 5 - 1 = 4$.

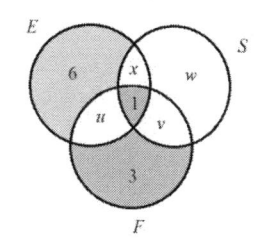

Figure 1 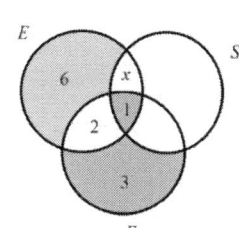   Figure 2 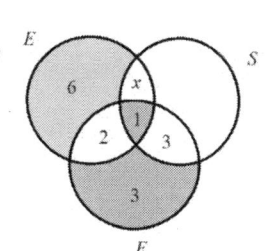   Figure 3 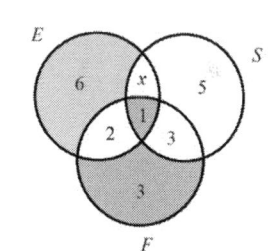   Figure 4

Problem 13. Solution: 10.
Let x be the number of people entered only tumbling competition.
$x - 7$ is the number of people entered tumbling competition.
By the formula, $n(A \cup B) = n(A) + n(B) - n(A \cap B)$, we have $48 - 18 = 20 + x + 7 - 7 \Rightarrow x = 10$.

Problem 14. Solution: 32.

Let x be the number of shoppers liked Brand Y only. $18 + x$ will be the number of shoppers liked Brand Y.

By the formula, $n(A \cup B) = n(A) + n(B) - n(A \cap B)$, we have

$60 - 12 = (16 + 18) + (18 + x) - 18 \Rightarrow x = 14$.

The answer is $x + 18 = 14 + 18 = 32$.

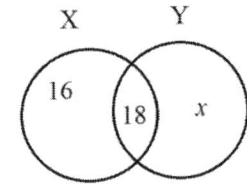

Problem 15. Solution: 122.

Let x be the number of students taking science only and y be the number of students taking history only.

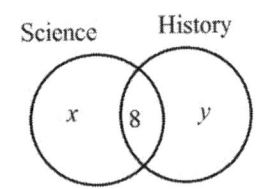

$8 = \dfrac{10}{100}(x+8) \Rightarrow 800 = 10x + 80 \Rightarrow x = 72$

$8 = \dfrac{16}{100}(y+8) \Rightarrow 800 = 16x + 128 \Rightarrow y = 42$.

The answer is $72 + 8 + 42 = 122$.

Problem 16. Solution: 14.

The Venn diagram is as follows and the answer is $60 - 46 = 14$.

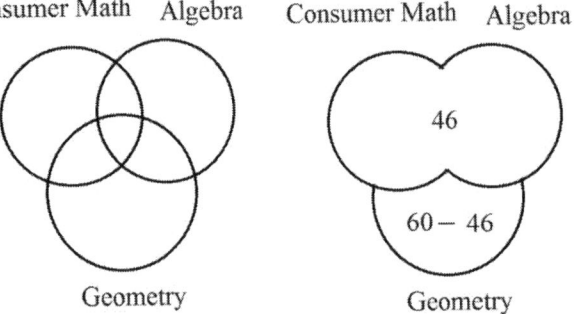

Problem 17. Solution: 10.

Let x be the number of consumers preferred neither game shows nor talk shows. By the formula, $n(A \cup B) = n(A) + n(B) - n(A \cap B)$, we have
$50 - x = 32 + 20 - 12 \Rightarrow x = 10$.

Problem 18. Solution: 11.
Let x be the number of students who have no pets
By the formula,
$n(A \cup B \cup C) = n(A) + n(B) + n(C) - n(A \cap B) - n(B \cap C) - n(C \cap A) + n(A \cap B \cap C) =$
$50 - x = 30 + 25 + 5 - 2 - 4 - 16 + 1 \Rightarrow x = 11$.

Problem 19. Solution: 5.
The number of students who did not pass is $250 \times (1 - \frac{80}{100}) = 50$.

The number of students who received a score below 60 is $50 \times \frac{1}{5} = 10$.

The number of students who r scored below 50 is $10 \times \frac{1}{2} = 5$.

Problem 20. Solution: 245,000.
Let x be the number of people who do not buy a newspaper at all in 100 people.
By the formula,
$n(A \cup B \cup C) = n(A) + n(B) + n(C) - n(A \cap B) - n(B \cap C) - n(C \cap A) + n(A \cap B \cap C) =$
$100 - x = 60 + 50 + 50 - 30 - 25 - 25 + 10 \Rightarrow x = 10$.
The number of people who do not buy a newspaper at all in 2,450,000 people is then $2,450,000 \times 10/100 = 245,000$.

Problem 21. Solution: 20
From the given, we can draw the Venn diagram (figure 1).
From the sentence "20 students had a fish" we know that $x = 20 - 12 - 3 - 2 = 3$ (figure 2).
From the sentence "50 students had a dog" we know that $u = 50 - 19 - 3 - 3 = 25$ (figure 3).

50 Lectures for Mathcounts Competitions   **(23) Venn Diagrams**

From the sentence "40 students had a cat" we know that $v = 40 - 19 - 3 - 2 = 16$ (figure 3).

The answer is then $100 - (50 + 16 + 2 + 12) = 20$.

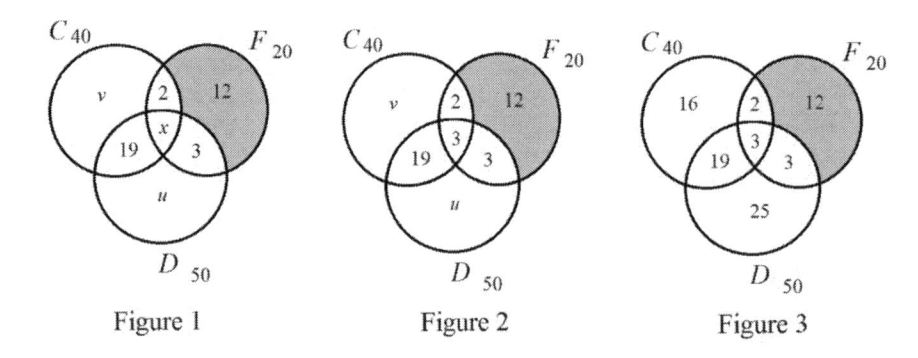

Figure 1   Figure 2   Figure 3

Problem 22. Solution: 16.

Let x be the number of students participated in both activities. By the formula, $n(A \cup B) = n(A) + n(B) - n(A \cap B)$, we have

$200 - 46 = 57 + 113 - x \quad \Rightarrow \quad x = 16$.

Problem 23. Solution: 25.

As shown in the figure, the answer is $(24 - 10) + 11 = 4 + 11 = 25$.

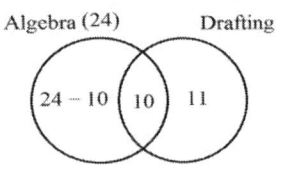

SOLUTIONS

Problem 1. Solution: 120(committees)
$\binom{10}{3} = 120$.

Problem 2. Solution: 60(ways)
Let three people be Alex, Bob, and Charles.
The first person has 5 choices. The next person has 4 choices. The last person has 3 choices.
By fundamental Counting principle, the answer is 5 × 4 × 3 = 60.

Problem 3. Solution: 24(sequences)
4! = 24.

Problem 4. Solution: 10 (combinations)
Any arrangement of WWWLL will do.
$\dfrac{5!}{3!2!} = 10$.

Problem 5. Solution: 60
$\binom{4}{1} \times \binom{6}{2} = 60$.

Problem 6. Solution: 8 (ways)
Case I: When these is no switch off:
ON   ON   ON   ON

Case II: When these is one switch off:
ON   ON   ON   OFF
ON   ON   OFF   ON
ON   OFF   ON   ON
OFF   ON   ON   ON
Case III: When there are two switches off:

ON	OFF	ON	OFF
OFF	ON	OFF	ON
OFF	ON	ON	OFF

Problem 7. Solution: 15(games)

$\binom{6}{2} = 15$.

Problem 8. Solution: 56(games)

$2 \times \binom{8}{2} = 56$.

Problem 9. Solution: 18(outcomes)

We have the following cases:
2 = 1 + 1
4 = 2 + 2 = 1 + 3 = 3 + 1
6 = 1 + 5 = 5 + 1 = 2 + 4 = = 4 + 2 = 3 + 3
8 = 2 + 6 = 6 + 2 = 3 + 5 = 5 + 3 = 4 + 4
10 = 4 + 6 = 6 + 4 = 5 + 5
12 = 6 + 6.

Total 18 ways.

Note that red 4 + green 6 is different from green 4 + red 6.

Problem 10. Solution: 8 (players)

Method 1: We see that $\binom{8}{2} = 28$. So the number of players is 8.

Method 2: Let the number of players be n.

$\binom{n}{2} = 28 \Rightarrow \frac{n(n-1)}{2} = 28 \Rightarrow n(n-1) = 56 \Rightarrow n(n-1) = 8 \times 7$.

So n is 8.

50 Lectures for Mathcounts Competitions (24) Combinatorics

Problem 11. Solution: 60 (flags)
We select 3 colors from 5 colors and arranger the 3 colors selected:
$\binom{5}{2} \times 3! = 60$.

Problem 12. Solution: 190 (contests)
The number of ways we are able to select a pair is the solution:
$\binom{20}{2} = 190$.

Problem 13. Solution: 12
Any arrangement of 4456 will do.
$\frac{4!}{2!} = 12$.

Problem 14. Solution: 190 (groups)
The number of ways we are able to select a pair of students is the solution.
When we select any two students, we form a group of two.
$\binom{20}{2} = 190$.

Problem 15. Solution: 63 (combinations)
The sum of the number of ways we are able to select 1, 2, 3, 4, 5, and 6 students each time is the solution.

$\binom{6}{0} + \binom{6}{1} + \binom{6}{2} + \binom{6}{3} + \binom{6}{4} + \binom{6}{5} + \binom{6}{6} = 2^6 = 64$.

$\binom{6}{1} + \binom{6}{2} + \binom{6}{3} + \binom{6}{4} + \binom{6}{5} + \binom{6}{6} = 64 - \binom{6}{0} = 64 - 1 = 63$.

Problem 16. Solution: 4970 (numbers)

Step 1: The thousand digits can be 3, 4, 5, 6, 7, 8, 9.

Step 2: The last digit can be 0 through 9.

Step 3: Then we find the number of ways such that $a \times b > 5$. a and b are digits among 1 to 9.

When $a = 1$, b can be 6, 7, 8, and 9.
When $a = 2$, b can be 3, 4, 5, 6, 7, 8, and 9.

When $a = 3$, b can be 3, 4, 5, 6, 7, 8, and 9.
When $a = 4$, b can be 4, 5, 6, 7, 8, and 9.
When $a = 5$, b can be 5, 6, 7, 8, and 9.
When $a = 6$, b can be 6, 7, 8, and 9.
When $a = 7$, b can be 7, 8, and 9.
When $a = 8$, b can be 8, and 9.
When $a = 9$, b can be 9.

We have $4 + 7 + 7 + 6 + 5 + 4 + 3 + 2 + 1 = 39$.
When we switch a and b we get $39 - 7 = 32$ more ways.

By the Fundamental Counting Principle, the final answer is
$7 \times (39 + 32) \times 10 = 4970$.

Note:
We minus 7 because when we switch (3, 3), (4, 4), (5, 5), (6, 6), (7, 7), (8, 8), and (9, 9), we do not get a difference way.

Problem 17. Solution: 528 (arrangements)
Method 1:
Without restriction we have 6! ways to seat 6 students (the faculty sponsor's position is fixed).
We treat two boys as a unit as shown in the figure. We have 4! ways to seat four girls.

We multiply 4! by 2 since we can switch the positions of two boys.
We multiply 4! × 2 by 2 again since we can switch the positions of two boys with G_1.
We multiply 4! × 2 × 2 by 2 one more time since we can switch the positions of two boys and G_1 with G_1, G_2, and G_3.

$$\boxed{B_1 \ B_2} \quad G_1 \quad F \quad G_2 \quad G_3 \quad G_4$$

So the answer is $6! - 4! \times 2 \times 2 \times 2) = 528$.

Method 2:
Case I:
We seat the faculty first. Then we select two girls (G_1, G_2, for example) to sit on the left. $\binom{4}{2}$. They can be arranged in 2! ways.

Then we seat 2 other girls $\binom{2}{2}$ and they can be arranged in 2! ways.

Then we select one boy (B1) from 2 $\binom{2}{1}$ to sit him on the left. He has 3 places to choose.

So we have $\binom{2}{1} \times 3$ ways to seat him.

Last step is to seat the B_1 and B_2. They have 3 places to be seated.
So we have $\binom{2}{1} \times 3 \times \binom{4}{2} \times 2! \times 3 = 432$

$$G_1 \quad G_2 \qquad F \qquad G_3 \quad G_4$$
$$\Uparrow \ \ \Uparrow \ \ \Uparrow \qquad\quad \Uparrow \ \ \Uparrow \ \ \Uparrow$$
$$B_1 \qquad\qquad\qquad B_2$$

Case II:
We seat the faculty first. Then we select one girl (G1) from the four in $\binom{4}{1}$ ways to be seated to the left..
Then we seat 3 other girls to the right and they can be arranged in 3! ways.

$$G_1 \quad F \quad G_2 \quad G_3 \quad G_4$$
$$\Uparrow \qquad \Uparrow$$
$$B_1 \ B_2$$

Then two boys can be seated in two ways .

Note that we can also seat G1 to the right and the rest of the girls to the left. So we multiply the result by 2:

$$2 \times \binom{4}{1} \times 3! \times 2 = 96.$$

The answer is $432 + 96 = 528$.

Problem 18. Solution: 560 (ways)

$$\binom{8}{2} \times \binom{6}{3} = 560.$$

Problem 19. Solution: 90 (games)

$$2 \times \binom{10}{2} = 90.$$

Problem 20. Solution: 24 (ways)

We calculate the number of ways to arrange DNNR: $\dfrac{4!}{2!} = 12$.

We see that we have two cases: I _ _ _ _ E and E _ _ _ _ I.
So the answer is $12 \times 2 = 24$.

Problem 21. Solution: 30 (games)

$$2 \times \binom{6}{2} = 30.$$

Problem 22. Solution: 30 (arrangements)

We see that we have the case: N _ _ _ _ S.

50 Lectures for Mathcounts Competitions (24) Combinatorics

We calculate the number of ways to arrange CIECE: $\dfrac{5!}{2!2!} = 30$.

Problem 23. Solution: 21(segments)

Any two points will form a line. So $\binom{7}{2} = 21$.

Problem 24. Solution: 240(gifts)

Each person brings 15 gifts. The answer is $16 \times 15 = 240$.

Problem 25. Solution: 63(committees)

$\binom{6}{1} + \binom{6}{2} + \binom{6}{3} + \binom{6}{4} + \binom{6}{5} + \binom{6}{6} = 6 + 15 + 20 + 15 + 6 + 1 = 63$.

Problem 26. Solution: 50(combinations)

$\binom{5}{2} \times \binom{5}{1} = 50$.

Problem 27. Solution: 1024(ways)

$\binom{11}{6} + \binom{11}{7} + \binom{11}{8} + \binom{11}{9} + \binom{11}{10} + \binom{11}{11}$

$= \binom{11}{5} + \binom{11}{4} + \binom{11}{3} + \binom{11}{2} + \binom{11}{1} + \binom{11}{11}$.

$= 462 + 330 + 165 + 55 + 11 + 1 = 1024$.

Problem 28. Solution: 240(ways)

$5 = 2 + 1 + 1 + 1$

$\binom{5}{2}\binom{3}{1}\binom{2}{1}\binom{1}{1} \times \dfrac{4!}{3!} = 240$

Problem 29. Solution: 3

Since we want the odd product, we are not albe to select the number 2.

The answer is $\binom{3}{2} = 3$.

Problem 30. Solution: 84

$3 \times \binom{8}{2} = 84$.

Problem 31. Solution: 20

$\binom{5}{1} \times \binom{4}{1} = 20$.

Problem 32. Solution: 150.

We have 6 colors to choose for flag 1, and 5 colors to choose fro flag 2 since flag 2 needs to have a different color from flag 1. We have 5 colors to choose for flag 3 since it only needs to be different from flag 2. So the answer is

$\binom{6}{1} \times \binom{5}{1} \times \binom{5}{1} = 150$. $\binom{6}{1} \times \binom{5}{1} \times \binom{5}{1} = 150$.

Problem 33. Solution: 12

The sum can be 3, 6, 9, 12.

3 = 1 + 2	2 ways
6 = 1 + 5 = 2 + 4 = 3 + 3	5 ways
9 = 3 + 6 = 4 + 5	4 ways
12 = 6 + 6	1 way.

Total 12 ways.

Problem 34. Solution: 60

Any arrangement of 445556 will do.

$\dfrac{6!}{2!3!} = 60$.

Problem 35. Solution: 36.

Method 1: Since we do not label each group, we think that if two groups have the same number of people, they are identical.

We know that each group has one man. So we have one way to place three men into 3 groups.

$4 = 2 + 1 + 1$. Now we have $\binom{4}{2} \times \binom{2}{1} \times \binom{1}{1}$ ways to place women.

After the placement, we order these groups and we have $\dfrac{3!}{2!1!}$ ways to do so. So the answer is $\binom{4}{2} \times \binom{2}{1} \times \binom{1}{1} \times \dfrac{3!}{2!1!} = 6 \times 2 \times 3 = 36$.

Method 2:

First we consider order and think all three groups are distinct.
$7 = 3 + 2 + 2$.
Let the number of ways to divided the groups be x.
Then $x \times 3! = P$

$$P = [\binom{4}{2} \times \binom{3}{1}] \times [\binom{2}{1} \times \binom{2}{1}] \times [\binom{1}{1} \times \binom{1}{1}] \times \dfrac{3!}{2!} == 216.$$

So $x = \dfrac{P}{3!} = \dfrac{216}{6} = 36$.

Problem 36. Solution: 42

$\binom{6}{3} + \binom{6}{4} + \binom{6}{5} + \binom{6}{6} = 20 + 15 + 6 + 1 = 42$.

Problem 37. Solution: 1440

Since one coach must be at each end, we arrange them first. We have two ways to arrange them.

Then we have 6! Ways to arrange 6 students.
So the answer is 2 × 6! = 1440.

Problem 38. Solution: 3498.
We have 3 cases: 12 = 8 + 4 = 7 + 5 = 6 + 6.

Case 1: $\binom{12}{8} \times \binom{4}{4} \times 2 = 990$

Case 2: $\binom{12}{7} \times \binom{5}{5} \times 2 = 1584$

Case 2: $\binom{12}{6} \times \binom{6}{6} = 924$

The answer is 990 + 1584 + 924 = 3498.

Problem 39. Solution: 90.
6 = 2 + 2 + 2
$\binom{6}{2} \times \binom{4}{2} \times \binom{2}{2} \times \frac{3!}{3!} = 90$.

Problem 40. Solution: 90.

First we consider order and think all three groups are distinct.
6 = 2 + 2 + 2.
Let the number of ways to divided the groups be x.
Then $x \times 3! = P$

$\binom{6}{2} \times \binom{4}{2} \times \binom{2}{2} \times \frac{3!}{3!} = 90$.

So $x = \frac{P}{3!} = \frac{90}{6} = 15$.

Problem 41. Solution: 105.
First we consider order and think all three groups are distinct.
7 = 3 + 2 + 2.

Let the number of ways to divided the groups be x.

Then $x \times 3! = P$

$$\binom{7}{3} \times \binom{4}{2} \times \binom{2}{2} \times \frac{3!}{2!} = 630.$$

So $x = \dfrac{P}{3!} = \dfrac{630}{6} = 105$.

Problem 42. Solution: 7560.

$9 = 2 + 3 + 4$.

Let the number of ways to divided the groups be x.

$$\binom{9}{2} \times \binom{7}{3} \times \binom{4}{4} \times \frac{3!}{1!1!1!} = 7560.$$

Problem 43. Solution: 1260

First we consider order and think all three groups are distinct.

$9 = 2 + 3 + 4$.

Let the number of ways to divided the groups be x.

Then $x \times 3! = P$

$$\binom{9}{2} \times \binom{7}{3} \times \binom{4}{4} \times \frac{3!}{1!1!1!} = 7560.$$

So $x = \dfrac{P}{3!} = \dfrac{7560}{6} = 1260$.

SOLUTIONS

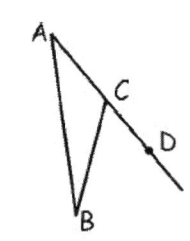

Problem 1. Solution: 23.
$\angle BCD = \angle ABC + \angle BAC \Rightarrow 55° = \angle ABC + 32° \Rightarrow 55° = \angle ABC = 55° - 32° = 23°$.

Problem 2. Solution: 130.
$70 + 5x + 6x = 180 \Rightarrow x = 10$.
Three angles are 50, 60, and 70. The answer is $60 + 70 = 130$.

Problem 3. Solution: 30. 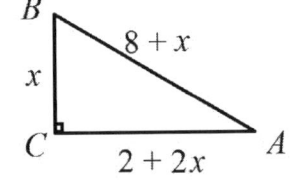
By Pythagorean Theorem,
$x^2 + (2+2x)^2 = (8+x)^2 \Rightarrow$
$x^2 + 4 + 8x + 4x^2 = 64 + 16x + x^2 \Rightarrow x^2 - 2x - 15 = 0$
$\Rightarrow (x+3)(x-5) = 0$
So x = 5. The perimeter is $5 + 12 + 13 = 30$.

Problem 4. Solution: 132.
Method 1:
Let the smallest angle be $4x$.
$4x + 5x + 6x = 180 \Rightarrow x = 12$.
The measure of the greatest supplement of these three angles is $180 - 4x = 132$.

Method 2:
The smallest angle is $\dfrac{4}{4+5+6} \times 180 = 48$
The measure of the supplement of it is $180 - 48 = 132$.

Problem 5. Solution: 117. 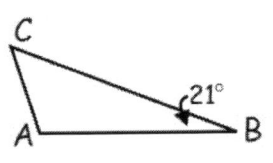
The measure of angle C is $21 \times 2 = 42$.
$\angle A = 180° - 21 - 42° = 117°$.

Problem 6. Solution: 140. 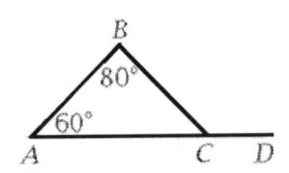
$\angle BCD = \angle CBA + \angle CAB = 180° + 60° = 140°$.

50 Lectures for Mathcounts Competitions (25) Angles And Triangles

Problem 7. Solution: 80°.

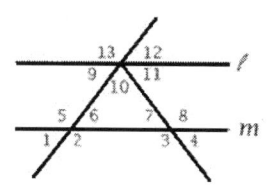

$\angle A = 180° - \angle 9 - \angle 11 = 180° - \angle 6 - 60°$
$= 180° - \angle 1 - 60° = 180° - 40 - 60° = 80°$.

Problem 8. Solution: 35.
$3x + 2x - 10 + x + 40 = 180 \Rightarrow x = 25$.
Three angles are 40, 65, and 75. The answer is $75 - 40 = 35$.

Problem 9. Solution: 102.
Method 1:
The third angle is $180 - 55 - 47 = 78$. Its supplement angle is $180 - 78 = 102$.

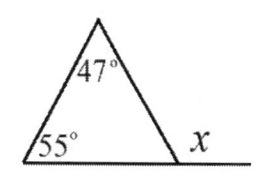

Method 2:
$x = 55 + 47 = 102$.

Problem 10. Solution: 90. 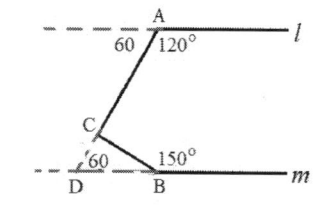
$\angle ACD = 60°$.
$\angle DCB = 150° - 60° = 90°$.
So $\angle C = 90°$.

Problem 11. Solution: 27.
$103 = \angle A + \angle ABC \Rightarrow 103 = 76 + \angle ABC \Rightarrow$
$\angle ABC = 27$.
Thus $x = 27$.

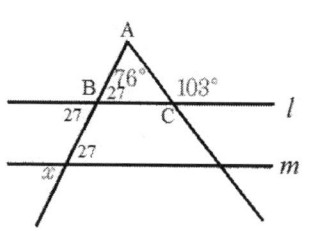

Problem 12. Solution: 45.
$130 = 85 + ? \Rightarrow ? = 130 - 85 = 45$.

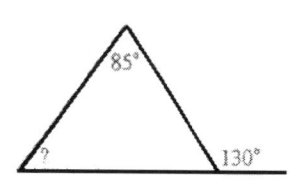

Problem 13. Solution: Obtuse.
The third angle is 180 – 31 – 58 = 91.
So the triangle is obtuse.

Problem 14. Solution: 70 (degrees).
Method 1:
Let the largest angle be 7*x*.
$5x + 6x + 7x = 180 \Rightarrow x = 10$.
The measure of the largest angle of the triangle is 7*x* = 70.

Method 2:
The largest angle is $\dfrac{7}{5+6+7} \times 180 = 70$.

Problem 15. Solution: 160 (degrees).
The largest angle is $\dfrac{3}{3+10+14} \times 180 = 20$
The measure in degrees of the largest exterior angle of the triangle is 180 – 20 = 160.

Problem 16. Solution: 45 (degrees).
Connect *CG*.
$BC = BG$ and $\angle BCG = \angle BGC = (180° - 60° - 90°) \div 2 = 15°$.
Thus $\angle GCE = \angle BCE - \angle BCG = 60° - 15° = 45°$.

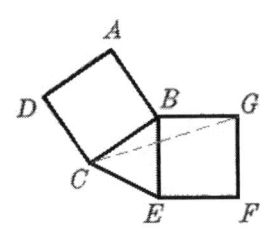

Problem 17. Solution: 98.
Let one base angle be *x*. The vertex angle is 16 + 2*x*.
$16 + 2x + x + x = 180 \Rightarrow 4x = 180 - 16 \Rightarrow x = 41$.
The vertex angle is 16 + 2*x* = 16 + 2 × 41 = 98.

Problem 18. Solution: 30 (degrees).
The middle angle is $\dfrac{4}{3+4+5} \times 180 = 60$
The measure of the complement of it is 90 – 60 = 30.

Problem 19. Solution: 15 (degrees).
We label each angle as shown in the figure.
$\beta = 2\alpha$
$\gamma = \alpha + \beta = 3\alpha$.
$120 + \alpha + \gamma = 180 \Rightarrow \alpha + \gamma = 60 \Rightarrow \alpha + 3\alpha = 60 \Rightarrow 4\alpha = 60 \Rightarrow \alpha = 15$.

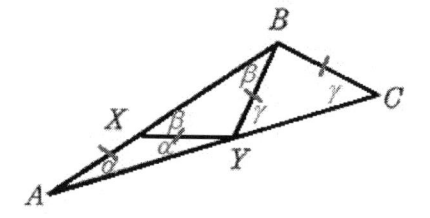

Problem 20. Solution: 100 (degrees).
We label each angle as shown in the figure.
For triangle *AEB*, we have $\beta = \alpha + 50$ (1)
For triangle *ACF* and triangle *DEF*, we have $\alpha + \angle C = 50 + \beta$ (2)
Substituting (1) into (2): $\alpha + \angle C = 50 + \alpha + 50 \Rightarrow \angle C = 50 + 50 = 100$.

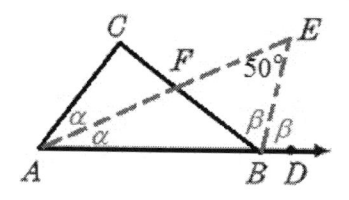

Problem 21. Solution: 3.
Since $\angle A \cong \angle B$, $BC = AC \Rightarrow 2x + 2 = 3x - 1 \Rightarrow 3 = 3x - 2x \quad x = 3$.

Problem 22. Solution: 91 (° or degrees).
The third angle is $180° - 28° - 61° = 91°$.

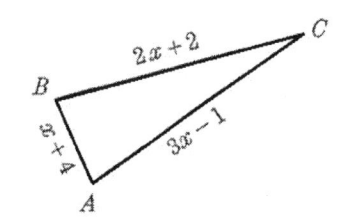

SOLUTIONS

Problem 1. 141.
$51 + \alpha + 51 + \alpha + \alpha + \alpha = 180 \Rightarrow 4\alpha = 78 \Rightarrow 2\alpha = 39$.
The answer is $51 + \alpha + 51 + \alpha = 102 + 2\alpha = 102 + 39 = 141$.

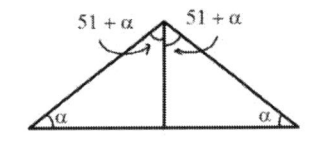

Problem 2. 45 (degrees).
We label each angle as follows:

In isosceles triangle ABC, we have: $2\alpha + \alpha + 180 - 2\gamma + \gamma = 180 \Rightarrow \gamma = 3\alpha$.
In isosceles triangle ABC, we also have: $\alpha + 180 - 2\gamma = \gamma \Rightarrow$
$3\gamma = 180 + \alpha \Rightarrow 9\alpha = 180 + \alpha \Rightarrow 8\alpha = 180 \Rightarrow$
$\angle A = 2\alpha = 180/4 = 45$.

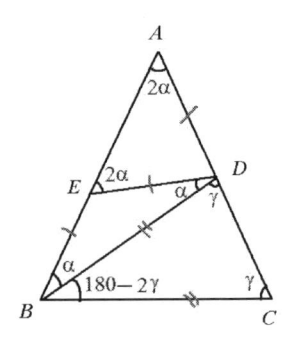

Problem 3. 40 (degrees).
Since $CD \parallel AB$, $\angle CBA = \angle DCB = 40°$ (alternate interior angles).
Since $AC = BC$, $\angle CAB = \angle CBA = 40°$.
Since $CD \parallel AB$, $\angle CAB = \angle ECD = 40°$ (corresponding angles).

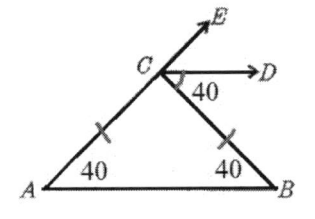

Problem 4. 28 (degrees).
Since $AB = BC$, $\angle BAC = \angle BCA = \alpha$.
Since $\overline{BC}$ is parallel to the segment through A, $x = \angle BCA = \alpha$ (alternate interior angles).
Thus $124 + \alpha + x = 180 \Rightarrow 124 + x + x = 180$
$\Rightarrow 2x = 180 - 124 = 56 \Rightarrow x = 28$.

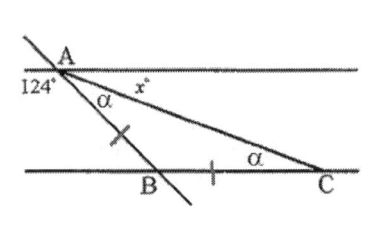

Problem 5. 20°.

$80 + 80 + \alpha = 180 \Rightarrow \alpha = 180 - 80 - 80 = 20$.

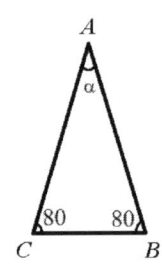

48

Problem 6. 54.

$2\alpha - 36 + \alpha + \alpha = 180 \quad \Rightarrow \quad 4\alpha = 180 + 36 \quad \Rightarrow \quad \alpha = 54.$

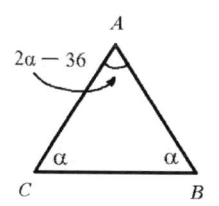

Problem 7. 28.

We label each angle as follows.
In triangle BCE, we have $\angle AEB = \angle C + \angle CBE \Rightarrow 84 = \alpha + 2\alpha \Rightarrow \angle C = \alpha = 28$.

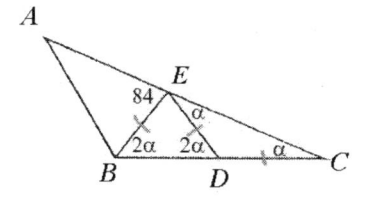

Problem 8. 360 (degrees).

$y + 82 = 180$ \hfill (1)
$x + 80 = 180$ \hfill (2)
$z = 80 + 82$ \hfill (3)
(1) + (2) + (3): $x + y + z = 180 + 180 + 82 - 82 - 80 - 80 = 360$.

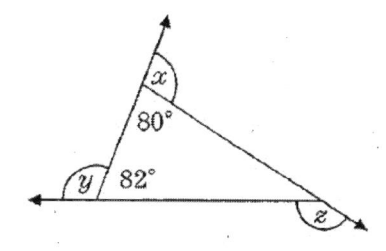

Problem 9. 80 (degrees).

The sum of three angles of a triangle is $180°$.

The measure of the largest angle facing the longest side 1/3 is $\dfrac{\frac{1}{3}}{\frac{1}{3}+\frac{1}{4}+\frac{1}{6}} \times 180° = 80°$.

Problem 10. $3\sqrt{3}$.

We draw the figure as follows.
The height of the equilateral triangle ABC is $r + r/2 = 2 + 1 = 3$.
$CD = \sqrt{3}$ and $CB = 2\sqrt{3}$.

The area is $\dfrac{1}{2} \times 2\sqrt{3} \times 3 = 3\sqrt{3}$.

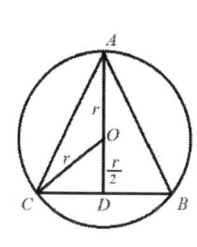

Problem 11. 30 cm.

49

Method 1:
This is a 5 – 12 – 13 right triangle. The perimeter is 5 + 12 + 13 = 30.

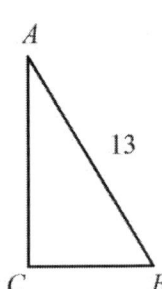

Method 2:
$\frac{1}{2} \times AB \times BC = 30 \implies AB \times BC = 60$ (1)

By Pythagorean Theorem, $AB^2 + BC^2 = 13^2$ (2)

(1) × 2 + (2): $(AB + BC)^2 = 17^2 \implies AB + BC = 17$.
The answer is $AB + BC + AC = 17 + 13 = 30$.

Problem 12. $15\sqrt{7}$.

The sides of the new triangle are 12, 8, and 10. Define $p = \frac{1}{2}(12 + 8 + 10) = 15$.

Using the Heron formula, we have:
$S_{\triangle ABC} = \sqrt{p(p-a)(p-b)(p-c)} = \sqrt{15(15-12)(15-8)(15-10)}$
$= \sqrt{15(3)(7)(5)} = 15\sqrt{7}$.

Problem 13. 28 cm².
Let the sides be a, b, and 12.
$a + b + 12 = 28 \implies a + b = 16$ (1)
By Pythagorean Theorem, $a^2 + b^2 = 12^2$ (2)
Squaring both sides of (1): $a^2 + 2ab + b^2 = 256$ (3)
(3) – (2): $2ab = 112$.
So the area is $\frac{2ab}{4} = \frac{112}{4} = 28$.

Problem 14. $2\sqrt{349}$.
The area of the original triangle is 9 × 40/2 = 180. Since the new triangle has one leg 4 × 9 = 36, another leg must be b and 36 × b/2 = 180. Thus $b = 10$. The new triangle should have the two legs of 10, 36, and hypotenuse $\sqrt{10^2 + 36^2} = 2\sqrt{349}$.

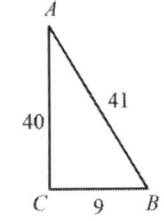

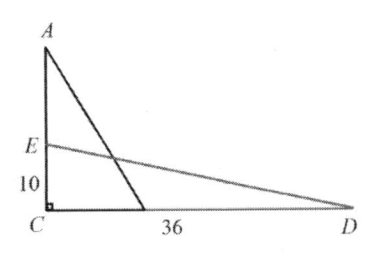

50 Lectures for Mathcounts Competitions   (26) Classification of Triangles

Problem 15. $1:\sqrt{2}+1$.

The ratio of the areas $\Delta ADE/\Delta ACB = [x/(x+y)]^2$.

Since $\Delta ADE = \frac{1}{2}\Delta ACB$, we have $\frac{1}{2} = (\frac{x}{x+y})^2$

$\Rightarrow \quad \frac{1}{\sqrt{2}} = \frac{x}{x+y} \quad \Rightarrow \quad \frac{x+y}{x} = \sqrt{2} \quad \Rightarrow \quad 1+\frac{y}{x} = \sqrt{2}$

$\Rightarrow \quad \frac{y}{x} = \sqrt{2}-1 \quad \Rightarrow \quad \frac{x}{y} = \frac{1}{\sqrt{2}-1} = \sqrt{2}+1$.

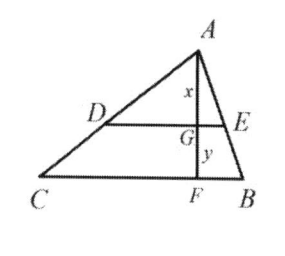

Problem 16. 36 cm.

The height of the triangle is h and $\frac{h \times 10}{2} = 60 \quad \Rightarrow \quad h = 12$

So triangle ACD is a 5 – 12 – 13 right triangle. So the perimeter is 13 + 13 + 10 = 36.

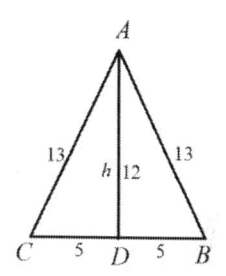

Problem 17. $12\sqrt{3}$ cm².

In the adjoining figure MV is an altitude of ΔAMV (a 30° – 60° – 90° triangle), and MV has length $2\sqrt{3}$. The required area of triangle ABV, therefore is

$\frac{1}{2}(AB)(MV) = \frac{1}{2} \times 12 \times 2\sqrt{3} = 12\sqrt{3}$.

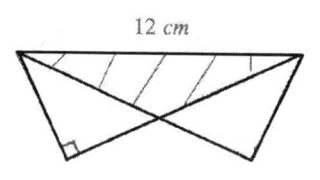

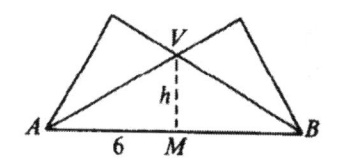

Problem 18. $2\sqrt{2}$ cm².

Let three sides be a, b, and c with $a \leq b \leq c$.
We have $a + b + c = 8$.
We see that $2 + 3 + 3 = 8$ (in fact this is the only way for the values of a, b, and c.

The height is $\sqrt{3^2 - 1^2} = 2\sqrt{2}$

The area of this triangle is $= \frac{1}{2} \times 2 \times 2\sqrt{2} = 2\sqrt{2}$ cm².

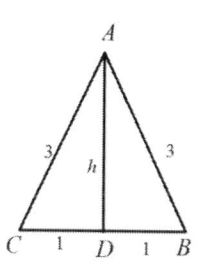

Problem 19. $\dfrac{\sqrt{400+a^2}}{a}$.

$\dfrac{1}{2} \times a \times b = 10 \Rightarrow \quad ab = 20 \quad \Rightarrow \quad b = \dfrac{20}{a}$

By Pythagorean Theorem, $a^2 + b^2 = c^2 \Rightarrow \quad a^2 + (\dfrac{20}{a})^2 = c^2 \Rightarrow$

$c = \sqrt{a^2 + (\dfrac{20}{a})^2} = \dfrac{\sqrt{400+a^2}}{a}$.

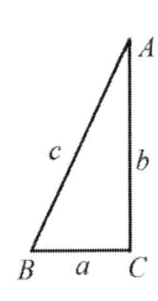

Problem 20. 210.
We have the following Pythagorean Triples:
a	b	c
20	21	29
12	35	37

The area of the right triangle is then $\dfrac{1}{2} \times 20 \times 21 = \dfrac{1}{2} \times 12 \times 35 = 210$.

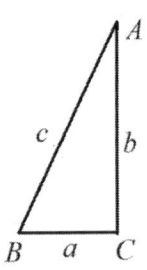

Problem 21. 2.
The sides of the triangle are a, b, and c.
Using the Heron formula and setting the area equal to the perimeter, we have:

$S_{\triangle ABC} = \sqrt{p(p-a)(p-b)(p-c)} = 2p$ \hfill (1)

Let $p-a=x$, $p-b=y$, and $p-c=z$

$x+y+z = 3p-(a+b+c) = p$

(1) becomes: $p(p-a)(p-b)(p-c) = pxyz = 4p^2$

Or $xyz = 4p$ \hfill (2)

Without loss of generality, we assume that $x \geq y \geq z$.

(2) becomes:

$xyz = 4(x+y+z) \leq 12x$ \hfill (3)

We also know that $yz \leq 12$, $z^2 \leq yz \leq 12 \quad \Rightarrow z \leq 3$.

When $z = 1$, (3) becomes:

$xy = 4(x+y+1) \quad \Rightarrow \quad x = 4 + \dfrac{20}{y-4}$

We get three solutions: (24, 5, 1), (14, 6, 1), and (9, 8, 1)
The corresponding triangles: (6, 25, 29), (7, 15, 20), and (9, 10, 17).

When $z = 2$, (3) becomes:

$2xy = 4(x+y+2) \Rightarrow x = 2 + \dfrac{8}{y-2}$

We get two triangles: (5, 12, 13) and (6, 8, 10).

When $z = 3$, since $yz \leq 12$, $y \leq 4$. But $y \geq z = 3$. So y can only be 3 or 4. For $y = 3$, there is no integral solution for x. For $y = 4$, there is no integral solution for x. Therefore, there are no solutions for $z = 3$.

We have five such triangles: (6, 25, 29), (7, 15, 20), (9, 10, 17), (5, 12, 13), and (6, 8, 10). Only the last two are right triangles.

SOLUTIONS

Problem 1. Solution: 27.5 units.

We know that $\triangle ABC \cong \triangle CED$ (AA). So we have

$\dfrac{P_{\triangle ABC}}{P_{\triangle DEC}} = \dfrac{10}{4} \quad \Rightarrow \quad P_{\triangle ABC} = \dfrac{10}{4} P_{\triangle DEC} = \dfrac{5}{2} \times (2+4+5) = \dfrac{55}{2} = 27.5$.

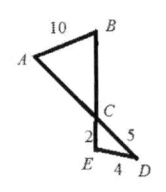

Problem 2. Solution: 60 units.

Applying Pythagorean Theorem to triangle ABD:
$AB^2 = AD^2 + BD^2 = 16^2 + 12^2 = 400$.
So $AB = 20$.
Applying Pythagorean Theorem to triangle BCD:
$BC^2 = DC^2 + BD^2 = 9^2 + 12^2 = 225$.
So $BC = 15$.
The perimeter is $20 + 15 + 9 + 16 = 60$.

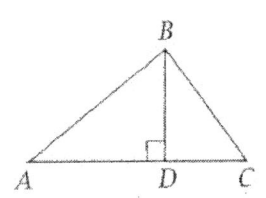

Problem 3. Solution: 27 cm.

Applying Pythagorean Theorem to triangle ABC: $BC^2 = AB^2 - AC^2 = 45^2 - 36^2 = 27^2$.
So $BC = 27$.

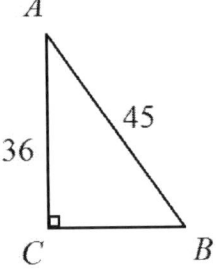

Problem 4. Solution: $\sqrt{3}$.

In triangle AMT, since $\angle ATM = 30$, $AM = \dfrac{1}{2} MT = 2$.

Applying Pythagorean Theorem to triangle AMT:
$AT = \sqrt{MT^2 - AM^2} = \sqrt{4^2 - 2^2} = 2\sqrt{3}$.

In triangle AHT, since $\angle T = 30$, $AH = \dfrac{1}{2} AT = \dfrac{2\sqrt{3}}{2} = \sqrt{3}$.

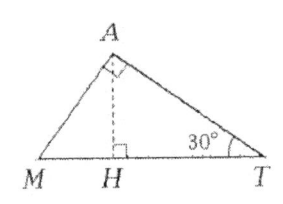

50 Lectures for Mathcounts Competitions   (27) Similar Triangles

Problem 5. Solution: $8\dfrac{1}{3}$ units.

Applying Pythagorean Theorem to triangle AED: $ED = \sqrt{AD^2 - AE^2} = \sqrt{5^2 - 4^2} = 3$.

$AE^2 = ED \times BE \quad \Rightarrow \quad 4^2 = 3BE \quad \Rightarrow \quad BE = \dfrac{16}{3}$.

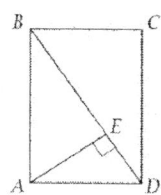

$BD = ED + BE = 3 + \dfrac{16}{3} = 3 + 5 + \dfrac{1}{3} = 8\dfrac{1}{3}$.

Problem 6. Solution: $\dfrac{1}{12}$.

We need to select one of the 6 line segments in order to get the second line segment collinear: AD, DB, AF, FC, CE, EB.

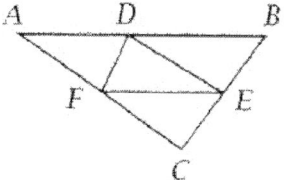

Since there are 9 line segments, this probability will be 6/9.
We have 1/8 probability to select the second line segment.

The probability is $\dfrac{6}{9} \times \dfrac{1}{8} = \dfrac{1}{12}$.

Problem 7. Solution: $\dfrac{25}{32}$.

We know that triangle ABC is a $6 - 8 - 10$ right triangle.
Let $ED = x$. $DC = 5 - x$.

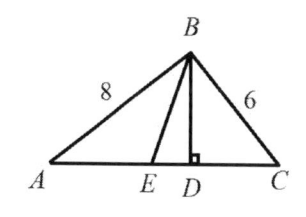

$\dfrac{1}{2} AB \times BC = \dfrac{1}{2} AC \times BD \quad \Rightarrow \quad \dfrac{1}{2} \times 8 \times 6 = \dfrac{1}{2} \times 10 \times BD$

$\Rightarrow \quad BD = \dfrac{24}{5}$.

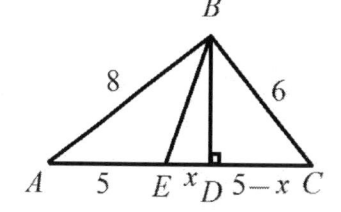

Applying Pythagorean Theorem to triangle BDC:

$DC = \sqrt{BC^2 - BD^2} = \sqrt{6^2 - \left(\dfrac{24}{5}\right)^2} = \dfrac{18}{5}$.

So $x = 5 - \dfrac{18}{5} = \dfrac{7}{5}$.

50 Lectures for Mathcounts Competitions   (27) Similar Triangles

The ratio of the area of $\triangle BEA$ to the area of $\triangle BDA$ is $\dfrac{5}{5+\dfrac{7}{5}} = \dfrac{5}{\dfrac{32}{5}} = \dfrac{25}{32}$.

Problem 8. Solution: 36.

We label each angle as shown.

In triangle ABC, γ is the exterior angle so $\gamma = 2\alpha$.

In triangle CBD, we have $2\gamma + \alpha = 180$ $\Rightarrow$ $4\alpha + \alpha = 180$ $\Rightarrow$ $5\alpha = 180 \Rightarrow$

$\alpha = 36$.

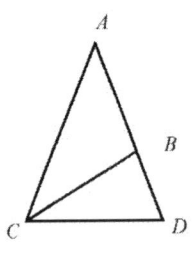

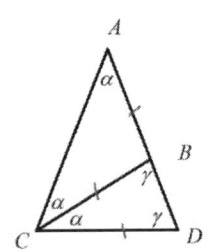

Problem 9. Solution: 9.

We label each angle as follows. We know that $\triangle PKR$ is similar to $\triangle QSR$. So we have

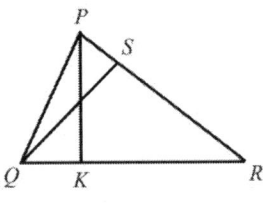

$\dfrac{PK}{QS} = \dfrac{PR}{QR}$ $\Rightarrow$ $\dfrac{6}{QS} = \dfrac{8}{12}$ $\Rightarrow$

$QS = 9$

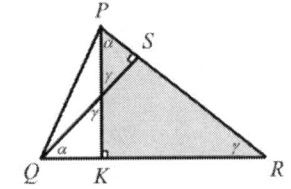

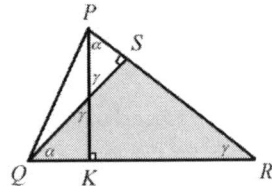

Problem 10. Solution: 27.

We have two cases.

Case 1: $2\alpha + 2\alpha + \alpha = 180$ $\Rightarrow$

$5\alpha = 180$ $\Rightarrow$ $\alpha = 36$.

The remaining angle is $2\alpha = 72$

Case 2: $2\alpha + \alpha + \alpha = 180$ $\Rightarrow$

$4\alpha = 180$ $\Rightarrow$ $\alpha = 45$.

The remaining angle is $\alpha = 45$

The answer is $72 - 45 = 27$.

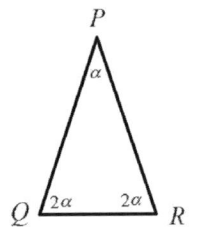

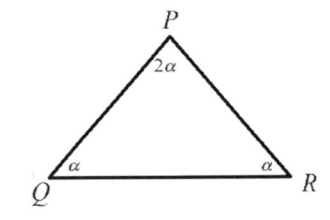

50 Lectures for Mathcounts Competitions   **(27) Similar Triangles**

Problem 11. Solution: $\frac{2}{3}$.

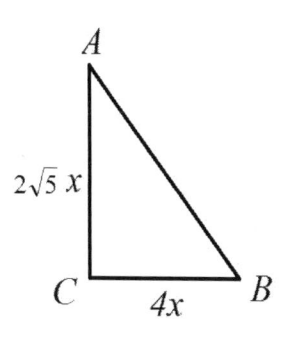

Let $AC = 2\sqrt{5}\,x$, $BC = 4x$.
Applying Pythagorean Theorem to triangle ABC:
$AB = \sqrt{AC^2 + BC^2} = \sqrt{20x^2 + 16x^2} = 6x$.
So $x = 5 - \frac{18}{5} = \frac{7}{5}$.

The ratio of BC to AB is $\frac{4x}{6x} = \frac{2}{3}$.

Problem 12. Solution: 46.8.

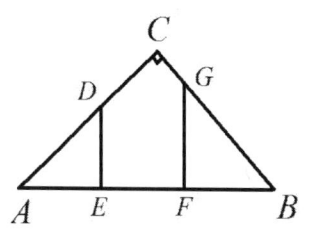

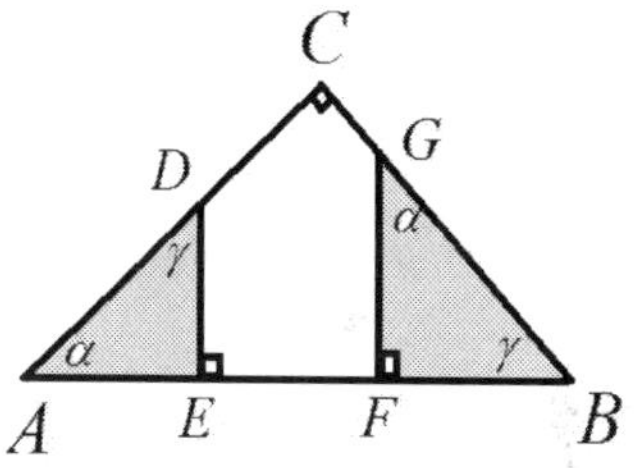

We label each angle as follows. We know that $\triangle AED$ is similar to $\triangle GFB$. So we have

$\frac{AE}{GF} = \frac{DE}{BF}$ $\Rightarrow$ $\frac{5}{18} = \frac{12}{BF}$ $\Rightarrow$ $BF = \frac{216}{5}$.

Applying Pythagorean Theorem to triangle BGF:

$GB = \sqrt{GF^2 + BF^2} = \sqrt{18^2 + (\frac{216}{5})^2} = 46.8$.

Problem 13. Solution: 10 (kilometers).

We draw $AF \parallel BD$ and $AF = BD$. Connect FD.
Applying Pythagorean Theorem to triangle AFE:
$AE = \sqrt{AF^2 + FE^2} = \sqrt{6^2 + 8^2} = 10$.

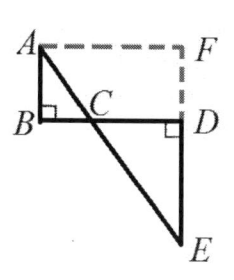

Problem 14. Solution: 8, 15, and 17.

57

50 Lectures for Mathcounts Competitions — (27) Similar Triangles

By the Triangle Inequality, if $P = a + b + c = 40$ and $a \le b \le c$, then $\frac{1}{3}P \le c < \frac{1}{2}P$

$\Rightarrow \quad \frac{40}{3} \le c < \frac{40}{2} \quad \Rightarrow \quad 14 \le c < 20$

The only Pythagorean Triple is (8, 15, 17).

Problem 15. Solution: 15

We know that $\triangle AEC$ is similar to $\triangle BDC$. So we have

$\frac{CB}{CD} = \frac{AB}{DE} \quad \Rightarrow \quad \frac{4}{CD} = \frac{6}{9} \quad \Rightarrow \quad CD = 6.$

The answer is $9 + 6 = 15$.

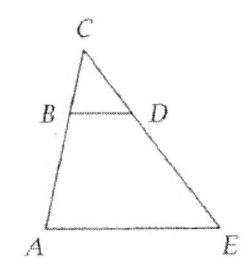

Problem 16. Solution: 35/12.

$EF = \frac{AB \times CD}{AB + CD} = \frac{7 \times 5}{7 + 5} = \frac{35}{12}.$

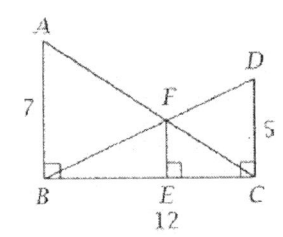

Problem 17. Solution: 16.

We know that $\triangle ADC$ is similar to $\triangle ACB$. So we have

$\frac{AC}{AB} = \frac{AD}{AC} \quad \Rightarrow \quad \frac{12}{AB} = \frac{9}{12} \quad \Rightarrow \quad AB = 16.$

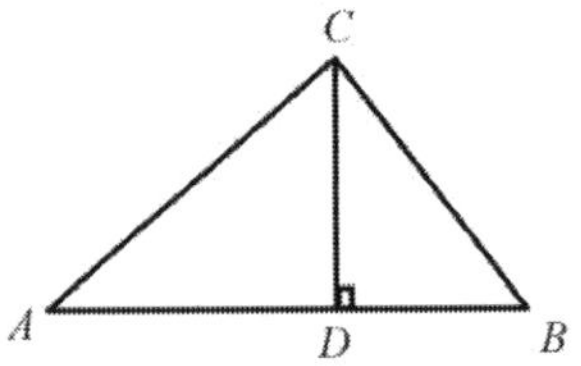

The answer is $9 + 6 = 15$.

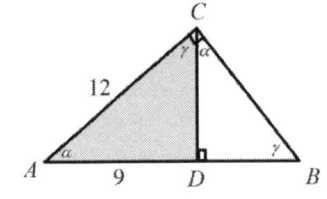

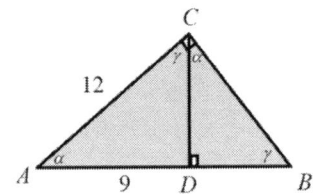

Problem 18. Solution: 40.

$\triangle QPR$ is a 16 – 30 – 34 right triangle with the perimeter $16 + 30 + 34 = 80$

50 Lectures for Mathcounts Competitions — (27) Similar Triangles

We know that $\triangle QPR$ is similar to $\triangle TSR$. So we have

$$\frac{P_{\triangle RST}}{P_{\triangle RPQ}} = \frac{QR}{RT} = \frac{1}{2} \implies P_{\triangle RST} = \frac{1}{2} \times P_{\triangle RPQ} = \frac{1}{2} \times 80 = 40.$$

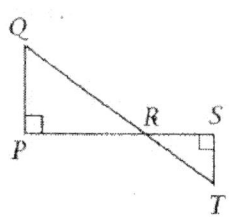

Problem 19. Solution: 24.

We know that $\triangle ABC$ is similar to $\triangle DFE$. So we have

$$\frac{AC}{DF} = \frac{BC}{EF} \implies \frac{10}{DF} = \frac{25}{60} \implies DF = 24.$$

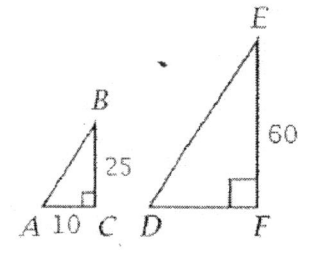

Problem 20. Solution: 21 units.

Connect AF. ADFE are cyclic. Since $\angle BAF = \angle DAF$, $EF = FD$.

Triangle AEF is congruent to triangle ADF. So $AE = 20$, and $EB = 9$. Triangle ABD is a 20 – 21 – 29 right triangle. So the answer is 21.

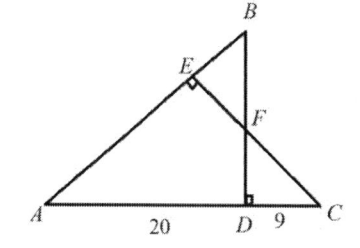

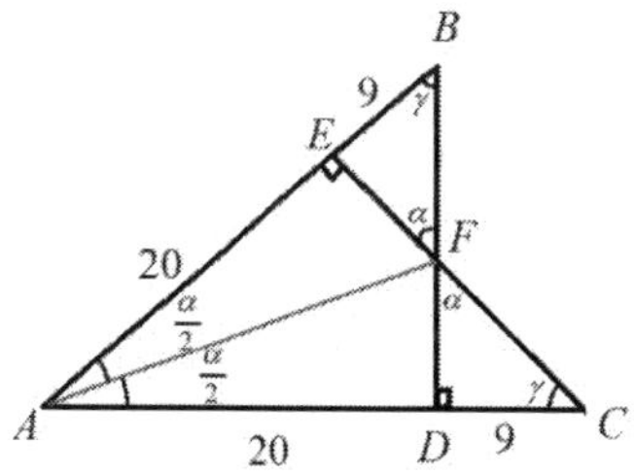

Problem 21. Solution: 15 units.

We know that $\triangle BCD$ is similar to $\triangle ABC$. So we have

$$\frac{BD}{AB} = \frac{BC}{AC} \implies \frac{12}{AB} = \frac{20}{25} \implies AB = 15.$$

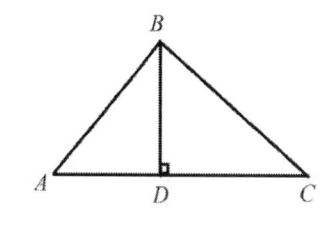

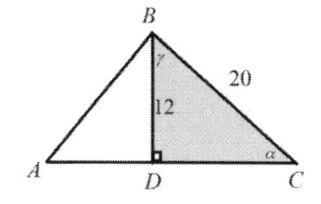

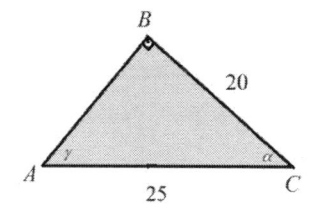

59

Problem 22. Solution: 3.375 (cm²)

The area of triangle ADE is $S_{\triangle ADE} = \dfrac{(3+1) \times 3}{2} = 6$

Triangle CEF is similar to triangle ADE.

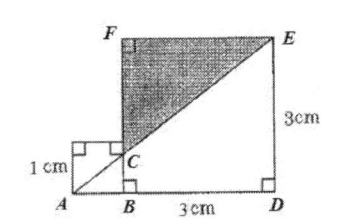

The area of triangle CEF can be obtained as following:

$\dfrac{S_{\triangle CEF}}{S_{\triangle ADE}} = \left(\dfrac{3}{4}\right)^2 = \dfrac{9}{16} \Rightarrow S_{\triangle CEF} = \dfrac{9}{16} S_{\triangle ADE} = \dfrac{9}{16} \times 6 = \dfrac{27}{8} = 3.375$

Method 2: Triangle CEF is similar to triangle ADE.

$\dfrac{ED}{CB} = \dfrac{AD}{AB} \Rightarrow CB = \dfrac{AB \times ED}{AD} = \dfrac{1 \times 3}{4} = \dfrac{3}{4}$

$S_{\triangle CEF} = \dfrac{FE \times FC}{2} = \dfrac{3 \times (3 - \frac{3}{4})}{2} = 3.375$.

Problem 23. Solution: 1/3.

Triangle FDC is similar to triangle ABC.

The area of triangle FDC can be obtained as following:

$\dfrac{S_{\triangle FDC}}{S_{\triangle ABC}} = \left(\dfrac{1}{3}\right)^2 = \dfrac{1}{9} \Rightarrow S_{\triangle FDC} = \dfrac{1}{9} S_{\triangle ABC} = \dfrac{1}{9} \times 3 = \dfrac{1}{3}$

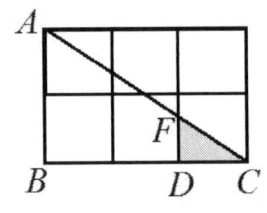

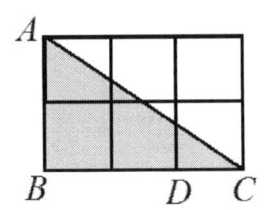

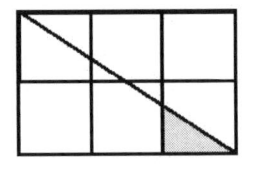

Problem 24. Solution: 250.

Case 1:

We know that $\triangle PQR$ is similar to $\triangle ABC$. So we have

$\dfrac{P_{\triangle PQR}}{P_{\triangle ABC}} = \dfrac{PQ}{AB} = \dfrac{50}{10} = 5 \Rightarrow P_{\triangle PQR} = 5 \times P_{\triangle ABC} = 5 \times 50 = 250$.

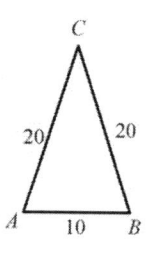

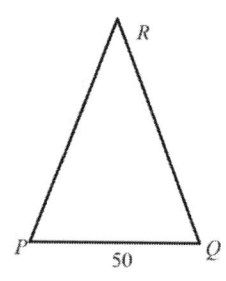

50 Lectures for Mathcounts Competitions (27) Similar Triangles

Case 2:

We know that $\triangle PQR$ is similar to $\triangle ABC$. So we have

$$\frac{P_{\triangle PQR}}{P_{\triangle ABC}} = \frac{PQ}{AB} = \frac{50}{10} = 5 \implies P_{\triangle PQR} = 5 \times P_{\triangle ABC} = 5 \times 50 = 250.$$

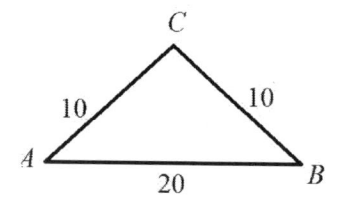

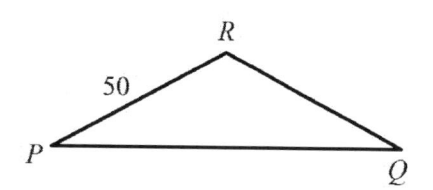

Problem 25. Solution: $6\sqrt{26}$

Applying Pythagorean Theorem to triangle AYB:
$AB^2 + AY^2 = BY^2 \implies 9n^2 + m^2 = 16^2$ \quad (1)

Applying Pythagorean Theorem to triangle ACX:
$AX^2 + AC^2 = XC^2 \implies n^2 + 9m^2 = 28^2$ \quad (2)

(1) + (2): $10n^2 + 10m^2 = 16^2 + 28^2 \implies$

$(n)^2 + (m)^2 = 104 \implies BC^2 = (3n)^3 + (3m)^2 = 9(n^2 + m^2) = 9 \times 104 \implies$

$BC = \sqrt{9 \times 104} = 3\sqrt{104} = 6\sqrt{26}$.

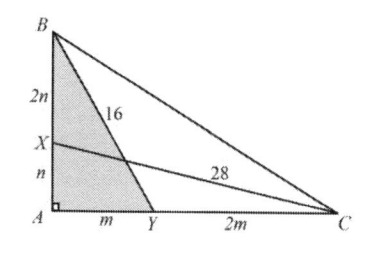

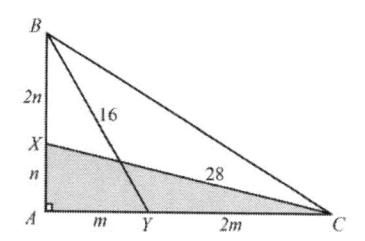

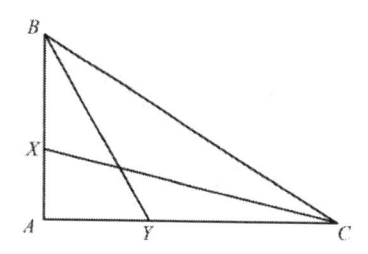

50 Lectures for Mathcounts Competitions (27) Similar Triangles

Problem 26. Solution: 2.155.

We know that $CE = DE = EF = s$.

We know that triangle EFB is a 30 – 60 – 90 right triangle. So we have $EB = 2BF = \dfrac{2\sqrt{3}}{3}$.

The ratio $t : s = \dfrac{s + \dfrac{2\sqrt{3}}{3}s}{s} = 1 + \dfrac{2\sqrt{3}}{3} \approx 2.1547 \approx 2.154$.

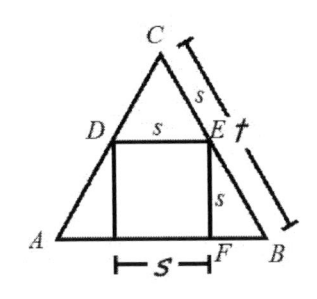

Problem 27. Solution: $\dfrac{6\sqrt{13}}{13}$.

Applying Pythagorean Theorem to triangle ABC:

$AB^2 + AC^2 = BC^2 \Rightarrow BC = \sqrt{2^2 + 3^2} = \sqrt{13}$.

We also have: $S_{\triangle ABC} = \dfrac{AB \times AC}{2} = \dfrac{BC \times AD}{2}$

$\Rightarrow \dfrac{2 \times 3}{2} = \dfrac{\sqrt{13} \times AD}{2} \Rightarrow AD = \dfrac{6\sqrt{13}}{13}$.

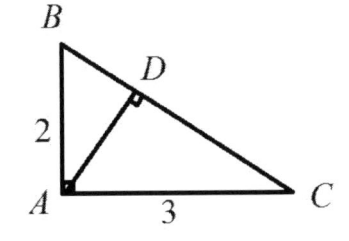

SOLUTIONS

Problem 1. Solution: 1.

By Pythagorean Theorem $c^2 = a^2 + b^2 \Rightarrow \quad (\sqrt{5})^2 = b^2 + 2^2$
$b^2 = 1 \Rightarrow \quad b = 1$.

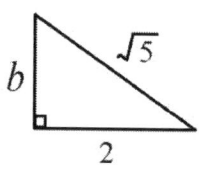

Problem 2. Solution: 10 cm.

By Pythagorean Theorem $c^2 = a^2 + b^2 \Rightarrow c^2 = 6^2 + 8^2 = 100 \Rightarrow c = 10$.

Problem 3. Solution: 36 sq units.

Triangle ADC is a 3 – 4 – 5 right triangle. Triangle ABC is a 5 – 12 – 13 right triangle.

The answer is

$\frac{1}{2} AD \times DC + \frac{1}{2} AC \times BC = \frac{1}{2} \times 3 \times 4 + \frac{1}{2} \times 5 \times 12 = 6 + 30 = 36$.

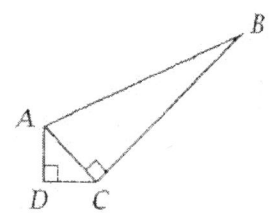

Problem 4. Solution: 35.

By Pythagorean Theorem $c^2 = a^2 + b^2 \Rightarrow c^2 = 21^2 + 28^2 = 35^2 \Rightarrow$
$AB = c = 35$.

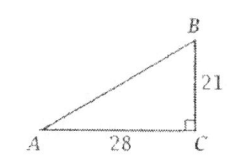

Problem 5. Solution: $\sqrt{38}$.

By Pythagorean Theorem $c^2 = a^2 + b^2 \Rightarrow$
$c^2 = 6^2 + (\sqrt{2})^2 = 38 \Rightarrow AC = c = \sqrt{38}$.

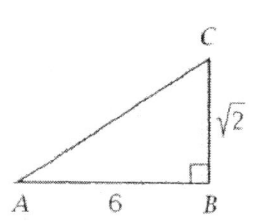

Problem 6. Solution: 8.6 units.

By Pythagorean Theorem $c^2 = a^2 + b^2 \Rightarrow c^2 = 5^2 + 7^2 = 74 \Rightarrow c = \sqrt{74} \approx 8.6$.

50 Lectures for Mathcounts Competitions (28) Pythagorean Theorem

Problem 7. Solution: $2\sqrt{2}$.
Since $m\angle CBD = 45$, $BC = CD = 4$. So $BD = 4\sqrt{2}$.
Since $m\angle ABD = 60$, $AB = \frac{1}{2}BD = \frac{1}{2} \times 4\sqrt{2} = 2\sqrt{2}$.

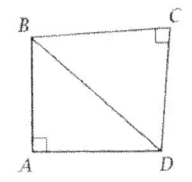

Problem 8. Solution: $10\sqrt{2}$.
Draw $BD \perp AC$.
Since $m\angle A = 30°$, $BD = \frac{1}{2}AB = \frac{1}{2} \times 20 = 10$.
Since $m\angle C = 45°$, $CD = BD = 10$ and $BC = 10\sqrt{2}$.

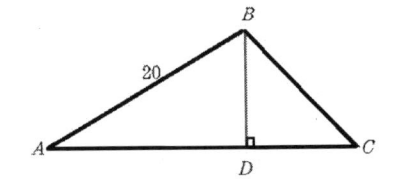

Problem 9. Solution: $5\sqrt{3}$.
Since $\angle RIT = 30°$, $RT = \frac{1}{2}RI = \frac{1}{2} \times 10 = 5$.
Thus $\overline{TI} = 5\sqrt{3}$.

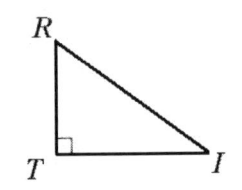

Problem 10. Solution: 41.
Let the lengths of the two legs be a and $a + 1$.
By Pythagorean Theorem $c^2 = a^2 + b^2$ $\Rightarrow$ $29^2 = a^2 + (a+1)^2$
$\Rightarrow 2a^2 + 2a + 1 - 841 = 0$ $\Rightarrow 2a^2 + 2a - 840 = 0$ $\Rightarrow a^2 + a - 420 = 0$ $\Rightarrow$
$(a - 20)(a + 21) = 0$.
Since a is a positive integer, $a = 20$.
The answer is $a + a + 1 = 20 + 20 + 1 = 41$.

Problem 11. Solution: $\frac{1}{3}$.

Since both a and d are positive numbers, $a + 2d$ must be the hypotenuse.
By Pythagorean Theorem, $a^2 + (a+d)^2 = (a+2d)^2$ $\Rightarrow$
$a^2 + a^2 + 2ad + d^2 = a^2 + 4ad + 4d^2$ $\Rightarrow$ $a^2 = 2ad + 3d^2$ $\Rightarrow$ $1 = \frac{2ad}{a^2} + \frac{3d^2}{a^2}$
$\Rightarrow$ $3(\frac{d}{a})^2 + 2(\frac{d}{a}) - 1 = 0$ (1)

Let $x = \dfrac{d}{a}$.

(1) becomes $3x^2 + 2x - 1 = 0 \Rightarrow (3x-1)(x+1) = 0$.

Thus $x = \dfrac{d}{a} = \dfrac{1}{3}$.

Problem 12. Solution: 841.

Let the lengths of the other leg be a and the hypotenuse be $a + 1$.

By Pythagorean Theorem $(a+1)^2 = a^2 + 29^2 \Rightarrow a^2 + 2a + 1 = a^2 + 841$

$\Rightarrow 2a = 840 \Rightarrow a = 420$

The answer is $a + a + 1 = 420 + 420 + 1 = 841$.

Problem 13. Solution: $40\sqrt{3}$.

Since $\angle A = 30°$, $BE = \dfrac{\sqrt{3}}{3} AE = 10\sqrt{3}$.

Since $\angle ADE = 30°$, $ED = AE\sqrt{3} = 30\sqrt{3}$.

The answer is $BD = BE + ED = 10\sqrt{3} + 30\sqrt{3} = 40\sqrt{3}$.

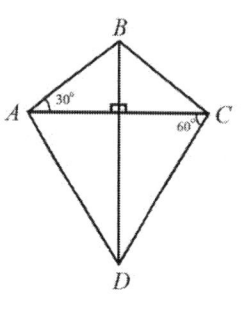

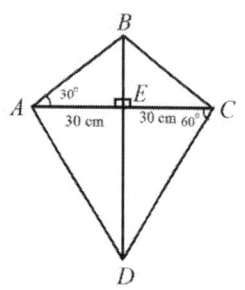

Problem 14. Solution: $3\sqrt{5}$.

We know that $EF = ED$. So $\angle EFD = \angle EDF = 45°$ and $FD = \sqrt{2} \times FE = 3\sqrt{2}$.

Since $DC = 3$ and $FD = 3\sqrt{2}$, by Pythagorean Theorem, in triangle FDC, $FC = \sqrt{3^2 + (3\sqrt{2})^2} = 3\sqrt{3}$.

By Pythagorean Theorem, in triangle CFB, $FB = \sqrt{3^2 + (3\sqrt{3})^2} = 6$.

By Pythagorean Theorem, in triangle AFB, $AF = \sqrt{6^2 + 3^2} = \sqrt{45} = 3\sqrt{5}$.

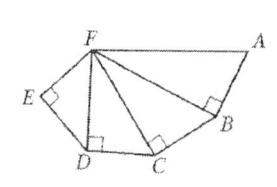

50 Lectures for Mathcounts Competitions (28) Pythagorean Theorem

Problem 15. Solution: 144 square inches.

Connect EC. Triangle CDE is a $6-8-10$ right triangle with the area $\dfrac{6\times 8}{2}=24$.

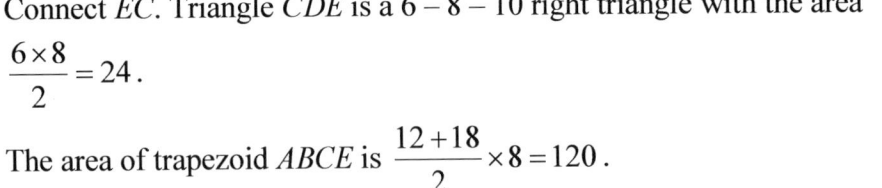

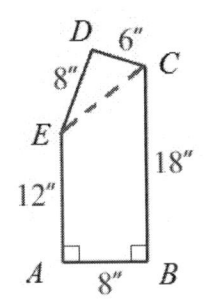

The area of trapezoid $ABCE$ is $\dfrac{12+18}{2}\times 8=120$.

The answer is $24+120=144$.

Problem 16. Solution: $3\sqrt{2}$.

If $\sqrt{5}\leq x$, by Pythagorean Theorem, we have $x=\sqrt{(\sqrt{5})^2+(\sqrt{3})^2}=\sqrt{8}=2\sqrt{2}$.

If $\sqrt{5}\geq x$, by Pythagorean Theorem, we have $x=\sqrt{(\sqrt{5})^2-(\sqrt{3})^2}=\sqrt{2}$.

The answer is $2\sqrt{2}+\sqrt{2}=3\sqrt{2}$.

Problem 17. Solution: 15.

The hypotenuse is $A(2-\sqrt{2})\times\sqrt{2}$.

So $A(2-\sqrt{2})+A(2-\sqrt{2})+A(2-\sqrt{2})\times\sqrt{2}=30 \Rightarrow$
$2A(2-\sqrt{2})+A(2-\sqrt{2})\times\sqrt{2}=30 \Rightarrow A(2-\sqrt{2})(2+\sqrt{2})=30 \Rightarrow A(4-2)=30$
$\Rightarrow A=15$.

Problem 18. Solution: $28\dfrac{4}{5}$.

Triangle ABC is a $5-12-13$ right triangle with $AB=13$.

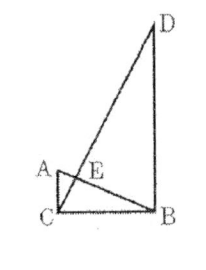

$AC^2=AB\times AE \Rightarrow AE=\dfrac{AC^2}{AB}=\dfrac{5^2}{13}=\dfrac{25}{13}$

$BC^2=AB\times BE \Rightarrow BE=\dfrac{BC^2}{AB}=\dfrac{12^2}{13}=\dfrac{144}{13}$.

We know that triangle ACE is similar to triangle BDE. So we have $\dfrac{AC}{BD}=\dfrac{AE}{BE} \Rightarrow$

$\dfrac{5}{BD}=\dfrac{\frac{25}{13}}{\frac{144}{13}}=\dfrac{25}{144} \Rightarrow \dfrac{1}{BD}=\dfrac{5}{144} \Rightarrow BD=\dfrac{144}{5}=28\dfrac{4}{5}$.

Problem 19. Solution: 11 (millimeters)

Let $AC = a$ and $CE = b$.

We have $a^2 - 4^2 = b^2 - 9^2$ (1)

$a^2 + b^2 = (4+9)^2$ (2)

(2) – (1): $2b^2 = 234$ ⇒ $b^2 = 117$ ⇒ $CE = b = \sqrt{117} \approx 10.817 \approx 11$.

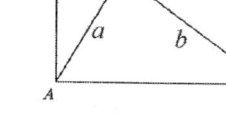

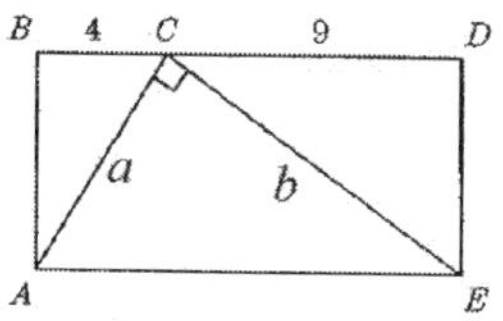

Problem 20. Solution: $3\sqrt{6}$ (inches).

Connect OD. We know that $OD = 6$. In triangle OCD, $CO = 3\sqrt{2}$.
By Pythagorean Theorem, in triangle ACO,

$AC = \sqrt{AO^2 + CO^2} = \sqrt{6^2 + (3\sqrt{2})^2} = \sqrt{36+18} = \sqrt{54} = 3\sqrt{6}$
(inches).

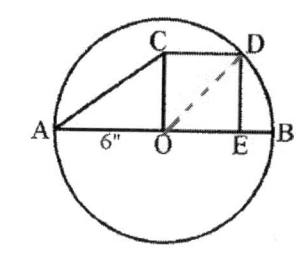

SOLUTIONS

Problem 1. Solution: 60°.
The sum of four interiro angles of a quadrilateral is 360.
The measure of the least angle is $\frac{3}{3+4+5+6} \times 360 = 60°$.

Problem 2. Solution: 3.75.
Since these quadrilaterals are similar., we have $\frac{x}{7.5} = \frac{8}{16} \Rightarrow x = 3.75$.

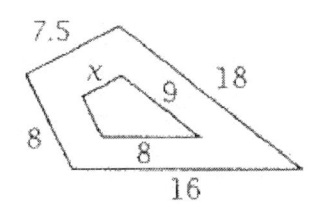

Problem 3. Solution: 130°.
We know that for a parallelogram, $\angle ABC + \angle BCD = 180°$.
So $\angle BCD = 180° - \angle ABC = 180° - 50° = 130°$.

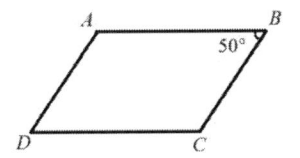

Problem 4. Solution: 4 units.
We label each line segments as follows.
$m + y = 12$ (1)
$y + x = 17$ (2)
$n + x = 9$ (3)
(1) – (2): $m - x = -5$ (4)
(4) + (3): $m + n = 4$.
The answer is 4.

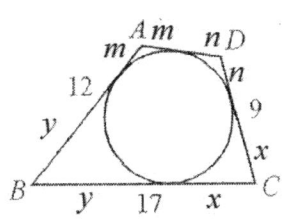

Problem 5. Solution: 8.
$ABCD$ is a rhombus and the area is $\frac{1}{2} AC \times BD = \frac{1}{2} \times 4 \times 4 = 8$.

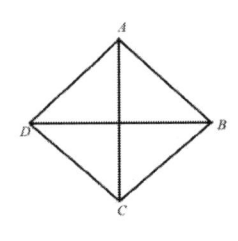

Problem 6. Solution: 68.
$\frac{1}{2} AB \times BC = 144.5 \quad \Rightarrow \quad AB^2 = 289 \quad \Rightarrow \quad AB = 17$.

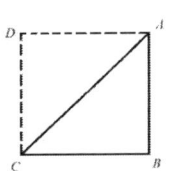

50 Lectures for Mathcounts Competitions (29) Quadrilaterals

The periemte is 4 × 17 = 68.

Problem 7. Solution: 50 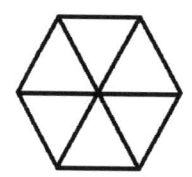
Total we have 12 quadrilaterals in the diagram and 6 of them are parallelograms. So the answer is 6/12 = 0.5 = 50%.

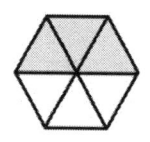

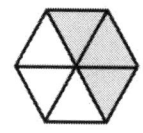

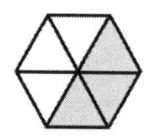

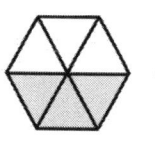

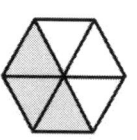

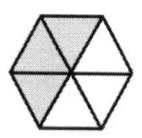

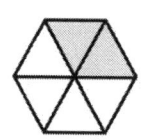

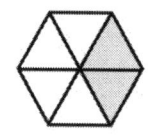

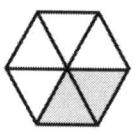

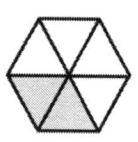

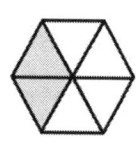

Problem 8. Solution: 7.5 (units).
We know that (1) *EF* is the perpendicular bisector of *BD* and (2) *EO = FO*. 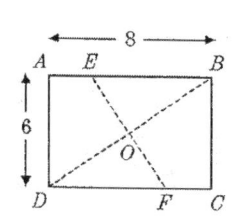
Since *AB* = 8 cm, *BC* = 6 cm, so *BD* = 10 cm and *BO* = 5 cm.
△*DOF*∽△*BCD* (because two angles are the same), so $\frac{OF}{BC} = \frac{DO}{DC}$.
Then $\frac{OF}{6} = \frac{5}{8}$ and *OF*=15/4.
EF = 2 × *OF* = 15/2 = 7.5.

Problem 9. Solution: 72 (degrees). 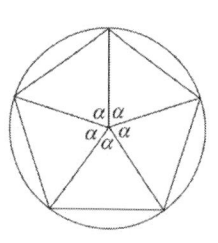
From the figure we see that 5α = 360°. So the answer is α = 360°/5 = 72°.

Problem 10. Solution: 36 (degrees).
The sum of four interiro angles of a quadrilateral is 360.
The measure of the smallest angle is $\frac{1}{1+2+3+4} \times 360 = 36$.

69

Problem 11. Solution: $14 + 2\sqrt{5}$ cm.

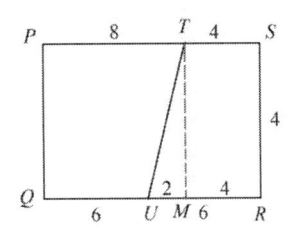

We draw the figure and draw $TM \perp QR$ at M.
$TU = \sqrt{TM^2 + UM^2} = \sqrt{4^2 + 2^2} = 2\sqrt{5}$.
The answer is $4 + 4 + 6 + 2\sqrt{5} = 14 + 2\sqrt{5}$ cm.

Problem 12. Solution: $8\sqrt{3}$.

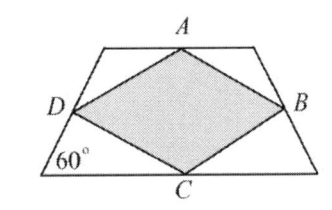

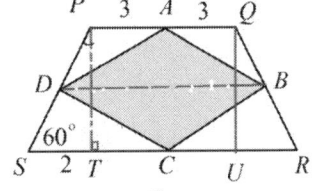

We connect DB. Draw $PT \perp SR$, $QU \perp SR$.
Thus we have $ST = (10 - 6)/2 = 2$.
In right triangle STP, $\angle SPT = 30°$. So $PT = 2\sqrt{3}$.
We also know that $DB = \dfrac{PQ + SR}{2} = \dfrac{6 + 10}{2} = 8$.
Then the area of quadrilateral $ABCD$ is
$\dfrac{DB \times AC}{2} = \dfrac{DB \times PT}{2} = \dfrac{8 \times 2\sqrt{3}}{2} = 8\sqrt{3}$.

Problem 13. Solution: 33.3%.

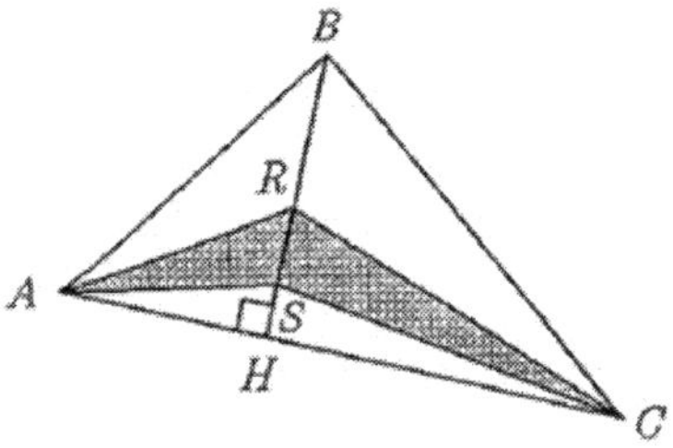

Let $BR = 3$, $RS = 2$, and $SH = 1$.
$\dfrac{S_{\triangle RCS}}{S_{\triangle ABC}} = \dfrac{RS}{BH} = \dfrac{2}{3+2+1} = \dfrac{1}{3} = 33.3\%$.

Problem 14. Solution: 25 cm².

Let a, b, and c represent the area of the region each letter is in. We know that FH and EG bisect each other ($AEIF \sim CGIH$, and $FBGI \sim HDEI$). 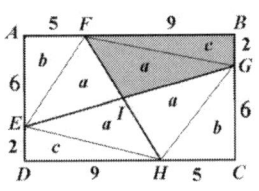
$2b + 2c + 4a = 14 \times 8$ and $b = 15$, $c = 9$.
We can conclude that $a = 16$.
The area of the shaded region is equal to $a + c = 16 + 9 = 25$.

Problem 15. Solution: 36 (units^2).
Connect *AC*. Triangle *ABC* is a 3 – 4 – 5 right triangle and
triangle *ACD* is a 3 – 12 – 13 right triangle.

The area is $\dfrac{AB \times BC}{2} + \dfrac{AC \times AD}{2} = \dfrac{3 \times 4}{2} + \dfrac{5 \times 12}{2} = 6 + 30 = 36$.

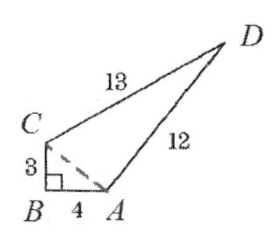

Problem 16. Solution: 13.
Let the length of the diagonal be x.
By Triangular Inequality, we have
$\begin{cases} 8 + 10 > x \\ 8 + x > 10 \end{cases} \Rightarrow \quad 2 < x < 18 \qquad (1)$

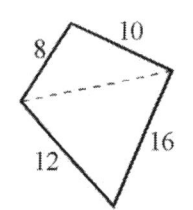

We also have $\begin{cases} 12 + 16 > x \\ 12 + x > 16 \end{cases} \Rightarrow \quad 4 < x < 28 \qquad (2)$

Combining (1) and (2), we get: $5 \leq x \leq 17$.
There are 17 – 5 + 1 = 13 values of x.

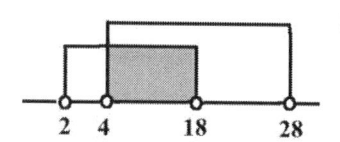

Problem 17. Solution: 60 (units^2).

The area is $\dfrac{EG \times FH}{2} = \dfrac{30 \times 4}{2} = 60$.

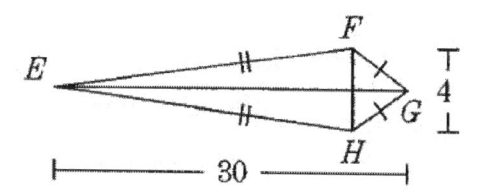

Problem 18. Solution: 70 (degrees).
The sum of four interiro angles of a quadrilateral is 360.
The measure in degrees of the fourth angle is 360 – 70 – 120 – 100 = 70.

Problem 19. Solution: 80 (degrees).
In triangle *AED*, x + y + 130 = 180 $\Rightarrow$ x + y = 50.
We know that $\angle AED$ = x + y + $\angle AFD$
$\Rightarrow \qquad \angle AFD = \angle AED - (x + y) = 130 - 50 = 80$.

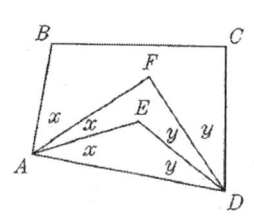

Problem 20. Solution: 234 (square inches).

Applying Pythagorean Theorem to triangle *BCD*: $BD = \sqrt{BC^2 + CD^2} = \sqrt{24^2 + 7^2} = 25$.

Applying Pythagorean Theorem to triangle *ABD*: $AD = \sqrt{BD^2 - AB^2} = \sqrt{25^2 - 20^2} = 15$.

The area is $\dfrac{AB \times AD}{2} + \dfrac{BC \times CD}{2} = \dfrac{20 \times 15}{2} + \dfrac{24 \times 7}{2} = 150 + 84 = 234$.

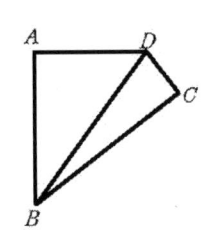

Problem 21. Solution: 11/3.

Extend sides *AD* and *BC* to meet at *V*, forming the original figure, triangle *ABV*.

In $\triangle ABV$, *AC* and *BD* are medians from vertices *A* and *B* that meet at point *E*, which divides the length of each in the ratio 2 : 1. This means that $EC = \dfrac{1}{3} AC = \dfrac{11}{3} = 3\dfrac{2}{3}$.

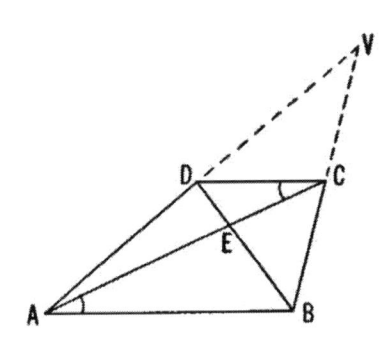

SOLUTIONS

Problem 1. Solution: 252 sq units.
We know that $AD = 18$. $AE = AD - DE = 18 - 8 = 10$.
So the area of trapezoid $ABCE$ is:
$$S_{ABCE} = \frac{(AE + BC)}{2} \times AB = \frac{10 + 18}{2} \times 18 = 252.$$

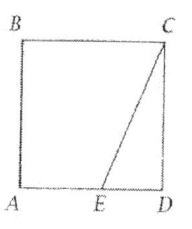

Problem 2. Solution: 110°.
Since $ABCD$ is an isosceles trapezoid, $\angle BAD + \angle BCD = 180°$
$\Rightarrow \quad \angle BCD = 180° - \angle BAD = 180° - 70° = 110°$.

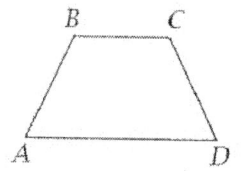

Problem 3. Solution: 48.
We draw the figure as follows. $DE = CF = 3$ and triangle ADE is a $3 - 4 - 5$ right triangle.

So the area of trapezoid $ABCD$ is:
$$S_{ABCD} = \frac{(AB + CD)}{2} \times AE = \frac{9 + 15}{2} \times 4 = 48.$$

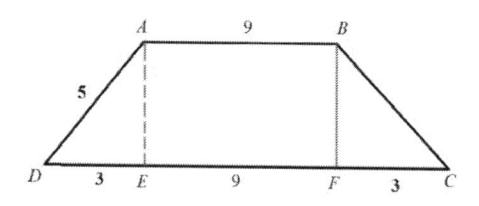

Problem 4. Solution: 135.
Since AD is a diagonal, $\angle ADB = 45°$.
Since $AD \parallel BC$, $\angle BDC = 90°$.
Thus $\angle ADC = \angle ADB + \angle BDC = 90° + 45° = 135°$.

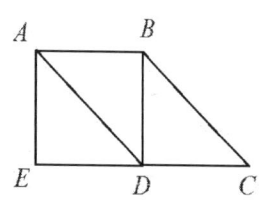

Problem 5. Solution: 124 units.
We know that AEF is a $7 - 24 - 25$ right triangle so $AE = 25$.
We draw $DG \perp AB$ at G. $DG = BC = 48$.
Triangle AEF is similar to triangle ADG.
So we have $\dfrac{AE}{AD} = \dfrac{EF}{DG} \quad \Rightarrow \quad \dfrac{25}{AD} = \dfrac{24}{48} \Rightarrow \quad AD = 50$

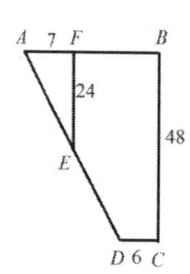

73

$$\frac{AF}{AG} = \frac{EF}{DG} \quad \Rightarrow \quad \frac{7}{AG} = \frac{24}{48} \Rightarrow \quad AG = 14.$$

The perimeter of trapezoid $ABCD$ is $AG + GB + BC + CD + DA = 14 + 6 + 48 + 6 + 50 = 124$.

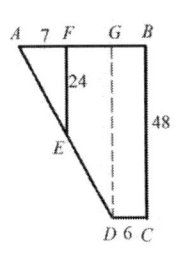

Problem 6. Solution: 5.

Let the other base be x.

Since the area of trapezoid is: $S = \frac{(7+x)}{2} \times 6 = 36 \Rightarrow x = 5$.

Problem 7. Solution: 28.

Since $3PQ \times PQ = 48$, $PQ = 4$ and $QR = 12$.
$PT = 8$ and $QU = 6$.
So the area of trapezoid $PQUT$ is:
$$S_{PQUT} = \frac{(PT + UQ)}{2} \times PQ = \frac{8+6}{2} \times 4 = 28.$$

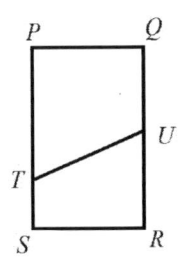

Problem 8. Solution: 13 units.

Draw $AF \perp DC$ at F, $BE \perp DC$ at E. We see that $EC = 5$. We also know that $BE = 12$.
Triangle CBE is a 5 – 12 – 13 right triangle. Thus $BC = 13$.

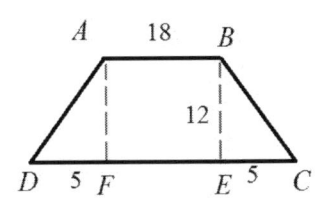

Problem 9. Solution: 15.

Draw $CE \perp AD$ at E. $AE = 4$ and $ED = 12$.
Triangle CDE is a 9 – 12 – 15 right triangle. Thus $CD = 15$.

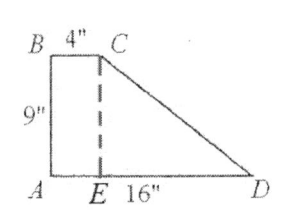

Problem 10. Solution: 6.3.

The area of trapezoid $ABCD$ is:
$$S_{ABCD} = \frac{(AB + CD)}{2} \times AF = \frac{8+16}{2} \times AF = 72 \Rightarrow AF = 6.$$

Thus $DF = 6$, $BE = 6$, and $CD = 16 – 6 – 8 = 2$.
Applying Pythagorean Theorem to triangle BCE:

50 Lectures for Mathcounts Competitions (30) Trapezoids

$$BC = \sqrt{BE^2 + CE^2} = \sqrt{6^2 + 2^2} = \sqrt{40} \approx 6.325 \approx 6.3$$

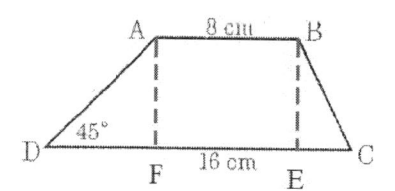

Problem 11. Solution: 48.

The area of the shaded trapezoid is $\frac{1}{6}$ of the area of the square.

So we calculate the area of the square to be $S = 6 \times 24 = 144$.

So one side will be $\sqrt{144} = 12$. Then the perimeter is $12 \times 4 = 48$.

Problem 12. Solution: 16(cm).

Let h be the height.

The area of trapezoid is: $S = \dfrac{(5+9)}{2} \times h = 112 \quad \Rightarrow \quad h = 16$.

Problem 13. Solution: 86 (cm).

Let b be the other base.

The area of trapezoid is: $S = \dfrac{(32+b)}{2} \times 11 = 649 \quad \Rightarrow \quad b = 86$.

Problem 14. Solution: 20 (cm).

Let b be the other base.

The area of trapezoid is: $S = \dfrac{(12+b)}{2} \times 8 = 128 \quad \Rightarrow \quad b = 20$.

Problem 15. Solution: 26 (cm^2).

The area of trapezoid is: $S = \dfrac{(4+9)}{2} \times 4 = 26$.

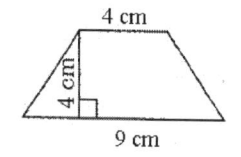

Problem 16. Solution: 88 (units^2).

Draw $AE \perp DC$ at E, $BF \perp DC$ at F. Since $AD = 8\sqrt{2}$, in right isosceles triangle ADE, $AE = DE = 8$.

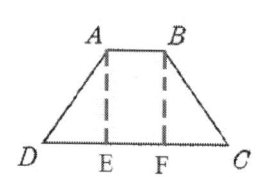

75

Triangle BCF is a 6 – 8 – 10 right triangle. So CF = 6. CD = DE + EF + CF = 8 + 4 + 6 = 18.

The area of trapezoid is: $S = \dfrac{(4+18)}{2} \times 8 = 88$.

Problem 17. Solution: 29 (cm)

Draw $AE \perp DC$ at E, $BF \perp DC$ at F.

Both triangles ADE and BCF are 3 – 4 – 5 right triangle. So AE = 4.

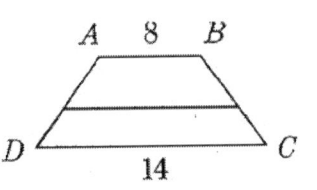

Triangle ADE is similar to triangle AGP.

So we have $\dfrac{DE}{GP} = \dfrac{AE}{AP} \Rightarrow \dfrac{3}{GP} = \dfrac{4}{4-PE} \Rightarrow$

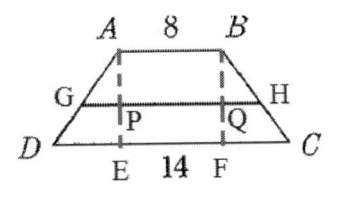

$\dfrac{3}{GP} = \dfrac{4}{4-1} \Rightarrow GP = \dfrac{9}{4}$

We also have $\dfrac{AD}{AG} = \dfrac{DE}{GP} \Rightarrow \dfrac{5}{AD-DG} = \dfrac{3}{\dfrac{9}{4}} \Rightarrow \dfrac{5}{5-DG} = \dfrac{4}{3} \Rightarrow DG = \dfrac{5}{4}$.

The perimeter is $GP + PQ + QH + HC + CD + DG = 2GP + 8 + 2DG + 14 =$

$= \dfrac{2 \times 9}{4} + \dfrac{2 \times 5}{4} + 22 = 29$.

Problem 18. Solution: 70 (degrees).

Extend CD as shown in the figure. We know that $\alpha = \angle DAB$ (alternate interior angles).
We also know that $\alpha + \angle ADC = 180°$. So $\alpha + 110 = 180° \Rightarrow$
$\alpha = \angle A = 180° – 110° = 70°$.

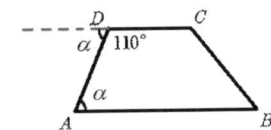

Problem 19. Solution: 22 (inches).

Draw $BF \perp DC$ at F.

Triangle ADE is a 30 – 60 – 90 right triangle. Thus DE = 2, AD = 4.

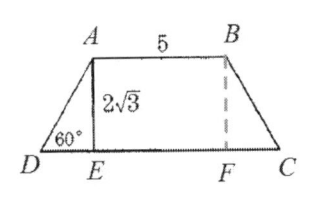

The perimeter is $AB + BC + DC + AD = 2AB + 2AD + 2DE = 2 \times 5 + 2 \times 4 + 2 \times 2 = 22$.

Problem 20. Solution: 4.

Triangle ABE is similar to triangle CDE.

So we have $\dfrac{DC}{AB} = \dfrac{CE}{AE} \Rightarrow \dfrac{a}{3a} = \dfrac{CE}{16 - CE}$

$\Rightarrow \dfrac{1}{CE} = \dfrac{4}{16 - CE} = \dfrac{4}{16} = \dfrac{1}{4} \Rightarrow CE = 4$.

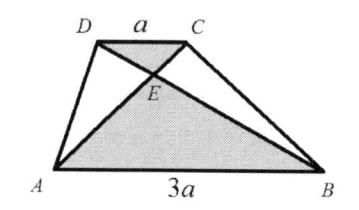

SOLUTIONS

Problem 1. Solution: 4 cm.
Let the height be x.
The area of $ABCD$ is $S_{ABCD} = DC \times x = 72 \Rightarrow 18 \times x = 72$
$\Rightarrow x = 4$.

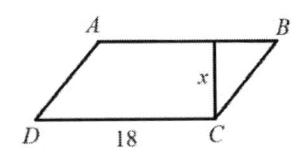

Problem 2. Solution: 3.
Let the other side be x.
The area of $ABCD$ is $S_{ABCD} = DC \times x = 36 \Rightarrow 12 \times x = 36$
$\Rightarrow x = 3$.

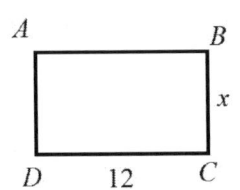

Problem 3. Solution: $8\sqrt{5}$ units.
Let $DB = 4\sqrt{5}$. Then $DE = 2\sqrt{5}$. $AD = 40/4 = 10$.
$AE = \sqrt{AD^2 - DE^2} = \sqrt{10^2 - (2\sqrt{5})^2} = \sqrt{100 - 20} = 4\sqrt{5}$.
The diagonal AC is $2 AE = 8\sqrt{5}$.

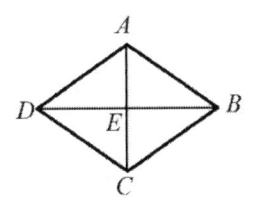

Problem 4. Solution: 65.
Extend CD as shown in the figure. We know that $x = \angle DAB$ (alternate interior angles). We also know that $x + \angle ADC = 180°$. So $x + 115 = 180° \Rightarrow x = \angle A = 180° - 115° = 65°$.

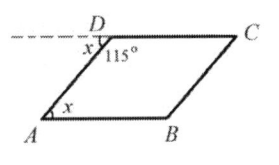

Problem 5. Solution: 12.
The square has the side length of $24/4 = 6$ and the area of $6^2 = 36$.
Let the length of the rectangle be x.
Since the rectangle's area is also 4, we have
$S_{ABCD} = AB \times BC = 36 \Rightarrow 3x = 36 \Rightarrow x = 12$.

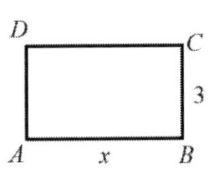

Problem 6. Solution: $4\sqrt{2}$ units.
Triangle ABD is an isoceles right triangle. So $8 = x\sqrt{2} \Rightarrow$

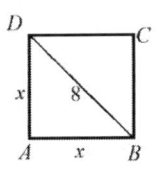

78

$x = \dfrac{8}{\sqrt{2}} = \dfrac{8\sqrt{2}}{2} = 4\sqrt{2}$.

Problem 7. Solution: 18 m.
Let the length and width of the rectangle be x and y.
$xy = 288$ \hfill (1)
$(x+2)y = 288 + 32 \Rightarrow xy + 2y = 320$ \hfill (2)
Substituting (1) into (2): $288 + 2y = 320 \Rightarrow$
$2y = 320 - 288 = 32 \Rightarrow y = 182$.

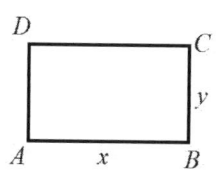

Problem 8. Solution: $3\sqrt{65}$.
Let the length and width of the rectangle be $4x$ and $7x$.
$4x \times 7x = 252 \Rightarrow x^2 = 9 \Rightarrow x = 3$.
The diagonal is $AC = \sqrt{AB^2 + BC^2} = \sqrt{21^2 + 12^2} = \sqrt{585} = 3\sqrt{65}$.

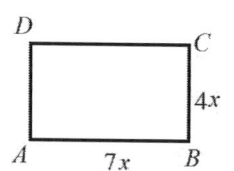

Problem 9. Solution: 46 units.
Triangle ABC is a $8 - 15 - 17$ right triangle. So the perimeter is
$2 \times 8 + 2 \times 15 = 46$.

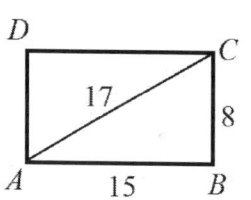

Problem 10. Solution: 1225 sq cm.
The greatest value of the area is $(144/4)^2 = 1296$.
The smallest value of the area is $[(144-2)/2] \times 1 = 71$.
The difference is $1296 - 71 = 1225$.

Problem 11. Solution: 26.
We need $6 \times 2 + 7 \times 2 = 12 + 14 = 26$.

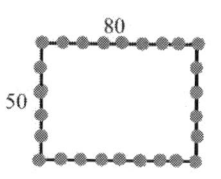

Problem 12. Solution: $6\sqrt{3}$ and $8\sqrt{3}$.
The area of the rectangle is $12 \times 12 = 144 = 4x \times 3x \Rightarrow x = 2\sqrt{3}$.
The dimensions, in inches, of the rectangle are $4x = 8\sqrt{3}$ and $3x = 6\sqrt{3}$.

Problem 13. Solution: $6\sqrt{3}$.
Triangle ABC is an equilateral triangle with the side length of 6.
The height of the triangle is $h = \frac{\sqrt{3}}{2}a = \frac{\sqrt{3}}{2} \times 6 = 3\sqrt{3}$.
The length of the other diagonal of the rhombus is $2h = 6\sqrt{3}$.

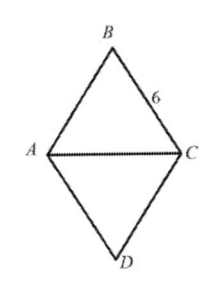

Problem 14. Solution: 90.
Extend BA as shown in the figure. We know that $x = \angle ADC$ (alternate interior angles). We also know that $x + \angle DAB = 180°$. So $x + 135 = 180°$ $\Rightarrow$ $x = 180° - 135° = 45°$.
The difference is $135° - 45° = 90°$.

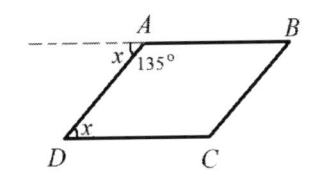

Problem 15. Solution: $7\sqrt{2}$.
Triangle ABD is an isoceles right triangle. So $x = x = 7\sqrt{2}$.

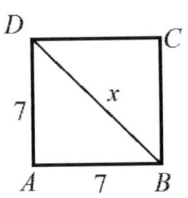

Problem 16. Solution: 26.
Let the length and width of the rectangle be $5x$ and $12x$.
$5x \times 12x = 240$ $\Rightarrow$ $x^2 = 4$ $\Rightarrow$ $x = 2$.
The diagonal is $AC = \sqrt{AB^2 + BC^2} = \sqrt{24^2 + 10^2} = \sqrt{676} = 26$.

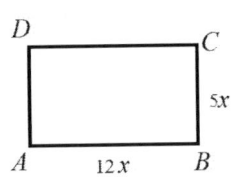

Problem 17. Solution: $3\sqrt{2}$.
Triangle ABC is an isoceles right triangle. So the diagonal is $AC = 6\sqrt{2}$.
We know that $BE = \frac{BD}{2} = \frac{AC}{2} = 3\sqrt{2}$.

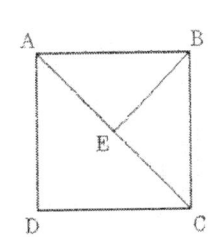

Problem 18. Solution: 118 (degrees).
Extend CD to E as shown in the figure. We know that $\angle ADE = \angle DAB = 62°$ (alternate interior angles). We also know that $x + \angle ADE = 180°$. So $x + 62 = 180°$ $\Rightarrow$ $x = 180° - 62° = 118°$.

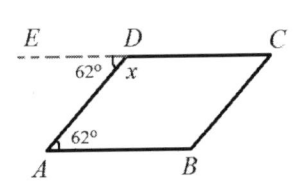

Problem 19. Solution: 26 (ft)
The sum of two adjacent sides is 39 + 52 = 91.
The diagonal is $\sqrt{39^2 + 52^2} = 65$.
The difference is 91 – 65 = 26.

Problem 20. Solution: 105 (degrees).
The sum of four interior angles of a parallelogram is 360.
The sum of two other opposite angles is 360 – 150 = 210.
One of the other angles IS 210/2 = 105.

Problem 21. Solution: 24 (in.)
Let the length and width of the rectangle be x and $3x$.
$2[(3x + 8) + (x + 8)] = 96 \quad \Rightarrow \quad x = 8$.
The length of the picture in inches is 24.

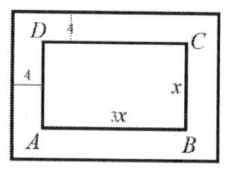

Problem 22. Solution: 50 : 29.
The ratio of the area of the larger square to the area of the smaller square is $\dfrac{10^2}{3^2 + 7^2} = \dfrac{50}{29}$.

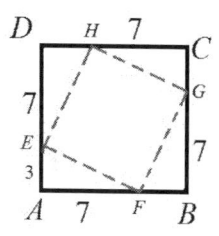

Problem 23. Solution: 6 (units).
Let x be the length of the other side.
$12\dfrac{1}{2} \times x = 75 \quad \Rightarrow \quad \dfrac{x}{2} = 3 \quad \Rightarrow \quad x = 6$.

Problem 24. Solution: 10 (cm).
The width is (28 – 8 × 2)/2 = 6.
The diagonal is $\sqrt{6^2 + 8^2} = 10$.

Problem 25. Solution: 29 (units).
Applying Pythagorean Theorem to triangle ABF:
$FB = \sqrt{AB^2 - AF^2} = \sqrt{25^2 - 15^2} = 20$

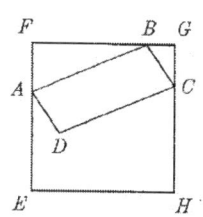

Applying Pythagorean Theorem to triangle *BCG*:
$BG = \sqrt{BC^2 - CG^2} = \sqrt{15^2 - 12^2} = 9$.
The answer is 20 + 9 = 29.

Problem 26. Solution: 130 (degrees).
Let the parallelogram be *ABCD*. Extend *CD* to *E* as shown in the figure. We know that $\angle ADE = \angle DAB = 50°$ (alternate interior angles). We also know that $x + \angle ADE = 180°$. So $x + 50 = 180°$ $\Rightarrow$ $x = 180° - 50° = 130°$.

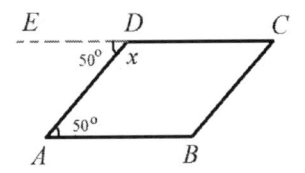

Problem 27. Solution: 4 (in.).
Let *x* be the length of the side.
$x^2 = 4x$ $\Rightarrow$ $x^2 - 4x =$ $\Rightarrow$ $x(x - 4) = 0$.
Since $x \neq 0$, $x = 4$.

Problem 28. Solution: 12 (cm).
Let x_1 be the length of the original rectangle and x_2 be the length of the new rectangle.
$\frac{S_2}{S_1} = (\frac{x_2}{x_1})^2$ $\Rightarrow$ $\frac{1.44 S_1}{S_1} = (\frac{x_2}{x_1})^2$ $\Rightarrow$ $1.44 = (\frac{x_2}{x_1})^2$ $\Rightarrow$ $\frac{x_2}{x_1} = 1.2$
$\Rightarrow$ $\frac{x_2}{10} = 1.2 \Rightarrow$ $x_2 = 12$.

Problem 29. Solution: $4 + 2\pi$ (units).
The perimeter the semicircular region is $\frac{2\pi \times 8}{2} + 8 \times 2$.

Let 4*x* be the perimeter the square and *x* be the length of a side of the square.
$4x = \frac{2\pi \times 8}{2} + 8 \times 2$ $\Rightarrow$ $x = 4 + 2\pi$ (units).

Problem 30. Solution: $\frac{3}{10}$.

The ratio is $\frac{3 \times 5}{5 \times 10} = \frac{3}{10}$.

Problem 31. Solution: $\frac{8}{3}$.

Since $\angle PMQ$ is a right angle, triangle PBM is similar to triangle MCQ.

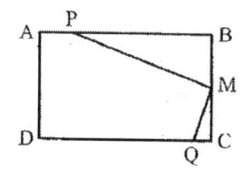

$$\frac{PM}{MQ} = \frac{PB}{MC} \Rightarrow \frac{PM}{MQ} = \frac{PB}{\frac{1}{2}BC} = \frac{2PB}{BC} = 2 \times \frac{4}{3} = \frac{8}{3}.$$

Problem 32. Solution: 27.

We know that $\angle DEC = 45°$. Since $\angle DEC + \angle AEF = 90°$, $\angle AEF = 90° - \angle DEC = 45°$. Similarly, all the triangles are isosceles right triangles ($\triangle AEF$, $\triangle FBH$, $\triangle CGH$).

Thus $CH = BH = BF = \sqrt{2} \times HG = 3\sqrt{2}$. $FH = \sqrt{2} \times BH = \sqrt{2} \times 3\sqrt{2} = 6$.

The area of rectangle $CEFG$ is $FG \times CG = (6+3) \times 3 = 27$.

We also know that $AE = AF = \frac{EF}{\sqrt{2}} = \frac{CG}{\sqrt{2}} = \frac{3}{\sqrt{2}} = \frac{3\sqrt{2}}{2}$.

The area of rectangle $ABCD$ is

$$AB \times BC = (AF + FB)BC = (\frac{3\sqrt{2}}{2} + 3\sqrt{2}) \times (3\sqrt{2} \times 2) = 54.$$

The answer is $54 - 27 = 27$.

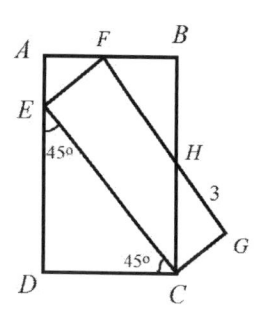

Problem 33. Solution: $\frac{1}{2}$.

Since $\angle ACD = \angle CAB = 45°$ and $\angle AOB = \angle COM$, triangle ABO is similar to triangle CMO.

$$\frac{AB}{CM} = \frac{OA}{OC} \Rightarrow \frac{OA}{OC} = \frac{AB}{\frac{CD}{2}} = \frac{AB}{\frac{AB}{2}} = \frac{1}{2}.$$

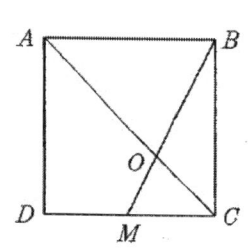

Problem 34. Solution: 12 (centimeters).

Let $DB = x$, $AC = y$
We have $x + y = 28$ (1)

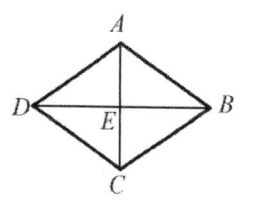

Since $\dfrac{DB \times AC}{2} = 96 \Rightarrow DB \times AC = 192 \Rightarrow xy = 192$ (2)

We see that x and y are the two roots of quadratic equation $t^2 - 28t + 192 = 0 \Rightarrow (t-12)(t-16) = 0$.

So $DB = 16$ and $AC = 12$. The answer is 12 since we want to find the length of the shorter diagonal.

50 Lectures for Mathcounts Competitions   (32) Angle Bisector And Median

SOLUTIONS

Problem 1. Solution: $3\sqrt{2}$.

Since CD is the perpendicular bisector of segment AB, $\angle ADC = 90°$. Since $\angle A = 45°$, $\angle ACD = 90° - 45° = 45°$ as well. So triangle ACD is a isosceles right triangle and $AC = \sqrt{2}AD = 3\sqrt{2}$.

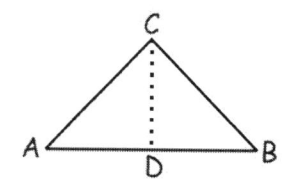

Problem 2. Solution: 16.

$BD = \dfrac{2}{3} BG = \dfrac{2}{3} \cdot 24 = 16$.

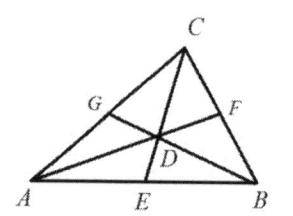

Problem 3. Solution: $12\sqrt{3}$.

In the adjoining figure MV is an altitude of ΔABV. Since ΔAMV is a $30° - 60° - 90°$ triangle, MV ha length $2\sqrt{3}$. The required area is, therefore, area

$\Delta ABV = \dfrac{1}{2}(AB)(MV) = \dfrac{1}{2} \cdot 12 \cdot 2\sqrt{3} = 12\sqrt{3}$.

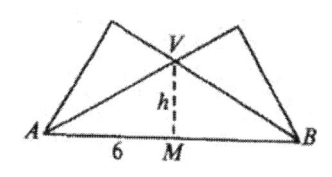

Problem 4. Solution: 8.

Applying Pythagorean Theorem to ΔBCE:

$CE^2 + BC^2 = BE^2 \quad \Rightarrow \quad CE^2 + BC^2 = (2\sqrt{11})^2 = 44$

$\Rightarrow \quad \dfrac{1}{4} AC^2 + BC^2 = 44$ \hfill (1)

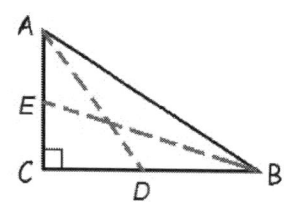

Applying Pythagorean Theorem to ΔDCA:

$AC^2 + CD^2 = AD^2 \quad \Rightarrow \quad AC^2 + CD^2 = 6^2 = 36 \quad \Rightarrow \quad AC^2 + \dfrac{1}{4} BC^2 = 36$ \hfill (2)

(1) + (2): $\dfrac{5}{4} AC^2 + \dfrac{5}{4} BC^2 = 80 \quad \Rightarrow \quad AC^2 + BC^2 = 64 = 8^2$ \hfill (3)

Applying Pythagorean Theorem to ΔBCA:

$AC^2 + BC^2 = AB^2$ \hfill (4)

Substituting (3) into (4): $8^2 = AB^2 \quad \Rightarrow \quad AB = 8$.

Problem 5. Solution: 10.06.

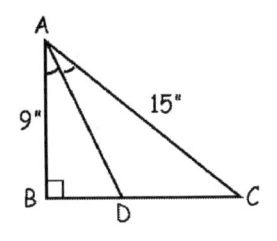

Right triangle ABC is a $9 - 12 - 15$ triangle.
Let $BD = x$.
By the angle bisector theorem,
$$\frac{AB}{BD} = \frac{AC}{CD} \Rightarrow \frac{9}{x} = \frac{15}{BC - BD} = \frac{15}{12 - x} = \frac{9 + 15}{12} \Rightarrow$$
$$\frac{9}{x} = \frac{24}{12} = 2 \Rightarrow x = \frac{9}{2}.$$
Applying Pythagorean Theorem to $\triangle ABD$:
$$AD = \sqrt{AB^2 + BD^2} = \sqrt{9^2 + (\frac{9}{2})^2} \approx 10.06.$$

Problem 6. Solution: 75. 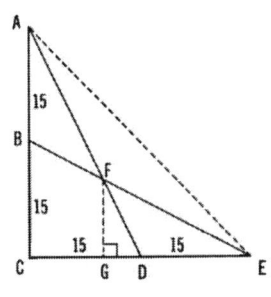
Method 1 (official solution):
Draw AE and the altitude FG to the base DE of triangle DEF.
Since F is the intersection point of the medians of a triangle
ACE, $FD = \frac{1}{3} AD$. $\therefore FG = \frac{1}{3} AC = \frac{1}{3} \cdot 30 = 10$.

$\therefore$ area $(\triangle DEF) = \frac{1}{2} \cdot 15 \cdot 10 = 75$.

The three medians of a triangle divide the triangle into six
triangles of equal area. Therefore, Area $(\triangle FDE) = 75$.

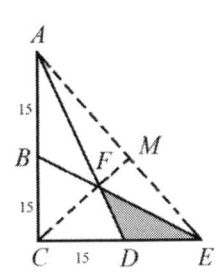

Method 2 (our solution):
Connect AE. Then connect CF and extend it to meet AE at M.
F is the centroid and triangle ACE is divided into six smaller triangles
with the same area.

The area of $(\triangle ACD) = \frac{1}{2} \cdot 30 \cdot 15 = 225$.

The area of $(\triangle FDE) = \frac{225}{3} = 75$.

Problem 7. Solution: 5:19.
Let the line through M parallel to side AB of the square intersect sides AD and BC in

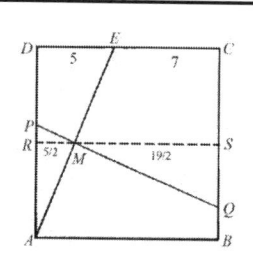

points R and S, respectively. Since M is the midpoint of AE, $RM = \frac{1}{2}DE = \frac{5}{2}$ inches, and therefore $MS = 12 - \frac{5}{2} = \frac{19}{2}$ inches. Since PMR and QMS are similar right triangles, the required ratio $PM:MQ = RM:MS = 5:19$ because corresponding sides of similar triangles are proportional.

Problem 8. Solution: $4\sqrt{2}$. 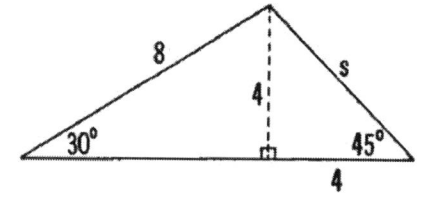
Let s denote the length of the side we want to figure out (see figure to the right). The altitude to the longest side, opposite the 30° angle, has length $\frac{8}{2} = 4$ and is also one leg of an isosceles right triangle with hypotenuse s, which therefore has length $4\sqrt{2}$.

Problem 9. Solution: $4K$. 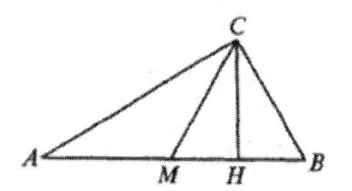
Right triangle CHM and CHB are congruent since their angles at C are equal. Therefore the base MH of $\triangle CMH$ is ¼ $\frac{1}{4}$ of the base AB of $\triangle ABC$, while their altitudes are equal.
Hence the area of $\triangle ABC$ is $4K$.

Problem 10. Solution: 36.

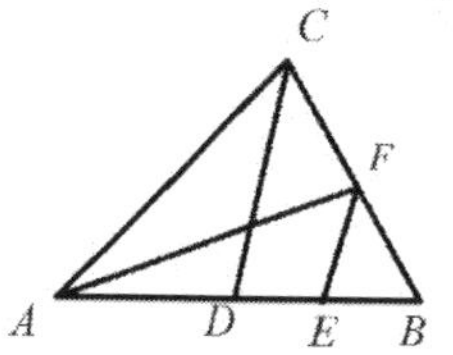

The area of $\triangle AFB$ is 48, $\frac{1}{2}$ the area of $\triangle ABC$.

$$\frac{S_{\triangle AFE}}{S_{\triangle AFB}} = \frac{AE}{AB} = \frac{3}{4} \quad \Rightarrow \quad S_{\triangle AFE} = \frac{3}{4}S_{\triangle AFB} = \frac{3}{4} \times 48 = 36.$$

Problem 11. Solution: a. 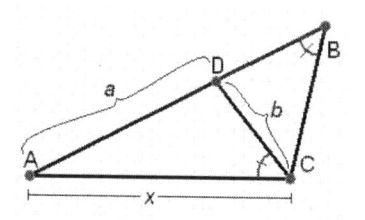
Let $BC = y$.
By the angle bisector theorem, we have
$$\frac{x}{a} = \frac{y}{b} \quad \Rightarrow \quad ay = bx \quad (1)$$
By the angle bisector length formula, we have

87

$b^2 = xy - ab \Rightarrow xy = ab + b^2$ (2)

(2) ÷ (1): $\dfrac{x}{a} = \dfrac{b^2 + ab}{bx} \Rightarrow x^2 = a(b+a) \Rightarrow x = \sqrt{a(b+a)}$.

Problem 12. Solution: $\sqrt[3]{2}$
Draw DG so that $DG \perp BC$ and G lies on BC. Let $AC = x$ and $GC = y$. Note that $BC = 2y$, since $\triangle BCD$ is isosceles.
Since $\triangle DCG \sim \triangle ACF \sim \triangle BCA$, we obtain the equal ratios:
$\dfrac{1}{y} = \dfrac{x}{1} = \dfrac{2y}{x}$.

Thus $y = \dfrac{1}{x}$ and $y = \dfrac{x^2}{2}$, implying that

$x^3 = 2$, or $x = \sqrt[3]{2}$.

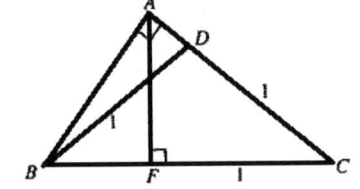

Problem 13. Solution: 23.
Method 1 (official solution):
Let the angle opposite to the side of length 25 be θ and the length of the third side be x.
Then the law of cosines tells us
$25^2 = 20^2 + 4x^2 - 80x \cos\theta$ and $19.5^2 = 20^2 + x^2 - 40x \cos\theta$.
Multiplying the second equation by negative two and adding the two equations gives
$25^2 - 2 \times 19.5^2 = -20^2 + 2x^2$.
Solving for x, $x = 11.5$. Hence the third side is 23.

Method 2 (our solution):

Let the length of the third side be $2x$.
By Theorem 5 (The median length formula):
$(19.5^2) + (19.5^2) = (20^2 - x^2) + (25^2 - x^2) \Rightarrow 760.5 = 1025 - 2x^2 \Rightarrow$
$2x^2 = 1025 - 760.5 = 264.5 \Rightarrow x^2 = 1025 - 760.5 = 132.25 \Rightarrow$
$(x - 11.5)(x + 11.5) = 0 \Rightarrow x = 11.5$.
The length of the third side is $2x = 2 \times 11.5 = 23$.

50 Lectures for Mathcounts Competitions   (32) Angle Bisector And Median

Problem 14. Solution: 26.

Let $OM = a$ and $ON = b$. Then $19^2 = (2a)^2 + b^2$ and $22^2 = a^2 + (2b)^2$.

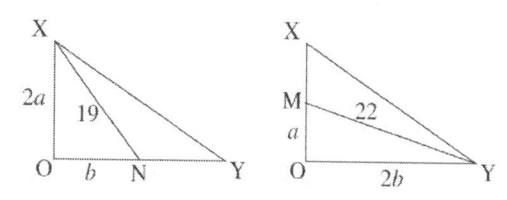

Hence
$5(a^2 + b^2) = 19^2 + 22^2 = 845$.

It follows that $MN = \sqrt{a^2 + b^2} = \sqrt{169} = 13$

$MN = \sqrt{a^2+b^2} = \sqrt{169} = 13$.

Since $\triangle XOY$ is similar to $\triangle MON$ and $XO = 2 \cdot MO$, we have $XY = 2 \cdot MN = 26$.

Problem 15. Solution: $14\sqrt{5}$.

By the angle-bisector theorem, $AB/BC = 9/7$. Let $AB = 9x$ and $BC = 7x$, let $m\angle ABD = m\angle CBD = \theta$, and let M be the midpoint of BC. Since M is on the perpendicular bisector of BC, we have $BD = DC = 7$.

Then $\cos\theta = \dfrac{\frac{7x}{2}}{7} = \dfrac{x}{2}$.

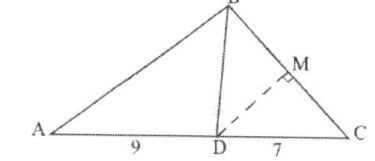

Applying the Law of Cosines to $\triangle ABD$ yields
$9^2 = (9x)^2 + 7^2 - 2(9x)(7)(x/2)$
from which $x = 4/3$ and $AB = 12$. Apply Heron's formula to obtain the area of triangle ABD as $\sqrt{14 \cdot 2 \cdot 5 \cdot 7} = 14\sqrt{5}$.

Problem 16. Solution: $\dfrac{\sqrt{5}-1}{2}$.

By the Pythagorean Theorem, $AC = \sqrt{5}$. By the Angle Bisector Theorem, $\dfrac{BD}{AB} = \dfrac{CD}{AC}$.

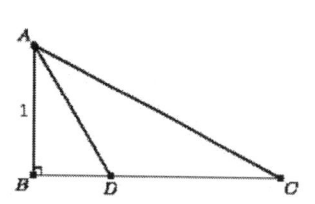

Therefore $CD = \sqrt{5}$ and $BD + CD = 2$. $BD = \dfrac{2}{1+\sqrt{5}} = \dfrac{\sqrt{5}-1}{2}$.

SOLUTIONS

Problem 1. Solution: 3.
We have $(n+2)^2 + (4n)^2 = (5n-2)^2 \Rightarrow n^2 + 4n + 4 + 16n^2 = 25n^2 - 20n + 4$.
$\Rightarrow 8n^2 - 24n = 0 \Rightarrow n^2 - 3n = 0 \Rightarrow n(n-3) = 0$.
Since $n \neq 0$, $n = 3$.

Problem 2. Solution: 60.
The first triangle is a $20 - 21 - 29$ right triangle.
Let the shortest side of the second triangle be x.
Since both similar triangles are similar, we have $\dfrac{29}{87} = \dfrac{20}{x} \Rightarrow x = \dfrac{87 \times 20}{29} = 60$.

Problem 3. Solution: 188.
We know that $AC < \dfrac{P}{2} = \dfrac{384}{2} = 192$. So at most $AC = 191$.
$BC = 190$. $AB = 384 - 191 - 190 = 3$.
The answer is $191 - 3 = 188$.

Problem 4. Solution: 3.
By the triangle inequality theorem, the sum of any two sides is greater than the third side. We can form three non-congruent triangles: (5, 5, 8), (5, 14, 14), and (8, 14, 14).

Problem 5. Solution: 24.
The least possible perimeter of the triangle should be greater than 21. We try 22. Since the sum of 3 prime numbers is eve, 2 must be one of them. The triangle with the sides 2, 7, 7 does not have a perimeter greater than 21. Next will be (2, 11, 11) and this one works. The perimeter is $2 + 11 + 11 = 24$. For the perimeter 23, we indeed have $5 + 7 + 11 = 23$ which is less than 21 but 23 is a prime. So 24 is our answer.

Problem 6. Solution: 11.
We notice that $3x - 13 > 0$ or $x > 13/3 > 4$. We see that $3x - 4 - (3x - 13) = 9 > 0$. We also see that $3x - 4 - (2x - 1) = x - 3 > 0$ as well. So we know that $3x - 4$ is the hypotenuse.

Applying Pythagorean Theorem, we have $(2x - 1)^2 + (3x - 13)^2 = (3x - 4)^2$.
Solving we get: $x = 11$ and $x = 7/2$ (ignored since x is less than 4).
So the answer is 11.

Problem 7. Solution: 4.
We know that we can have (3, 4, 5), (6, 8, 10), (9, 12, 15), and (5, 12, 13).

Problem 8. Solution: $3\sqrt{2}$.
If $x \geq \sqrt{5}$, we have $(\sqrt{3})^2 + (\sqrt{5})^2 = x^2$ $\Rightarrow$ $8 = x^2 \Rightarrow x = 2\sqrt{2}$.
If $x < \sqrt{5}$, we have $(\sqrt{3})^2 + x^2 = (\sqrt{5})^2$ $\Rightarrow$ $2 = x^2 \Rightarrow x = \sqrt{2}$.
The answer is $2\sqrt{2} + \sqrt{2} = 3\sqrt{2}$.

Problem 9. Solution: 23.
We see that
$3 + 5 + 7 = 15$ (The perimeter is not a prime number)
$3 + 5 + 11 = 19$ (The perimeter is a prime number but 3. 5.11 will not be able to form a triangle).

$5 + 7 + 11 = 23$ (The perimeter is a prime number and 5, 7, 11 will be able to form a triangle).

So 23 is the answer.

Problem 10. Solution: 84.
$(7a)^2 + (7b)^2 = (7c)^2$
The smallest Pythagorean triple (a, b, c) is (3, 4, 5).
The smallest possible perimeter is $7(3 + 4 + 5) = 7 \times 12 = 84$.

Problem 11. Solution: 2.
If $10 - n$ is the longest side, by Triangle Inequality Theorem, $2n + 3n > 10 - n \Rightarrow n > 5/3$.

If $3n$ is the longest side, by Triangle Inequality Theorem, $2n + 10 - n > 3n \Rightarrow n < 5$.

So n can only be 2, 3, or 4.

If $10-n$ is the longest side, we have $(2n)^2 +(3n)^2 < (10-n)^2 \Rightarrow n(3n+5) < 25$.

So $n = 2$ and 1 (ignored since it is not one of three numbers: 2, 34, and 4).

If $3n$ is the longest side, we have $(2n)^2 +(10-n)^2 < (3n)^2 \Rightarrow n(n+5) > 25$.

So $n = 4$ is the only solution.

The answer is 2.

Problem 12. Solution: 15.

The hypotenuse is $\sqrt{2}\ A(2-\sqrt{2}) = A(2\sqrt{2}-2)$.

So we have $A(2-\sqrt{2}) + A(2-\sqrt{2}) + A(2\sqrt{2}-2) = 30 \Rightarrow$

$A(2-\sqrt{2}+2-\sqrt{2}+2\sqrt{2}-2) = 30 \quad\Rightarrow\quad 2A = 30 \quad\Rightarrow\quad A = 15$.

Problem 13. Solution: 81.

By Triangle Inequality Theorem, we have $9 - 5 < n < 9 + 5 \Rightarrow 4 < x < 14$. So the answer is $5 + 6 + 7 + 8 + 9 + 10 + 11 + 12 + 13 = 81$.

Problem 14. Solution: 7.

Let a, $a + 2$, and b be the three sides.

By Triangle Inequality Theorem, $a + b > a + 2 \quad\Rightarrow\quad b > 2$.

The perimeter is $P = a + a + 2 + b = 2a + 2 + b$.

Since $b > 2$, $P > 2a + 2 + 2$. The smallest value of a is 1. Thus $P > 6$. The least possible perimeter of the triangle is 7.

Problem 15. Solution: 13.

By Triangle Inequality Theorem, we have $13 - 8 < n < 13 + 8 \Rightarrow 5 < x < 21$. So the possible values are 6, 7, 8, 9, 10, 11, 12, 13, 14, 15, 16, 17, 18, 19, 20.
The median is 13.

Problem 16. Solution: 14.

By Triangle Inequality Theorem, we have $36 - 8 < n < 36 + 8 \Rightarrow 28 < x < 44$. So the greatest possible whole number length could be 43 and the least possible whole number length could be 29.

The positive difference is 43 – 29 = 14.

Problem 17. Solution: 1192.
The perimeter is $6x + 40 + 4x + 104 + 7x - 23 = 17x + 121$.
If $6x + 40 = 4x + 104$, $x = 32$ and $P = 17x + 121$

The perimeter is $6x + 40 + 4x + 104 + 7x - 23 = 17x + 121$.
If $6x + 40 = 4x + 104$, $x = 32$.
If $6x + 40 = 7x - 23$, $x = 63$.
If $4x + 104 = 7x - 23$, x is not integer.
So the greatest possible perimeter is $P = 17 \times 63 + 121 = 1192$.

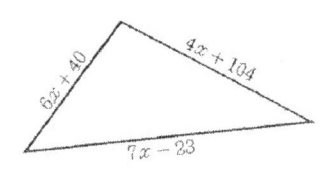

Problem 18. Solution: 7.
$m^2 + n^2 = 29$ (1)
$2mn = 20$ (2)
$m^2 - n^2 = 21$ (3)
(1) + (2): $(m+n)^2 = 49$ $\Rightarrow$ $m + n = 7$.

Problem 19. Solution: 80 (degrees).
The sum of three angles of a triangle is 180°.

The measure of the largest angle facing the longest side 1/3 is $\dfrac{\frac{1}{3}}{\frac{1}{3}+\frac{1}{4}+\frac{1}{6}} \times 180° = 80°$.

Problem 20. Solution: $24 - 8\sqrt{3}$.
$AB = 2BC = 2 \times 12 = 24$.
$ED = 2\,ED = \dfrac{2FD}{\sqrt{3}} = \dfrac{24}{\sqrt{3}} = 8\sqrt{3}$.
The answer is $24 - 8\sqrt{3}$.

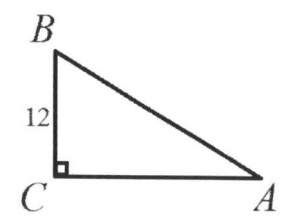

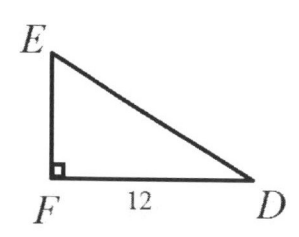

50 Lectures for Mathcounts Competitions (34) Area Method

SOLUTIONS

Problem 1. Solution: 50 (percent). 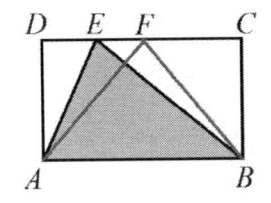
Method 1:
The shaded area / the rectangle area

$$= \frac{\frac{1}{2} L \times H}{LH} = 0.5 = 50\%.$$

Method 2:
Let F be the midpoint of DC. Connect FA and FB.

Then $S_{\triangle ABE} = S_{\triangle ABF} = \frac{1}{2} S_{\triangle ABCD}$. $\frac{S_{\triangle ABF}}{S_{\triangle ABCD}} = \frac{1}{2} = 50\%$

Problem 2. Solution: 16 sq units 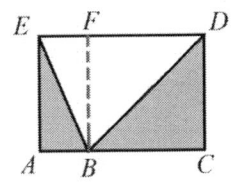
Draw $FB \perp AC$. We know that $S_{\triangle ABE} = S_{\triangle FBE}$ and $S_{\triangle BCD} = S_{\triangle BFD}$.

Thus the area of the shaded region is $\frac{1}{2} S_{ABCD} = \frac{1}{2} \times 4 \times 8 = 16$.

Problem 3. Solution: 36. 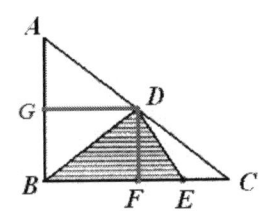
The area of triangle ABC is $12 \times 16/2 = 96$.
Let G be the midpoint of AB. Connect DG, DF.

The area of triangle BDF is $\frac{1}{4} S_{\triangle ABC} = 24$.

The area of triangle DEF is $\frac{1}{2} S_{DEF} = \frac{1}{8} S_{\triangle ABC} = 12$.

The answer is $24 + 12 = 36$.

Problem 4. Solution: $\frac{1}{3}$.

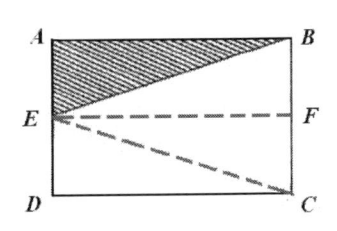

Draw $EF \parallel CD$. Connect CE. The four triangles in the figure shown have the congruent area.

94

The answer is then $\frac{1}{3}$.

Problem 5. Solution: Solution: 16 (units²).
Since triangles *ABD* and *ACD* have the same height and the same base, their areas are the same. $A_{\triangle ABC} = A_{\triangle ABD} + A_{\triangle ADC} = 8 + 8 = 16$

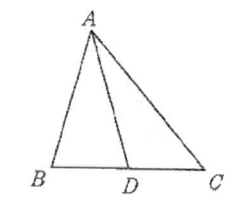

Problem 6. Solution: 1/4.
Since triangles *ABE* and *BED* have the same height and the same base, their areas are the same. Triangles *ABD* and *BCD* have the same areas as well.
The answer is then $\frac{1}{4}$. 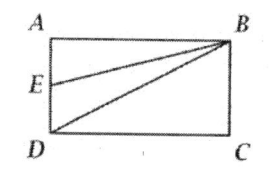

Problem 7. Solution: 60.
The triangle is a 8 – 15 – 17 right triangle with two legs 8 and 15. The area is 8 × 15 / 2 = 60.

Problem 8. Solution: $\frac{\sqrt{3}}{4}$.
The folded region is the triangle *MNP*. The area of triangle *MNP* is
$\frac{1}{4} S_{\triangle ABC} = \frac{1}{4} \times \frac{\sqrt{3}}{4} \times (2)^2 = \frac{\sqrt{3}}{4}$.

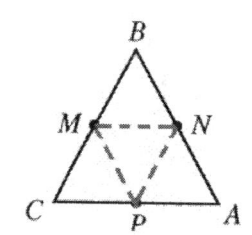

Problem 9. Solution: $\frac{1}{3}$.
$\dfrac{S_{\triangle ACE}}{S_{ABCD}} = \dfrac{\frac{1}{2} \times 2a \times CD}{3a \times cd} = \dfrac{2}{6} = \dfrac{1}{3}$.

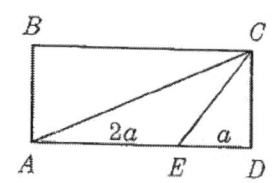

Problem 10. Solution: $\frac{1}{3}$.
Let *F* be the midpoint of *ED*. Connect *BF*.

Triangles *BCF, BEF,* and *BFD* have the same areas, and each is 1/6 of the area of *ABCD*.

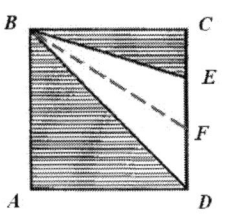

So $\dfrac{S_{\triangle BED}}{S_{ABCD}} = \dfrac{2}{6} = \dfrac{1}{3}$.

Problem 11. Solution: $\dfrac{2}{3}\sqrt{3}$ (cm^2).

Method 1:

Connect *CE*. Label each region as shown in figure 1.

$\dfrac{S_{\triangle ACE}}{S_{\triangle BCE}} = \dfrac{AE}{EB} = 1 \quad \Rightarrow \quad S_{\triangle ACE} = S_{\triangle BCE} = x + z.$

$\dfrac{S_{\triangle BEC}}{S_{\triangle DCE}} = \dfrac{BC}{CD} = 1 \quad \Rightarrow \quad S_{\triangle BCE} = S_{\triangle DCE} = x + z = y + z.$ So $y = x$.

Connect *BF*. Label each region as shown in figure 2.

We know that $y = x$. So all four triangles have the same area.

We know that $x = \dfrac{1}{3} \times \dfrac{2^2}{4}\sqrt{3} = \dfrac{1}{3}\sqrt{3}$.

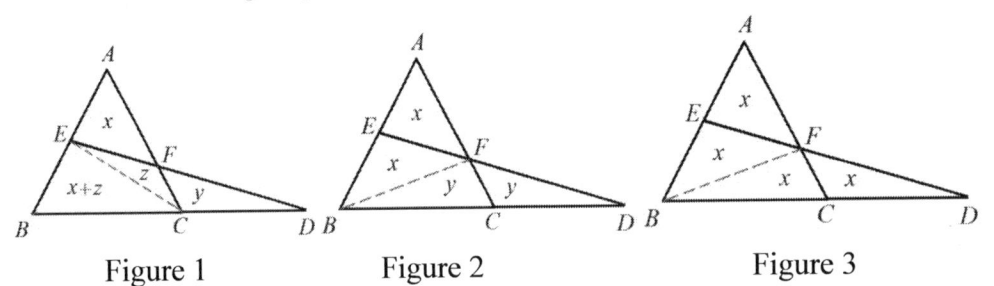

Figure 1 Figure 2 Figure 3

Method 2:

Connect *AD* and *BG*. *F* is the centroid and six smaller triangles have the same area.

So $3x = \dfrac{2^2}{4}\sqrt{3} = \sqrt{3} \Rightarrow x = \dfrac{\sqrt{3}}{3} \Rightarrow 2x = \dfrac{2\sqrt{3}}{3}$.

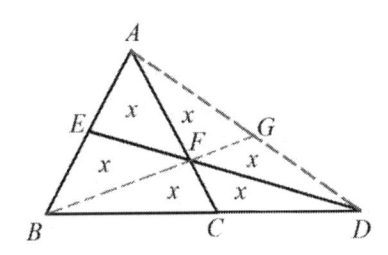

Problem 12. Solution: $\frac{45}{2}$ (units^2).

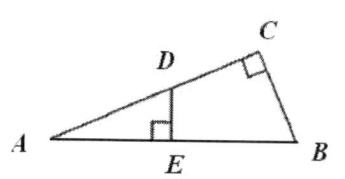

Let the area of triangle ABC be $S_{\triangle ABC}$, the area of ADE be $S_{\triangle ADE}$, and the area of quadrilateral $EBCD$ be $S_{\triangle EBCD}$.

The triangle ABC is a 5-12-13 right triangle and it is similar to triangle ADE, so:

$$\frac{S_{\triangle ADE}}{S_{\triangle ABC}} = \left(\frac{AE}{AC}\right)^2 = \left(\frac{6}{12}\right)^2 = \frac{1}{4} \Rightarrow S_{\triangle ADE} = \frac{1}{4} \times S_{\triangle ABC} = \frac{1}{4} \times \frac{5 \times 12}{2} = \frac{15}{2}$$

$$S_{EBCD} = S_{\triangle ABC} - S_{\triangle ADE} = \frac{5 \times 12}{2} - \frac{15}{2} = \frac{60-15}{2} = \frac{45}{2}.$$

Problem 13. Solution: 24 (units^2).

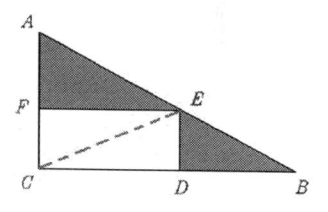

The area of triangle ABC is $\frac{1}{2} \times 8 \times 12 = 48$.

Connect CE. The four triangles in the figure shown have the congruent area.

The answer is then $\frac{48}{2} = 24$.

Problem 14. Solution: 12 sq units.

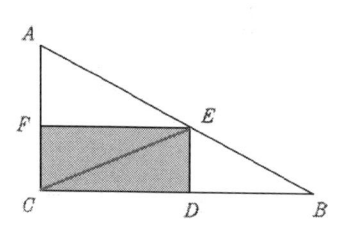

The area of triangle ABC is $\frac{1}{2} \times 8 \times 6 = 24$.

Connect CE. The four triangles in the figure shown have the congruent area.

The answer is then $\frac{24}{2} = 12$.

Problem 15. Solution: 24 (units^2).

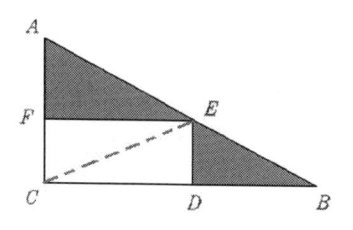

The area of triangle ABC is 48.

Connect CE. The four triangles in the figure shown have the congruent area.

The answer is then $\frac{48}{2} = 24$.

50 Lectures for Mathcounts Competitions   **(34) Area Method**

Problem 16. Solution: 12 sq units.
The area of triangle *ABC* is 24.
Connect *CE*. The four triangles in the figure shown have the congruent area.
The answer is then $\frac{24}{2} = 12$.

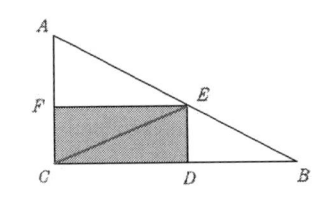

Problem 17. Solution: 75 (%).
Triangle *ABE* is $\frac{1}{4}$ of rectangle *ABCD* and *ADC* is $\frac{1}{2}$ of rectangle *ABCD*. The shaded area is $\frac{1}{4} + \frac{1}{2} = \frac{3}{4}$ of rectangle *ABCD*. $\frac{3}{4}$ = 75 (%).

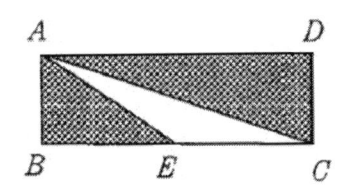

Problem 18. Solution: 20 (square centimeters).

The area of rectangle *ABCD* is 16 × 5 = 80.
Draw $PQ \perp DC$.
We see that the two shaded areas have the same area.
So the given figure can be converted in to the figure below.
The shaded area is 2/8 = 1/4. 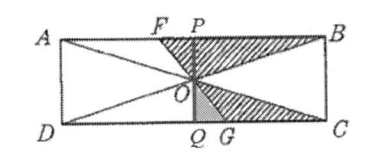
The answer is then 2/8 = 1/4 of the area of rectangle *ABCD*. So the answer is $\frac{1}{4}$ × 80 = 20.

Problem 19. Solution: 10.
The area of square *ABCD* is 6 × 6 = 36.
Triangles *ABE* is 36/3 = 12 = $\frac{6 \times BE}{2}$. So *BE* = 4. Thus *CF* = 4 as well. We then know that *EC* = *CF* = 2.
The area of triangle *CEF* is $\frac{1}{2} \times 2 \times 2 = 2$.
The area of $\triangle AEF$ is 12 − 2 = 10.

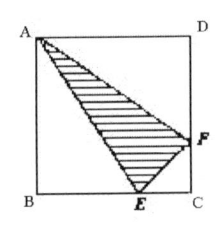

98

Problem 20. Solution: 2/3.
Connect BD.
Since triangle ABC and triangle ABD share the same height, and $DC = \frac{2}{3} AC$, $\triangle BDC$ have the same area 2/3.

Similarly, $\triangle BDC$ and $\triangle CDE$ have the same area. So the area of triangle CDE = 2/3.

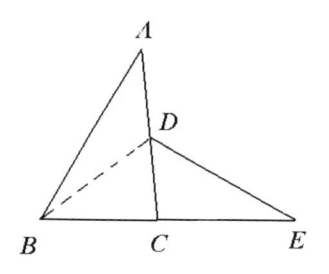

Problem 21. Solution: 18.

$\dfrac{S_{\triangle BDE}}{S_{\triangle ADE}} = \dfrac{5x}{x} = 5 \quad \Rightarrow \quad S_{\triangle BDE} = 5 \times S_{\triangle ABC} = 5 \times 1 = 5$

$\dfrac{S_{\triangle CBE}}{S_{\triangle ABE}} = \dfrac{2y}{y} = 2 \quad \Rightarrow \quad S_{\triangle CBE} = 2 \times S_{\triangle ABE} = 2 \times 6 = 12$.

The answer is $1 + 5 + 12 = 18$.

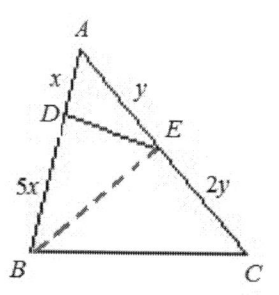

Problem 22. Solution: 2.

$S_{\triangle ABD} = \dfrac{2}{3} S_{\triangle ABC} = \dfrac{2}{3} \times 5 = \dfrac{10}{3}$. $S_{\triangle ACD} = 5 - \dfrac{10}{3} = \dfrac{5}{3}$.

Connect DF. Let x denote the area of $\triangle AEF$ and y denote the area of $\triangle DCF$.
Then we have $2x + y = 5/3$ \hfill (1)

Since $BD = \dfrac{2}{3} BC$, $\dfrac{BD}{BC} = \dfrac{2}{3}$ and $\dfrac{BD}{DC} = \dfrac{2}{1} = 2$

$x + 5/3 = 2y$ \hfill (2)

Solving the system of equations (1) and (2): $x = 1/3$.

The answer is $x + \dfrac{5}{3} = \dfrac{1}{3} + \dfrac{5}{3} = 2$.

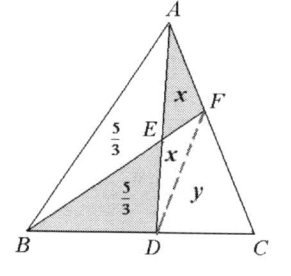

Problem 23. Solution: 75/8.
Method 1:
Triangle ABC is a 6 – 8 – 10 right triangle. So $AM = AC/2$

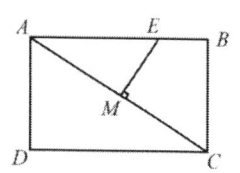

99

= 10/2 = 5.
Triangle *ABC* is similar to triangle *AME*.

$$\frac{S_{\triangle AME}}{S_{\triangle ABC}} = (\frac{AM}{AB})^2 = (\frac{5}{8})^2 = \frac{25}{64} \Rightarrow S_{\triangle AME} = \frac{1}{4}S_{\triangle ABC} = \frac{25}{64} \times \frac{1}{2} \times 6 \times 8 = \frac{78}{8}.$$

Problem 24. Solution: 315.
Method 1 (Official Solution):
Let the areas of two unknown triangles be *x* and *y*.
By Theorem 9:

$$\frac{40}{30} = \frac{40 + y + 84}{30 + 35 + x} \quad (1)$$

$$\frac{35}{x} = \frac{35 + 30 + 40}{x + 84 + y} \quad (2)$$

$$\frac{84}{y} = \frac{84 + x + 35}{y + 40 + 30} \quad (3)$$

Solving we get: $x = 70$, $y = 56$.

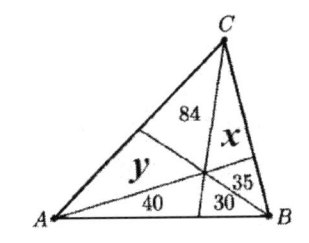

The area is then $30 + 35 + 70 + 84 + 56 + 40 = 315$.

Method 2 (our solution):
We label the points *D* and *E* as shown in the figure.
Looking at triangles *ADC* and *BDC*, by the Theorem 5, we have

$$\frac{84 + m}{n + 35} = \frac{40}{30} \quad (1)$$

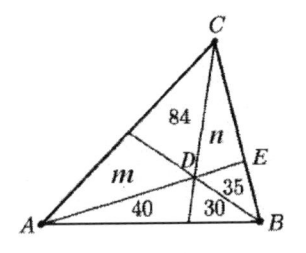

Looking at triangles *ADB* and *DEB*, by the Theorem 3, we have

$$\frac{AD}{DE} = \frac{40 + 30}{35} = 2.$$

Looking at triangles *ADC* and *DEC*, by the Theorem 3, we have

$$\frac{m + 84}{n} = \frac{AD}{DE} = 2 \Rightarrow 84 + m = 2n \quad (2)$$

Substituting (2) into (1), we get: $\frac{2n}{n + 35} = \frac{4}{3} \Rightarrow 6n = 4n + 140 \Rightarrow n = 70$.

Substituting $n = 70$ into (2), we get $m = 56$.
Therefore the area of $\triangle ABC$ is $84 + 40 + 30 + 35 + 126 = 315$.

50 Lectures for Mathcounts Competitions   (35) Polygons

SOLUTIONS:

Problem 1. Solution: 144°.
A decagon has 10 sides. Since the decagon is a regular decagon, each angle will be the same. Each interior angle is $a = 180 - \dfrac{360}{10} = 180 - 36 = 144°$.

Problem 2. Solution: 108.
A decagon has 10 sides. Since the decagon is a regular decagon, each angle will be the same. Each interior angle is $a = 180 - \dfrac{360}{10} = 180 - 36 = 144°$.

Problem 3. Solution: 54 units.
The perimeter is $9 + 11 + 12 + 10 + 4 + 8 = 54$.

Problem 4. Solution: 15.
We need 4 points to form a quadrilateral. The number of quadrilaterals will be
$\dbinom{6}{4} = \dbinom{6}{2} = 15$.

Problem 5. Solution: 16.
An octagon has 10 sides. Since the octagon is a regular octagon, each side will be the same length. Each side is $\dfrac{128}{8} = 16$ units long.

Problem 6. Solution: $\dfrac{1}{7}$. 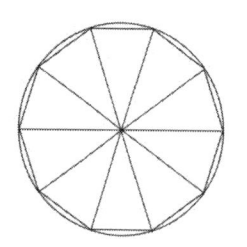
The number of diagonals of a convex n-gon is d_n:
$d_n = \dbinom{n}{2} - n = \dfrac{n(n-3)}{2}$. So we have
$d_{10} = \dbinom{10}{2} - 10 = 45 - 10 = 35$.

101

Among these 35 diagonals, 5 of them are diameter. So the probability is $P = \frac{5}{35} = \frac{1}{7}$.

Problem 7. Solution: 54 .
$d_{12} = \binom{12}{2} - 12 = 66 - 12 = 54$.

Problem 8. Solution: 24 .
We need 4 equilateral triangles to fill 1/6 of the hexagon. The answer is $4 \times 6 = 24$.

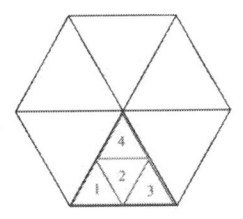

Problem 9. Solution: 36°.
Each interior angle of the regular pentagon is
$a = 180 - \frac{360}{5} = 180 - 72 = 108°$. $\angle PCD = \angle PDC) = 180° - 108° = 72°$.
The answer is $\angle P = 180° - (\angle PCD + \angle PDC) = 180° - 2 \times 72° = 36°$.

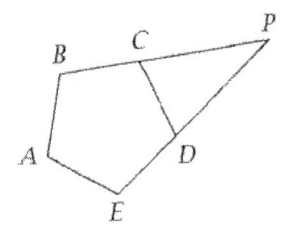

Problem 10. Solution: $\sqrt{3}$.
Draw $BG \perp AC$ at G. Triangle ABG is a 30 – 60 – 90 right triangle. $BG = \frac{1}{2} AB = \frac{1}{2}$ and $AG = \sqrt{3} BG = \frac{\sqrt{3}}{2}$. $AC = 2AG = \sqrt{3}$.

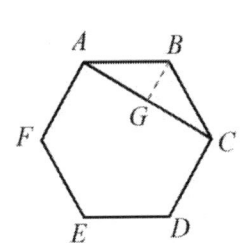

Problem 11. Solution: 2 .
We connect the vertices to from six congruent equilateral triangles as shown in the figure. $AD = 2AB = 2$.

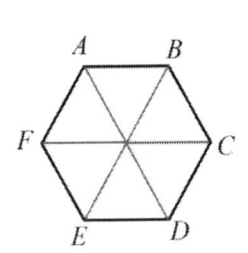

102

Problem 12. Solution: 8.
$d = \frac{n(n-3)}{2} \Rightarrow 20 = \frac{n(n-3)}{2} \Rightarrow 40 = n(n-3) \Rightarrow 8 \times (8-3) = n(n-3)$.
Thus $n = 8$.

Problem 13. Solution: 9.
$d_6 = \binom{6}{2} - 6 = 15 - 6 = 9$.

Problem 14. Solution: $54\sqrt{3}$.
We connect the vertices to from six congruent equilateral triangles as shown in the figure. $AB = \frac{1}{2}AD = 6$.

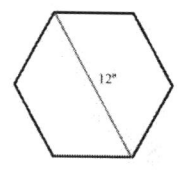

The area of equilateral triangle ABG is $\frac{\sqrt{3}}{4}(AB)^2 = 9\sqrt{3}$.
The area of the regular hexagon is $6 \times 9\sqrt{3} = 54\sqrt{3}$.

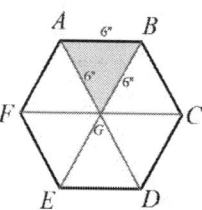

Problem 15. Solution: 108π.
Let G be the center of the circle and the hexagon.
Draw $PG \perp AB$ at G. Triangle APG is a 30 – 60 – 90 right triangle.

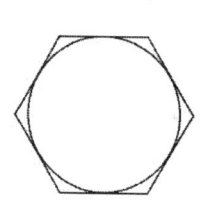

$AP = \frac{1}{2}AB = \frac{12}{2} = 6$ and $PG = \sqrt{3}AP = 6\sqrt{3}$.

The area of the circle is $\pi(PG)^2 = \pi \times (6\sqrt{3})^2 = 108\pi$.

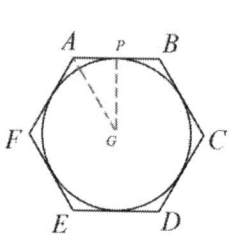

Problem 16. Solution: $\frac{8}{5}$.

103

50 Lectures for Mathcounts Competitions (35) Polygons

Let x be the side length of a regular pentagon and y be the side length of the regular octagon.

We know that $5x = 8y$ $\Rightarrow$ $\dfrac{x}{y} = \dfrac{8}{5}$.

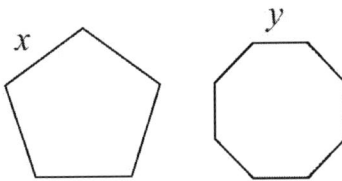

Problem 17. Solution: $\dfrac{3}{4}$.

Let x be the side length of a regular hexagon and y be the side length of the regular octagon.

We know that $6x = 8y$ $\Rightarrow$ $\dfrac{y}{x} = \dfrac{6}{8} = \dfrac{3}{4}$.

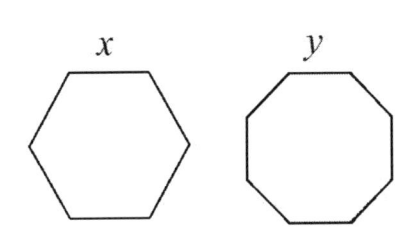

Problem 18. Solution: $36 + 36\sqrt{3}$.

Since the perimeter is 36, each side is $AB = \dfrac{36}{6} = 6$. We connect the vertices to from six congruent equilateral triangles as shown in the figure.

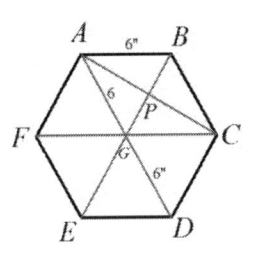

We have a total of 9 diagonals.
We see that there two types of diagonals: (1) $AD = BE = CF = 12$; (2) $AC = BD = CE = DF = EA = FB$.

Draw $BP \perp AC$ at P. Triangle ABP is a 30 – 60 – 90 right triangle. $BP = \dfrac{1}{2}AB = 3$ and $AP = \sqrt{3}BP = 3\sqrt{3}$.

$AC = 2AP = 6\sqrt{3}$.

The answer is $3 \times AD + 6 \times AC = 3 \times 12 + 6 \times 6\sqrt{3} = 36 + 36\sqrt{3}$.

Problem 19. Solution: 18.

Connect OE. Triangle COE is an isosceles triangle.

$\angle COE = \dfrac{2}{5} \times 360 = 144$.

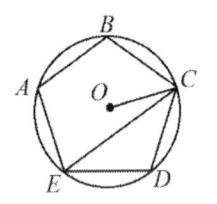

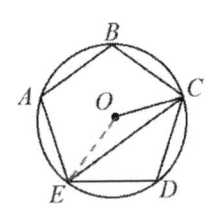

$\angle OCE = \dfrac{180-144}{2} = 18$.

Problem 20. Solution: 60.

We label some vertices as shown.

The interior angle $\angle ABD = 180 - \dfrac{360}{6} = 180 - 60 = 120°$.

The exterior angle $\angle DBC = 180 - 120 = 60°$.

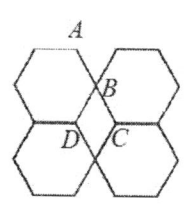

Problem 21. Solution: 8.

We place two polygons side-by-side as shown and extend CB to E.

We know that $\angle ABE = 45°$. Thus $\angle ABC = 180 = 45 = 135°$.

$135 = 180 - \dfrac{360}{n} \Rightarrow \dfrac{360}{n} = 45 \Rightarrow n = \dfrac{360}{45} = 8$.

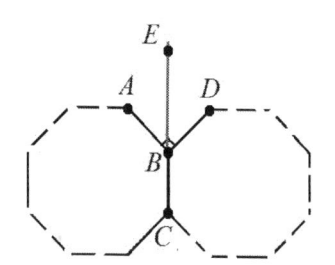

Problem 22. Solution: 36.

The sum of the measures of angles A, B, C, D, and E in the accompanying figure is 180°. Since each of the five angles are congruent, $\angle A = 180/5 = 36$.

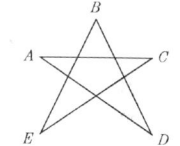

Problem 23. Solution: 252.

$d_{24} = \dbinom{24}{2} - 24 = 276 - 24 = 252$.

Problem 24. Solution: 60.

Each pentagonal face has $d_5 = \dbinom{5}{2} - 5 = 10 - 5 = 5$ face diagonals

The answer is $12 \times 5 = 60$.

Problem 25. Solution: 36.

Let the angle be x.

We know that each interior angle of the regular pentagon is

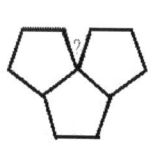

$180 - \dfrac{360}{5} = 180 - 72 = 108°$.

$108 + 108 + 108 + x = 360° \quad \Rightarrow \quad x = 36°$.

Problem 26. **Solution:** 9

$d_6 = \dbinom{6}{2} - 6 = 15 - 6 = 9$.

Problem 27. **Solution:** 360 (degrees).
We draw the circumscribed pentagon and label each angle as shown.
We have $\angle 1 + \angle 2 + \angle 3 + \angle 4 + \angle 5 + \angle 6 + \angle 7 + \angle 8 + \angle 9 + \angle 10 + \angle\alpha + \angle\beta + \angle\gamma + \angle\lambda + \angle\theta = 180(5-2) = 540°$ \quad (1)

We also have
$(\angle 1 + \angle 2 + \angle F) + (\angle 3 + \angle 4 + \angle G) + (\angle 5 + \angle 6 + \angle H) + (\angle 7 + \angle 8 + \angle M) + (\angle 9 + \angle 10 + \angle N) = 180(5) = 900°$ \quad (2)

(2) − (1): $(\angle F + \angle G + \angle H + \angle M + \angle N) - (\angle\alpha + \angle\beta + \angle\gamma + \angle\lambda + \angle\theta) = 900 - 540 = 360$.

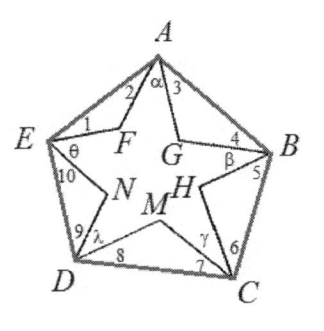

Problem 28. **Solution:** 14.
$x + 1 + x + 15 + 13 + 13 + 8 + 17 = 95 \quad \Rightarrow \quad 2x + 67 = 95$
$\Rightarrow \quad x = 14$.

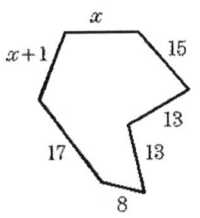

Problem 29. **Solution:** 48 (triangles).
For a pentagon (5 sides), we get $5 - 2 = 3$ triangles.
For a hexagon (6 sides), we get $6 - 2 = 4$ triangles.
The pattern s that for a n-gon (n sides), we get $n - 2$ triangles.
The answer is then $50 - 2 = 48$.

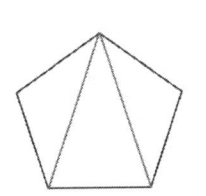

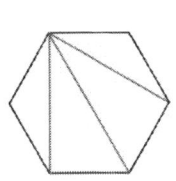

Problem 30. **Solution:** 35 (diagonals).
$d_{10} = \dbinom{10}{2} - 10 = 45 - 10 = 35$.

50 Lectures for Mathcounts Competitions (35) Polygons

Problem 31. Solution: 39
Looking at the figure on the right,
We know that $SN = SM = 4$. By Pythagorean's Theorem, $MN = 4\sqrt{2}$.
We can also find out that $SP = 2\sqrt{2}$, $SU = 8\sqrt{2}$, and $OU = r\sqrt{2}$.
$SU - SP - r = r\sqrt{2}$
$\Rightarrow 8\sqrt{2} - 2\sqrt{2} - r = r\sqrt{2} \Rightarrow r = \dfrac{6\sqrt{2}}{1+\sqrt{2}}$.

The area of the circle inscribed is equal to
$\pi r^2 = \pi(\dfrac{6\sqrt{2}}{1+\sqrt{2}})^2 = 38.81 \approx 39$.

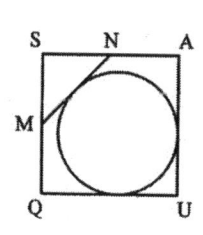

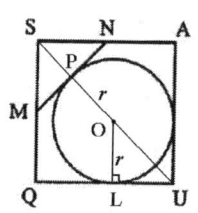

Problem 32. Solution: 15 (units).
$6(x + 5) = 8x \Rightarrow 2x = 30 \Rightarrow x = 15$.

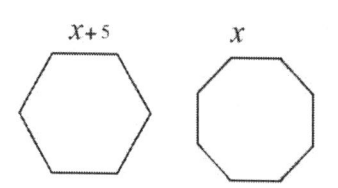

Problem 33. Solution: 135(degrees).
Each interior angle of the regular octagon is $180 - \dfrac{360}{8} = 180 - 45 = 135°$.

Problem 34. Solution: 12 (units).
We know that the first arrangement will produce the maximum perimeter of such a polygon (18).

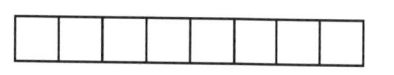

We know that the second arrangement will produce the minimum perimeter of such a polygon (12).

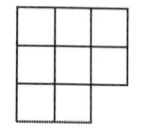

Problem 35. Solution: 15 (sides).
$d = \dfrac{n(n-3)}{2} \Rightarrow 90 = \dfrac{n(n-3)}{2} \Rightarrow 180 = n(n-3) \Rightarrow n^2 - 3n - 180 = 0$
$\Rightarrow (n-15)(n+12) = 0$. Thus $n = 15$.

Problem 36. Solution: 20 (diagonals)

$d_8 = \binom{8}{2} - 8 = 28 - 8 = 20$.

Problem 37. Solution: $\frac{1}{3}$.

Since $\triangle ABC$ is an isosceles right triangle,

$AB = BC = \dfrac{AC}{\sqrt{2}} = \dfrac{8}{\sqrt{2}} = 4\sqrt{2}$.

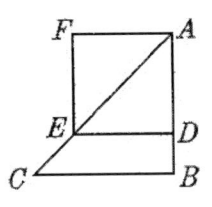

The area of the trapezoid $EDBC$ is $\dfrac{(ED+BC)DB}{2} = \dfrac{(4+4\sqrt{2})(4\sqrt{2}-4)}{2} = \dfrac{32-16}{2} = 8$.

The area of $\triangle ADE$ and the area of $\triangle AEF$ are all equal to $4 \times 4/2 = 8$.

So the answer is $\dfrac{1}{3}$.

Problem 38. Solution: 540 (degrees).

$d = \dfrac{n(n-3)}{2} \Rightarrow n = \dfrac{n(n-3)}{2} \Rightarrow 2n = n(n-3) \Rightarrow n^2 - 5n = 0 \Rightarrow n = 5$.

The number of degrees in the sum of all interior angles of the polygon $180(n-2) = 180(5-2) = 180 \times 3 = 540°$.

Problem 39. Solution: 150 (degrees).

The number of degrees in the sum of all interior angles of the pentagon is $180(n-2) = 180(5-2) = 180 \times 3 = 540°$.

$\dfrac{5}{3+3+3+4+5} \times 540 = 150$.

Problem 40. Solution: $96\sqrt{3}$ (square feet).

The regular hexagon consists of 6 congruent equilateral triangles of the area of

$\dfrac{\sqrt{3}}{4}(8)^2 = 16\sqrt{3}$ each.

The area of the regular hexagon is $6 \times 16\sqrt{3} = 96\sqrt{3}$.

50 Lectures for Mathcounts Competitions (35) **Polygons**

Problem 41. Solution: 13 (hexagons).

The side length of the hexagon is $\sqrt{3}$. Let n be the number of hexagons used to form the figure.

We see that the pattern for the number of sides of the resulting figure is $6n - 2(n-1) = 4n + 2$.

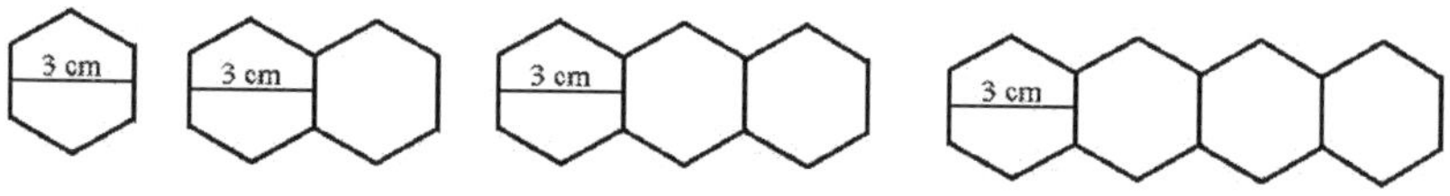

| 6 | 6 + 6 − 2 | 6 + 6 + 6 − 2×2 | 6 + 6 + 6 + 6 − 2×3 |

We have $(4n + 2) \times \sqrt{3} < 100$ $\Rightarrow$ $n < 13.93$

Since n is a positive integer, $n = 13$.

Problem 42. Solution: $\dfrac{27\pi}{16}$ (square inches).

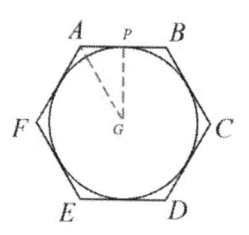

Let G be the center of the circle and the hexagon.
Draw $PG \perp AB$ at G. Triangle APG is a 30 – 60 – 90 right triangle. $AP = \dfrac{1}{2}AB = \dfrac{1}{2} \times \dfrac{3}{2} = \dfrac{3}{4}$ and $PG = \sqrt{3}AP = \dfrac{3\sqrt{3}}{4}$.

The area of the circle is $\pi(PG)^2 = \pi \times (\dfrac{3\sqrt{3}}{4})^2 = \dfrac{27\pi}{16}$.

Problem 43. Solution: $32\sqrt{3}$ (square inches).

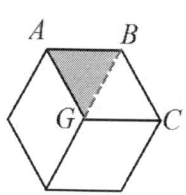

The regular hexagon consists of 6 congruent equilateral triangles of the area of

$\dfrac{\sqrt{3}}{4}(8)^2 = 16\sqrt{3}$ each.

The area of the rhombus is $2 \times 16\sqrt{3} = 32\sqrt{3}$.

Problem 44. Solution: 1 (side).

Let n be the number of sides for polygon 1 and m be the number of sides for polygon 2.
We have $180(n - 2) + 180(m - 2) = 1890$ $\Rightarrow$ $n + m = 15$ (1)

$$\binom{n}{2} - n + \binom{m}{2} - m = 34 \quad \Rightarrow \quad \binom{n}{2} + \binom{m}{2} = 34 + (n+m) = 49.$$

Since 49 is a small number, we see that $n = 7$ and $m = 8$.
The answer is $8 - 7 = 1$.

Problem 45. Solution: 8 (lines).

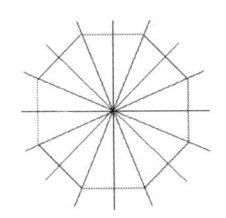

Problem 46. Solution: 9 (inches).
The regular hexagon consists of 6 congruent equilateral triangles.
So the answer is $AD - AB = 2AB - AB = AB = 9$.

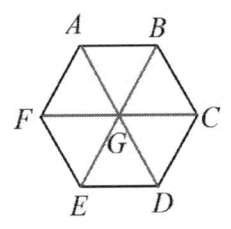

Problem 47. Solution: 8 (sides).
One of the interior angle will be $180 - 45 = 135$.

By the formula, each interior angle of the regular polygon of n sides is $180 - \dfrac{360}{n} = 135°$

$\Rightarrow \quad n = 8$.

50 Lectures for Mathcounts Competitions (36) Circles

SOLUTIONS

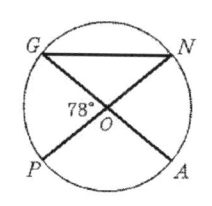

Problem 1. Solution: 39 (degrees).
Since $m\angle GOP = m\angle AON$ (vertical angles), $m\angle AON = 78°$.
Since angle AGN and AON face the same arc AN,
$$m\angle AGN = \frac{1}{2}m\angle AON = \frac{78°}{2} = 39°.$$

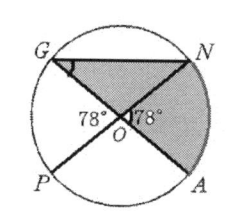

Problem 2. Solution: 11.2 (units) 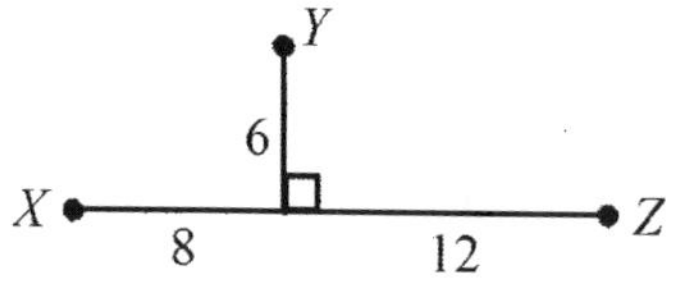
Draw the circumcircle of triangle AYZ.
Draw two diameter of the circle. Label all the line segments as shown in the figure.
We see that $TM = NO = 2$
$XT \times TZ = YT \times TP \implies 8 \times 12 = 6 \times TP \implies TP = 16$. Then $YP = 22$ and $NP = 11$.
Applying Pythagorean Theorem to triangle NPO:
$OP^2 = NO^2 + NP^2 = 2^2 + 11^1 = 125$
$OP = \sqrt{125} = 5\sqrt{5} \approx 11.2$.

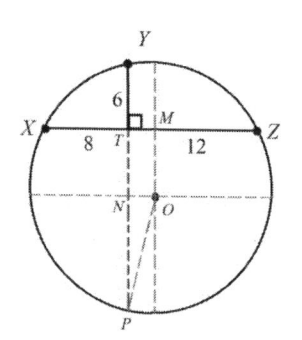

Problem 3. Solution: 10 (feet).

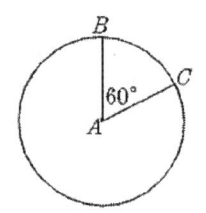

$$\frac{2\pi r}{360°} = \frac{\widehat{BC}}{60°} \implies \frac{60}{360°} = \frac{\widehat{BC}}{60°} \implies \widehat{BC} = 10$$

Problem 4. Solution: $12 + 6\pi$ or $6\pi + 12$ (inches)
$$\frac{2\pi \cdot 10}{2 \cdot 3} \times \frac{1}{2} + \frac{2\pi \cdot 26}{2 \cdot 3} \times \frac{1}{2} + \frac{10}{3} + \frac{26}{3} = 6\pi + 12.$$

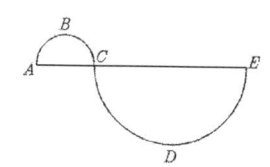

111

Problem 5. Solution: 3π (meters)

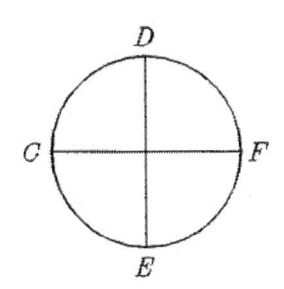

$$\frac{2\pi r}{360°} = \frac{\widehat{DF}}{90°} \Rightarrow \frac{2\pi \times \frac{12}{2}}{360°} = \frac{\widehat{DF}}{90°} \Rightarrow \widehat{DF} = \frac{2\pi \times 6}{4} = 3\pi.$$

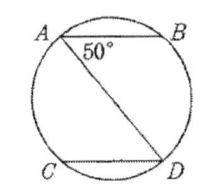

Problem 6. Solution: 8π (inches).
Connect OB, where O is the center. $\angle BOD = 2\angle BAD = 100°$.
So $\angle AOB = 180° - 100° = 80°$.

$$\frac{2\pi r}{360°} = \frac{\widehat{AB}}{80°} \Rightarrow \frac{2\pi \times \frac{36}{2}}{360°} = \frac{\widehat{AB}}{80°} \Rightarrow \widehat{AB} = 8\pi.$$

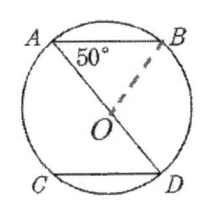

Problem 7. 9 (centimeters).
Connect OS as shown.
Since OS and RQ are the diagonals of rectangle OQSR, OS = RQ = 9 cm.

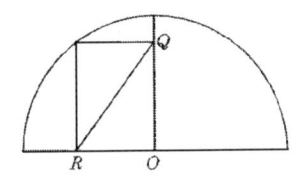

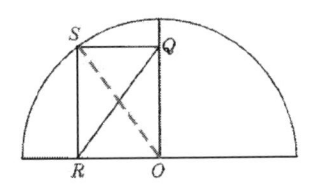

Problem 8. Solution: 11.7 (inches).
The side length of the large square is 14 and the side of the smaller square is 4.
Draw both AD and BE perpendicular to DE as shown in the figure.
Connect the centers of A and B. Draw BC // DE.
Applying Pythagorean Theorem to triangle ABC:
$AB^2 = AC^2 + BC^2 = (AD - CD)^2 + (8+2)^2$ 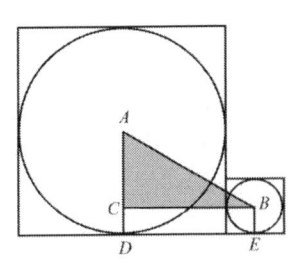
$= (8-2)^2 + (8+2)^2 = 36 + 100 = 136$ $AB = \sqrt{136} = 2\sqrt{34} = 11.7$.

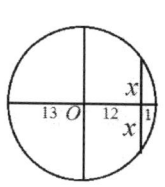

Problem 9. 10 (centimeters).
The figure is as shown. Let the length of the chord be $2x$.
We have $x \times x = 1 \times (13 + 12) \quad \Rightarrow \quad x = 5$.
$2x = 10$.

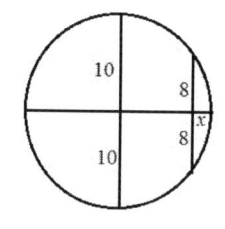

Problem 10. Solution: 6 (centimeters)
The figure is as shown. Let the distance from the midpoint of the chord to the center of the circle be $10 - x$.
We have $x \times (10 - x + 10) = 8 \times 8 \quad \Rightarrow$
$$x^2 - 20x + 64 = 0.$$
$x = 4$ or $x = 12$ (ignored since the chord cannot be longer than the diameter).
The answer is $10 - x = 10 - 4 = 6$.

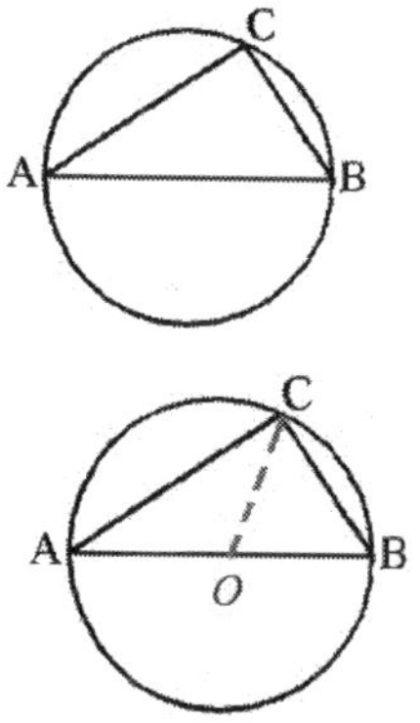

Problem 11. $\dfrac{5\pi}{3}$ centimeters)

Connect the center O and C as shown.

$\triangle COB$ is an equilateral triangle. $\angle COB = 60°$.

$\dfrac{2\pi r}{360°} = \dfrac{\overparen{BC}}{60°} \quad \Rightarrow \quad \dfrac{2\pi \times 5}{360°} = \dfrac{\overparen{BC}}{60°} \quad \Rightarrow \quad \overparen{BC} = \dfrac{5\pi}{3}$

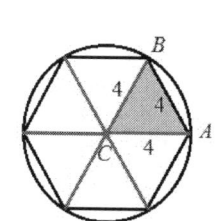

Problem 12. 16π sq units.
We draw the figure as shown. We see that triangle ABC is an equilateral triangle.
Thus the radius of the circle is 4 and the area is 16π.

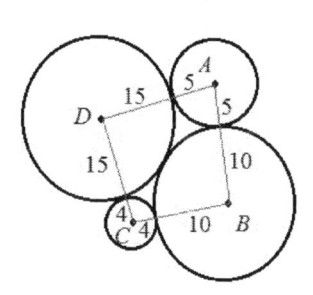

Problem 13. 68.
The radius of circles A, B, C, and D are 5, 10, 4, and 15, respectively.
Thus the perimeter of quadrilateral $ABCD$ is $2(5 + 10 + 4 + 15) = 68$.

50 Lectures for Mathcounts Competitions   (36) Circles

Problem 14. Solution: 33.
Note that 5-12-13 and 12-16-20 are Pythagorean triples.
The answer is 20 + 13 = 33.

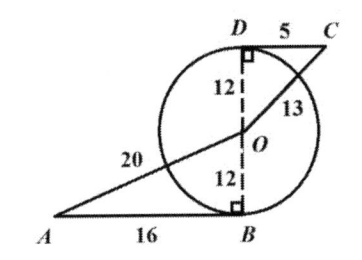

Problem 15. Solution: 10.
The radius of the circle is $DC + CE = AB + CE = 6 + 4 = 10$.
Connect DB as shown.
Since both DB and AC are the diagonals of rectangle $ABCD$, $AC = DB = 10$ cm.

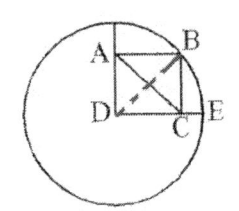

Problem 16. Solution: 12.
Draw $BD \perp AC$ at D. Triangle ABD is a 3-4-5 right triangle. Its area is $3 \times 4/2 = 6$.
The number of square units in the area of $\triangle ABC$ is $2 \times 6 = 12$.

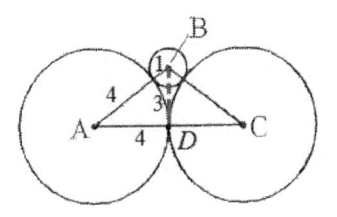

Problem 17. Solution: 6

We have $x \times 4 = 3 \times 8 \qquad \Rightarrow \qquad x = 6$.

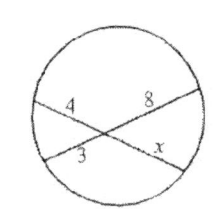

Problem 18. Solution: $5\sqrt{3}$.
Let the radius of circle P be x.
Connect PO and extend it to meet the circle O at B.
We have $AP^2 = 3x \times x \qquad \Rightarrow \qquad 15^2 = 3x^2$
$\Rightarrow \qquad x^2 = 75$
$x = 5\sqrt{3}$.

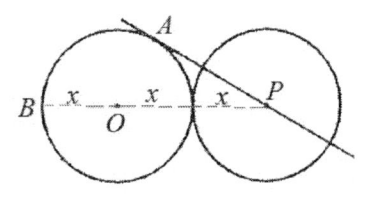

Problem 19. Solution: 4.
Extend AO to C and BP to D as shown.
We have $AP \times PC = BP \times PD \qquad \Rightarrow 2 \times (3 + 2 + 3) = BP^2$
$\Rightarrow BP^2 = 16 \Rightarrow BP = 4$

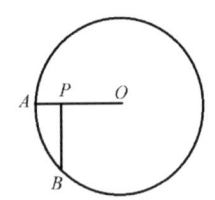

Problem 20. Solution: $\frac{1}{9}$.

Let the radius of the circle O be R, the radius of the circle Q be r_1, and the radius of the circle S be r_2. We know that $r_1 = \frac{R}{2}$.

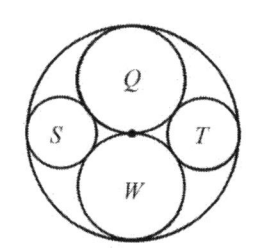

By the Pythagorean Theorem,
$(R - r_2)^2 = r_1^2 + (r_1 + r_2)^2 \Rightarrow R^2 - 2Rr_2 = 2r_1 r_2 \Rightarrow$

$R^2 - 2Rr_2 = 2r_1 r_2 \Rightarrow r_2 = \frac{R}{3}$

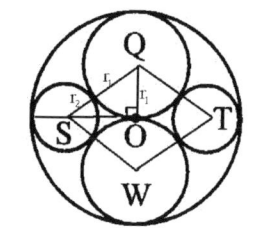

The ratio of the areas of the smallest circle and largest circle is

$\frac{\pi r_2^2}{\pi R^2} = \frac{r_2^2}{R^2} = \frac{(\frac{R}{3})^2}{R^2} = \frac{1}{9}$

Problem 21. Solution: 0.17.

Connect OP and extend OP to C. Connect the tangent points with P (PA, and PB as shown in the figure). $PA = OA = PB = r$. Triangle OAP is an isosceles right triangle. So $OP = \sqrt{2}r$

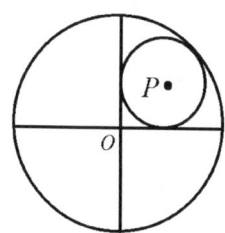

Let $OC = 1$. So $\sqrt{2}r + r = 1$

$\Rightarrow r(\sqrt{2} + 1) = 1 \Rightarrow r = \frac{1}{\sqrt{2} + 1} \Rightarrow r^2 = \frac{1}{3 + 2\sqrt{2}}$.

The answer is $\dfrac{\pi \cdot \frac{1}{3 + 2\sqrt{2}}}{\pi \cdot (1)^2} = \frac{1}{3 + 2\sqrt{2}} \approx 0.17$.

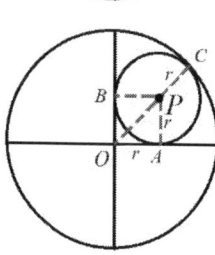

Problem 22. Solution: 32.6 (meters)

The length of the chord AB is equal to

$AB = 2AE = 2 \times \sqrt{90^2 - 45^2} \approx 2 \times 77.94 \approx 155.88$.

The length of the arc $AB = \dfrac{120^0 \times 2\pi \times 90}{360^0} = 188.49$.

The distance saved walking along chord AB instead of walking from A to B along the semicircular path $CABD$ is $188.49 - 155.88 \approx 32.6$.

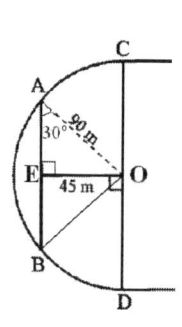

Problem 23. Solution: 9.6 (inches).
Let the center of the circle be O. Connect BO and AO.
Draw $BC \perp CO$. 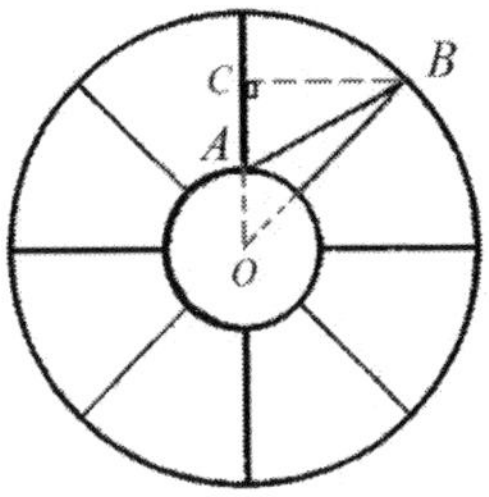
The area of the inner circular pane is $\pi \times r^2 = 16\pi$
Since all nine regions have the same area, the area of the large circle is $16\pi \times 9$ and the radius $OB = 12$.
The acute angle of O will be $360°/8 = 45°$.
Therefore triangle OCB is an isosceles right triangle and $\sqrt{2}\ OC = OB \Rightarrow OC = \dfrac{12}{\sqrt{2}} = 6\sqrt{2}$.

$CA = OC - AO = 6\sqrt{2} - 4$.
Applying Pythagorean Theorem to triangle ABC:
$AB^2 = AC^2 + BC^2 = (6\sqrt{2} - 4)^2 + (6\sqrt{2})^2 \approx 9.6$.

Problem 24. Solution: $300\pi + 50$. 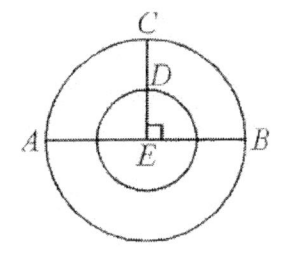
The diameter of the outer circle is 200 and the circumference is 200π.
The diameter of the inner circle is 100 and the circumference is 100π.
So the answer is $200\pi + 100\pi + 50 = 300\pi + 50$.

Problem 25. Solution: 20π. 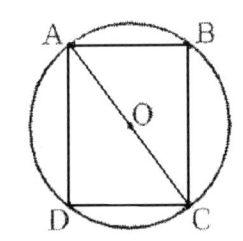
Triangle ADC is a 30°-60°-90° right triangle.
So $AC = 2DC = 2 \times 10 = 20$.
The circumference is $\pi d = 20\pi$.

Problem 26. Solution: 44.2. 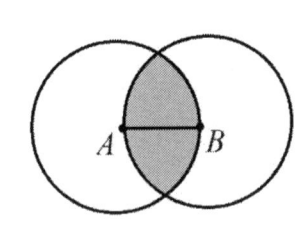
Let E be the point of intersection of circles A and B. Connect AE and BE.

The area of the equilateral triangle AEB: $y = \dfrac{\sqrt{3}}{4} \times 6^2 = 9\sqrt{3}$.

50 Lectures for Mathcounts Competitions (36) Circles

The area of the sector AEB: $y + x = \frac{1}{6} \times \pi \times 6^2 = 6\pi$.

Substituting the value of y into the above equation:
$x = 6\pi - 9\sqrt{3}$ and $2x = 12\pi - 18\sqrt{3}$.

The answer is $2(y + 2x)$
$= 2(9\sqrt{3} + 12\pi - 18\sqrt{3}) = 24\pi - 18\sqrt{3} \approx 44.2$

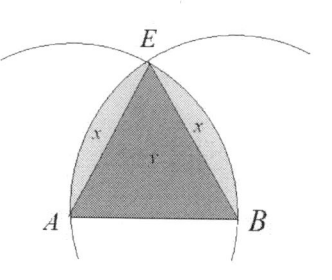

Problem 27. Solution: 98π (square inches)
Draw AB and CD as shown.
AB is the diameter of the inner circle. So $AB = 2 \times 7 = 14$.
CD is the diagonal of the square $CEDF$ and
$$CD = \sqrt{2}DF = \sqrt{2}AB = 14\sqrt{2}.$$
The area of the outer circle is $\frac{\pi(CD)^2}{4} = \frac{\pi}{4}(14\sqrt{2})^2 = 98\pi$.

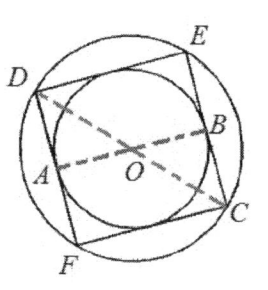

Problem 28. Solution: 3.27 (centimeters).
Let the radius of the semicircle be r.
The area is $\pi r^2/2$
The number of centimeters in the perimeter of a semicircle is $2\pi r/2 + 2r$.

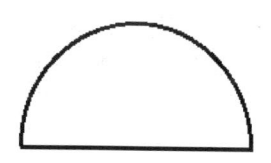

We set up the equation: $\pi r^2/2 = 2\pi r/2 + 2r$ $\Rightarrow$ $\pi r = 2\pi + 4$ $\Rightarrow r = 2 + \frac{4}{\pi} = 3.27$.

Problem 29. Solution: $\frac{5}{2}\pi$ (meters)

For the straight line from A to B, the runners run the same distance. To calculate the difference in meters ran, we can push the two semicircles together and calculate the difference in the circumferences of the two concentric circles with radius R_L and R_S.

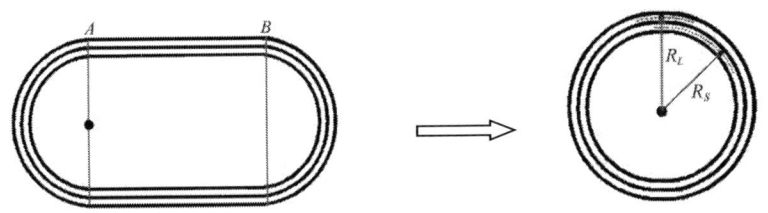

The circumference of the longer lane is $2\pi R_L$ and the circumference of the shorter lane is $2\pi R_S$. The difference is $2\pi R_L - 2\pi R_S = 2\pi(R_L - R_S) = 2\pi \times 1.25 = \frac{5}{2}\pi$.

Problem 30. Solution: 4.

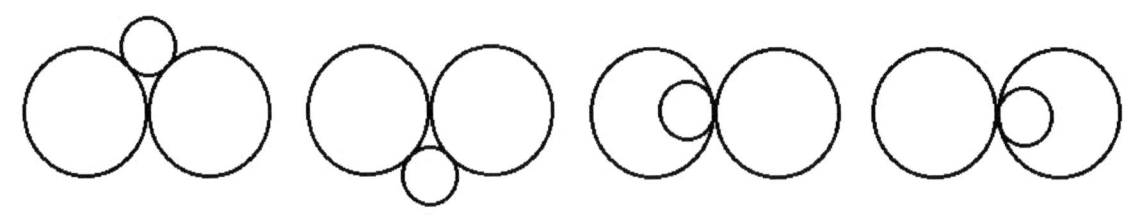

Problem 31. Solution: 2.
Let the radius of the semicircle be r.
The area is πr^2.
The number of centimeters in the circumference is $2\pi r$.
We set up the equation: $\pi r^2 = 2\pi r \quad \Rightarrow \quad r = 2$.

Index

A

acute angle, 116
alternate interior angles, 48, 76, 78, 80, 82
angle, 44, 45, 46, 47, 48, 49, 56, 57, 68, 69, 71, 86, 87, 88, 89, 93, 101, 102, 105, 106, 107, 110, 111, 116
arc, 111, 115
area, 25, 49, 50, 51, 52, 56, 60, 66, 68, 70, 71, 72, 73, 74, 75, 76, 78, 79, 81, 83, 85, 86, 87, 89, 94, 95, 96, 97, 98, 99, 100, 103, 107, 108, 109, 113, 114, 116, 117, 118
arithmetic mean, 24

B

base, 46, 74, 75, 86, 87, 95
bisect, 70

C

center, 103, 109, 112, 113, 116
chord, 113, 115
circle, 103, 107, 109, 111, 113, 114, 115, 116, 117
circumference, 116, 118
collinear, 55
composite number, 12
concentric, 117
congruent, 59, 87, 90, 94, 97, 98, 102, 103, 104, 105, 108, 109, 110
convex, 101
corresponding angles, 48

D

diagonal, 71, 73, 78, 79, 80, 81, 84, 117
diameter, 102, 111, 113, 116, 117
difference, 36, 79, 80, 81, 93, 117, 118
digit, 7, 8, 9, 10, 11, 12, 13, 36
Divisibility, 3
divisible, 7, 8, 9, 10, 11, 12, 13, 14

E

equation, 16, 21, 84, 88, 117, 118
equilateral, 49, 80, 102, 103, 104, 108, 109, 110, 113, 116
equilateral triangle, 49, 80, 102, 103, 104, 108, 109, 110, 113, 116
even number, 7, 13

F

face, 105, 111
formula, 27, 28, 29, 30, 31, 32, 50, 52, 87, 88, 89, 110

H

hexagon, 102, 103, 104, 106, 108, 109, 110
hypotenuse, 50, 64, 65, 66, 87, 90, 92

I

inequality, 3, 90
integer, 8, 15, 22, 23, 24, 25, 64, 93, 109
integers, 15, 18, 25
intersection, 86, 116
isosceles, 48, 73, 75, 83, 85, 87, 88, 104, 108, 115, 116
isosceles triangle, 48, 75, 104

L

Law of Cosines, 89
least common multiple, 12
line, 39, 55, 68, 86, 111, 117
line segment, 55, 68, 111

M

median, 88, 92
midpoint, 87, 89, 94, 95, 113

O

octagon, 101, 104, 107
odd number, 7

P

parallel, 48, 86
parallelogram, 68, 81, 82
pentagon, 102, 104, 105, 106, 108
percent, 27, 94
perimeter, 44, 50, 51, 52, 54, 58, 74, 75, 76, 79, 82, 90, 91, 92, 93, 101, 104, 107, 113, 117
perpendicular, 69, 85, 89, 112
point, 72, 86, 116
polygon, 107, 108, 109
positive number, 64
prime number, 8, 10, 90, 91
probability, 55, 102
product, 40
Pythagorean Theorem, 3, 44, 50, 52, 54, 55, 57, 61, 62, 63, 64, 65, 66, 67, 71, 74, 81, 82, 85, 86, 89, 91, 111, 112, 115, 116
Pythagorean Triple, 52, 58

Q

quadrilateral, 68, 69, 70, 71, 97, 101, 113

R

radius, 113, 114, 115, 116, 117, 118
ratio, 51, 56, 57, 62, 72, 81, 82, 87, 115
rectangle, 78, 79, 80, 81, 82, 83, 94, 98, 112, 114
regular polygon, 110
relatively prime, 24
rhombus, 68, 80, 109
right angle, 83
right triangle, 50, 51, 52, 53, 55, 58, 59, 62, 63, 66, 70, 71, 73, 74, 76, 78, 79, 80, 83, 85, 87, 90, 95, 97, 99, 102, 103, 104, 108, 109, 114, 115, 116
root, 20

S

semicircle, 117, 118
set, 117, 118
similar, 56, 57, 58, 59, 60, 61, 66, 68, 73, 76, 77, 83, 87, 89, 90, 97, 100
solution, 16, 22, 35, 53, 86, 88, 92, 100
square, 14, 22, 25, 66, 71, 75, 78, 81, 82, 86, 98, 108, 109, 112, 114, 117
sum, 8, 9, 10, 12, 13, 19, 24, 26, 35, 40, 49, 68, 69, 71, 81, 90, 93, 105, 108

T

trapezoid, 66, 73, 74, 75, 76, 108
triangle, 46, 47, 49, 50, 51, 52, 54, 55, 56, 57, 59, 60, 61, 62, 63, 65, 66, 67, 71, 72, 73, 74, 76, 77, 80, 81, 82, 83, 85, 86, 87, 89, 90, 91, 92, 93, 94, 95, 97, 98, 99, 100, 111, 112, 113, 115, 116

V

vertex, 46
vertical angles, 111

W

whole number, 13, 22, 25, 92
whole numbers, 13, 22

Made in the USA
Lexington, KY
30 January 2019

Made in United States
North Haven, CT
15 May 2023

Now that you've finished this 21 day journey- I want you to acknowledge the deeply transformative work you immersed yourself in. Healing can often feel isolating, lonely, and like no one is on your side. But, remember, YOU are your own greatest healer. You are highly capable, worthy, and enough. Healing is available to you and you are not alone as you navigate this path. There are hundreds of people who have completed this work along with you.

You might be wondering, what's next? If so, there are many ways to get involved and continue your healing work with me and the Uncensored Empath community.

For all resources mentioned in the book visit: theuncensoredempath.com/ 21daysofhealing

If you have questions or would like to share your 21 Days experience with the online community, join the free Facebook group: https://www.facebook.com/ groups/1477095185932809/

If you feel called to work with me 1:1 email me at sarah@theuncensoredempath.com

If you are curious what the 21 Days of Healing live experience is like check out theuncensoredempathcourses.com, the course is hosted twice a year.

If you want to experience even more healing and conversations around being an empath with chronic illness make sure you subscribe to my podcast, Healing Uncensored. Available on iTunes and all other platforms!

And be sure to follow me on Instagram @the_uncensored_empath to stay up to date on everything happening behind the scenes!

All the best to you on your healing path!!

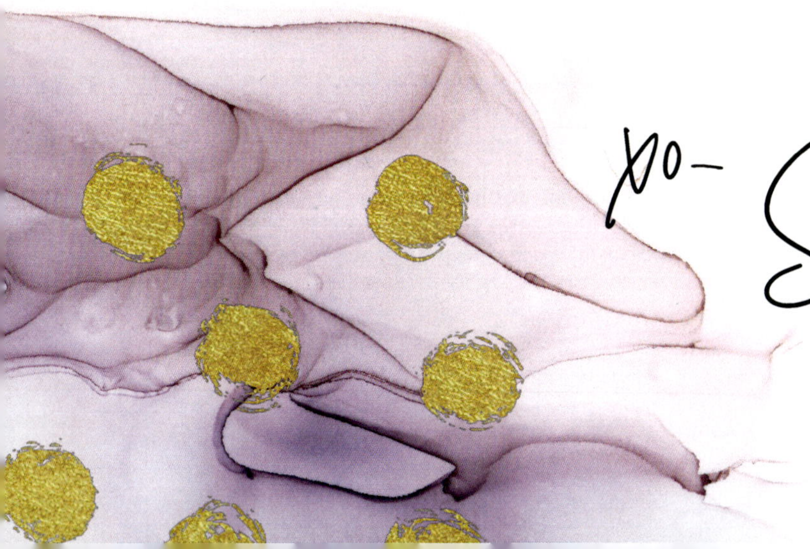

xo- Sarah ♡

out of the muck that we find ourselves in, and start to ask ourselves questions that empower and inspire us to begin our ascension. This work is also part of the process of integrating your shadow into your light. It is by allowing yourself to witness and change your old habits that you give yourself permission to change.

If you want to change, something's got to give.

We can all start this process of change by asking more empowering questions.

As a final (bonus) exercise in this 21 Days of Healing process, I offer you the following empowering questions, which you can ask whenever you feel like you are in a slump or in a state of dis-ease:

HOW IS THIS EXPERIENCE LEADING ME TOWARDS MY HIGHER PURPOSE?

$\triangledown$

WHAT POSITIVE/HEALING THINGS ARE EMERGING THROUGH THIS EXPERIENCE?

$\triangledown$

celiac disease here to teach me?" Seeing an issue from this perspective allows us to rise out of the victim mentality and provides more opportunities to really listen.

In reframing the question, I received an empowering answer:

Celiac disease is here to wake you up to the broken food system. It's just the first step in enhancing your awareness of where your food is sourced, how it is made, who made it, and how it was processed. Now that your eyes are open to all these things you can make more empowering decisions around all the other foods in your diet as well.

The answers and deeper level of understanding that you are seeking may not, and don't have to always come through the process of journaling. These messages may also arrive through intuitive nudges, dreams, signs, symbols, a book, or another sign.

I invite you to take a moment and consider the questions you've been asking yourself about your life— to determine whether they are empowering or disempowering.

I am emphasizing the importance of asking the right type of questions today, because I often see individuals with chronic illness fall into this trap of disempowerment and I have come to understand that asking these disempowering questions lowers your vibration. And, when you lower your vibration your organs do not function as effectively, you feel stressed, overwhelmed, broken, stuck, sick, or even hopeless.

In order to heal, something must change.

If you continue to ask the same questions that got you here, you can't expect them to get you anywhere different. That is how Albert Einstein defined insanity- doing the same thing over and over again and expecting different results.

If you are always asking questions like: why me? These types of thoughts will keep pulling you further into a downward spiral. To heal we must rise

When you ask empowering questions, the Universe answers. An empowering question is a question that seeks deeper understanding and meaning. It leaves your egoic, fear-based thoughts at the door so that your soul can evolve and learn.

These questions differ from disempowering questions that put you in the victim role.

The following are some examples of disempowering questions:

Why me?

How can I numb this pain?

What did I do to deserve this?

Who is to blame?

Sometimes when we feel backed into a corner, tough situations can cause us revert to disempowering questions, which can lead us to make excuses. Instead of falling back on disempowering feelings, or even self-sabotage, my challenge for you is to seek deeper understanding through empowering questions, such as:

How is this leading me towards my purpose?

What can I share?

What is trying to emerge through this?

What is the deeper lesson here?

I used to ask the following disempowering question all the time:

Who is to blame for this celiac disease I am experiencing?

And of course, my mind made up a ton of things I could potentially blame this disease on, like the ways the food industry processes grains, the impacts of my mom having me via C-section, or the Universe for "cursing" me.

Instead, I chose to sit down with my journal and ask empowering questions which allowed the answers flow more easily. An example of an empowering question that helped me a lot was, "What message is this

After hosting the *21 Days of Healing* live course for hundreds of women I've discovered that each individual inevitably has different ah-ha moments and breakthroughs while using the assorted healing tools and exercises. I encourage you to think about the tools that have been MOST helpful for you and list them below. Please feel free to look back on the previous pages as a refresher.

1. _____

2. _____

3. _____

4. _____

5. _____

The items that you listed above may serve as the main tools in your healing toolbox moving forward and you can certainly reuse them over and over again. In fact, I encourage you to utilize at least one tool from this book every day as you continue moving forward on your healing journey. The tools that you revisit could be as simple as tapping your thymus or singing to stimulate your vagus nerve or listening to one of the meditations. Now it's your chance to choose your own healing adventure!

Even though you're likely feeling pretty cracked open after this experience, I want to give you one last tool that you can turn to if or when everything feels like it's coming down on you at any point in your future.

This particularly potent activity invites you to ask yourself empowering questions.

Moving Forward

It is my sincere hope that you have experienced some big shifts in the past 21 days. I invite you to reflect on where you were three weeks ago, and revisit the goals and vision you wrote on Day One.

I'd also like to encourage you to reflect on how were you feeling 21 days ago and how that compares to how you are feeling now!

DAY TWENTY ONE

MOVING FORWARD

"She understood that the hardest times in life to go through were when you were transitioning from one version of yourself to another."

-Sarah Addison Allen

After you've listened to the meditation, I invite you to write about your experience.

What messages did you receive from the past generations? What messages did you receive from the future generations? What would you like to release moving forward?

▽

Messages

She told me later that she was sitting by my Grandma as she took her last breath and it was an even more intense experience for her than what I experienced from afar.

Being an inquisitive soul, I wondered if there was any meaning to all of this. Often individuals pass on their own birthdays, almost as if to exit and enter a worm hole that exists in this Universe on the same day. But, I'd never heard of whether or not there was meaning behind a family member passing away on your birthday, so I did some research.

Through my research I discovered that when a maternal ancestor passes on your birthday, it represents a chain breaking. I learned that this severing of past female lineages releases the energy, beliefs, and patterns that are no longer serving the current and future generations.

I interpreted it as any and all of the negative stories, patterns, and beliefs that my grandmother had carried with her from previous generations and continued to pass on to current generations would STOP RIGHT HERE and right now, with me.

I told myself, *I will not carry the weight of the past and I will not pass the weight on.*

Instead, I will break free of the old stories, oppression, and limiting beliefs to live a life filled with more magic, freedom, and unapologetic authenticity.

Now it's your turn to consider all the ways you've been impacted by your own lineage. This includes all of the stories passed down, all of the memories in your DNA, and the fear of war or oppression.

I invite you to participate in a powerful meditation to gather wisdom from all generations, both past and future. Through this process you will not only be able to understand this energy more clearly, but you will also be able to let go of what is no longer needed.

THEUNCENSOREDEMPATH.COM/21DAYSOFHEALING

Generational Wisdom

Today, I want you to consider how much energy you carry from the past.

Have you considered the ancestors who walked before you and the long line of lineage in your family? Have you ever done any research on your family tree or personal heritage?

November 30th, 2017 I turned 30 years old and that same day my mom's mother (my grandmother) passed away at 80 years old.

Surrounded by her four kids, she transitioned into the spirit world around 6:30pm.

I felt her pass.

I was sitting at our high-top kitchen table finishing up some work for the evening when I was overcome by this tingling sensation and a voice inside my head told me to stop what I was doing.

I had known since the night before that my Grandma had lost consciousness and that she would likely pass the next day, on my golden birthday.

So, I stopped to acknowledge the sensation and closed my eyes. I saw my grandmother laying on her hospital bed and this big wave of golden light rolling over her body, like a blanket. I said over and over inside my head, *It's okay Grandma, I won't be mad, it's okay to go, go be with Jordan.*

A few minutes later, the sensations were gone.

My Mom called me 30 minutes later.

"Grandma passed away about a half hour ago."

DAY TWENTY

GENERATIONAL WISDOM

"We all carry, inside us, people who came before us."

-Liam Callanan

All of this _____
It makes me feel _____
It's just so _____
I don't like to feel _____
That time _____
And _____
It brought up _____
I just feel so _____

_____ was there
And _____
I remember _____
I didn't like _____
I felt _____
And _____
All of this _____
I feel it in my _____

It feels like _____
And the sensation is _____
It's just so _____
And _____
It still feels _____
In my _____
All from that time _____
And now I feel _____

As a result of this _____
And _____
And _____
And I feel _____
All of this _____
From that time _____
I wish _____
Because _____

Maybe _____
What if _____
I guess I could _____
What if _____
I wish _____
And _____
I learned _____
And _____

Next time _____
Maybe I could release _____
And _____
So that _____
Yes, releasing all of this _____
I no longer _____
And I'm grateful for _____
Finally releasing this _____

Once you've filled in the blanks, start with tapping point 2 as you say one phrase, and then move on to the next meridian point and say the next phrase until you go through the whole script.

9.

Now that you've completed the tapping, I encourage you to rate the intensity of your emotion one more time to see how this activity worked for you.

| 1 | 2 | 3 | 4 | 5 | 6 | 7 | 8 | 9 | 10 |

7. Next, list 2-4 things that you wished would have happened during that experience instead. Also think of how this wound could have been healed or what was gained or learned from this experience.

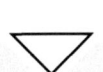

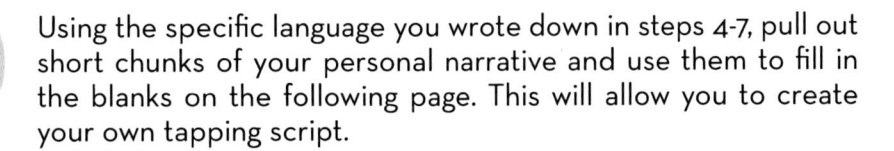

▽

8. Using the specific language you wrote down in steps 4-7, pull out short chunks of your personal narrative and use them to fill in the blanks on the following page. This will allow you to create your own tapping script.

If for any reason what you want to say doesn't fit into the script you can just fill in the blanks in your own creative way. These prompts are simply here to guide you and help you along as you go. You can edit this script in whatever ways you want, using excerpts from step 4-7 above.

5. How does this instance feel right now in your body? Get specific about any sensations, colors, visuals, shapes, or textures when explaining how your body feels when re-experiencing this emotion. (As an example, you might say my left shoulder feels, blue, hot, itchy, and tight).

▽

6. Think of how you were impacted short and/or long term by this experience. What were 2-4 negative things that happened because of this experience?

▽

Sometimes this simple exercise does the trick and it sends a signal to the brain that the body can release this emotion, but other times we must get more specific. If you rated the negative emotion you are working through higher than a 5, proceed to step four.

4. Using the same emotion you've been working with, name an instance when you felt this way. Be as specific and detailed as possible when writing out the memories surrounding this emotion and include answers to the following questions: Who was there? What was said? How did you feel? What was the outcome? What stands out to you?

▽

Now, I invite you to write out a few set-up statements of your own:

Even though _____, I _____.

Even though _____, I _____.

Even though _____, I _____.

3. THIS STEP IS CALLED THE REMINDER PHRASE.

This is a short phrase that will remind you of the negative emotion while you go through the tapping sequence. It serves to keep you focused on the specific issue you're working through.

The simplest way to do this is to fill in the blank with a word that best describes this feeling.

All of this _____ (Examples include: stress, anger, perfectionism, anxiety, fear, disbelief, worry, etc.)

Using the tapping points from Day 8, simply repeat this set-up statement while tapping on each of your eight energy meridians.

INNER EYE- All of this

_____

OUTER EYE- All of this

_____

UNDER EYE- All of this

_____

UNDER NOSE- All of this

_____

CHIN- All of this

_____

CHEST- All of this

_____

UNDER ARM- All of this

_____

TOP OF HEAD- All of this

_____

Try 3-5 rounds of this.

Then, rate the intensity of this feeling again on a scale of 0-10, using the scale below:

| 1 | 2 | 3 | 4 | 5 | 6 | 7 | 8 | 9 | 10 |

Now that you have reflected on the negative emotions you've experienced, which one stands out to you?

PICK ONE AND WRITE IT HERE:

_____

Perfect, you'll use this emotion in the steps below.

1. CONSIDER THE INTENSITY OF THIS FEELING AND RATE IT ON A SCALE OF 1-10.

1	2	3	4	5	6	7	8	9	10

2. NEXT WE WILL WORK ON THE SETUP STATEMENT.

In tapping we bring the problem to the surface so it can be released. This statement literally "sets up" the negative emotion you'd like to work on releasing.

This process includes two parts: 1) exposing yourself to the problem and 2) a self-acceptance statement.

EXAMPLE: Even though I feel this anger (exposure to problem), I deeply accept and love myself (self-acceptance statement).

In some ways this process is similar to exposure therapy, because you are exposing yourself to your negative experiences. Rather than avoiding them, you are going to confront them and recondition your response to them through tapping. It's also nice to drop into the discomfort instead of trying to be positive ALL of the time.

There is a duality when we experience pain and therefore all other negative feelings. We feel uncomfortable when we experience them, yet we need this discomfort to be able to contrast the light and dark in our lives. We need to acknowledge this shadow side so we can either release it, or integrate it into our light. So, like we discussed yesterday, oftentimes amidst immense discomfort, we also experience growth. As that discomfort surfaces we eventually come to realize that we have the opportunity to react and respond in a million possible ways.

Your challenge today is to consciously respond to negative emotions by using tapping.

I'm going to teach you how build your own tapping (BYOT) practice.

I'm going to assume you have some experience with negative emotions, and to begin the process of developing your own tapping practice, I encourage you to write down some of these negative emotions below:

DAY NINETEEN

BYOT

"As my sufferings mounted I soon realized that there were two ways in which I could respond to my situation - either to react with bitterness or seek to transform the suffering into a creative force. I decided to follow the latter course."

-Martin Luther King Jr.

WHAT MESSAGES HAVE YOU RECEIVED THROUGH YOUR CHALLENGES?

WHAT LIFE LESSONS HAVE SURFACED THROUGH YOUR STRUGGLE?

LOVE NOTE: YOU'RE DOING GREAT. I'M SO PROUD OF YOU FOR MAKING IT THIS FAR AND FOR PERFORMING ALL THIS INCREDIBLY LIBERATING WORK. YOUR BEST LIFE IS JUST ON THE OTHER SIDE OF ANY FEAR, CONSTRICTION, OR JUDGEMENT THAT HAS SURFACED THROUGH THIS EXPERIENCE AND I ENCOURAGE YOU TO KEEP GOING!!

WHAT HAVE YOU LEARNED FROM THE CHALLENGES YOU LISTED
ON THE FIRST PAGE OF THIS CHAPTER?

WHAT HAVE YOUR PHYSICAL SYMPTOMS TAUGHT YOU?

We can either look at our life challenges (like having to cope with an autoimmune disease) and think about how much stress they've caused, how painful they are, or how hard they are to cope with, OR we can choose to change how we look at these challenges and see them as our biggest teachers and opportunities for growth. We can choose, instead, to see that these challenges often push us into action, provide us with tools for connecting with other people, or give us reasons to explore our body's needs.

Let me give you some examples of events that have happened in my life that, at least on the surface, seemed shitty:

-My parents got divorced
-I was diagnosed with multiple chronic illnesses
-A man stalked me for years
-I had $25K in credit card debt when I started my business
-I lost my brother to suicide

Upon reflection, I have come to see that these events were my greatest teachers. Here is how I came to see them in a different light:

- My parent's divorce taught me fierce independence and responsibility.
- Chronic illness taught me to love my body and find a deep sense of gratitude for it.
- Experiencing a stalker made me trust the people who were closest to me in my life.
- Having debt when I started my business helped me heal my relationship with money and to take ownership of my finances.
- Losing my brother to suicide helped me to heal all the buried emotions of my past and encouraged me to step into my own truth.

Now, I invite you to give this process a try. As you work through the following questions, reflect and see if you can find whether you have earned any new wisdom through your past suffering. Below are a few questions to help you think deeper about the trials you've faced as an act of healing.

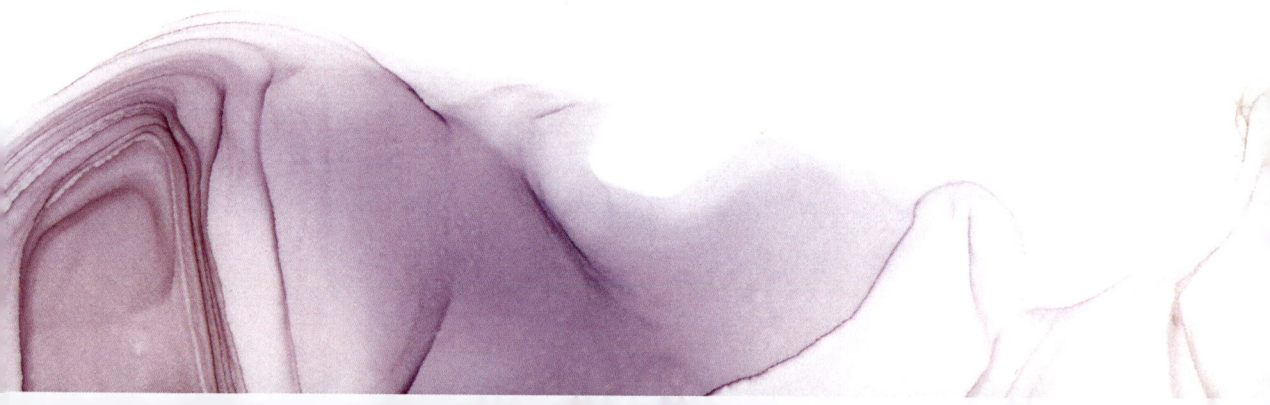

Discover Wisdom

For today's activity, start by answering the question below.

What's been hard, challenging, sticky, or frustrating for you in your life?

Good. Now that we got the juices flowing, it's easy to see how reflecting on the negative parts of life can cause you to feel pretty down in the dumps. But, you know that this is a healing journey, and my challenge for you today is to find the wisdom in the challenging, sticky, angry moments of discomfort.

To start reframing your thoughts, repeat after me:

The Universe has my back. I am supported. I am safe. I am protected. The things that show up in my life show up in perfect timing. These stumbling blocks transform into stepping stones that lead me down the path of my greatest self. Everything is always working out for me.

DAY EIGHTEEN

DISCOVER WISDOM

"When you follow your bliss... doors will open where you would not have thought there would be doors, and where there wouldn't be a door for anyone else."

-Joseph Campbell

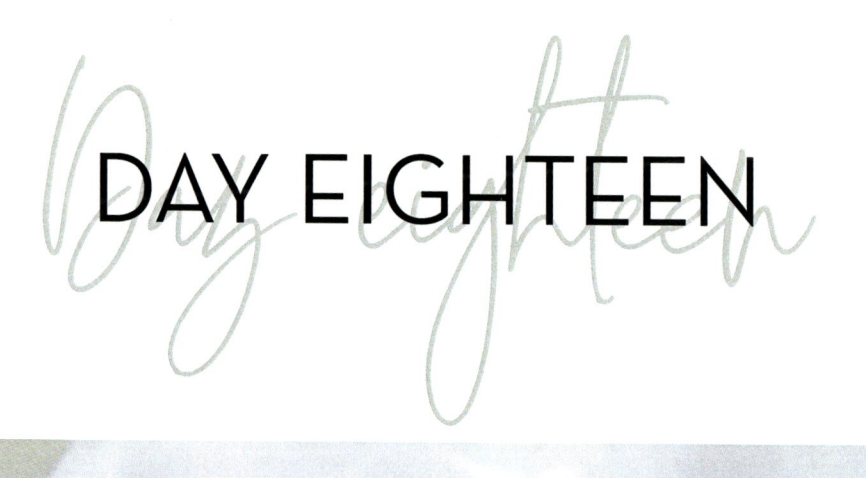

This practice is also effective for acute issues you face day to day, like anger or frustration you may experience when someone cuts you off while you're driving in traffic. It's helpful to resolve that negative energy before it turns into anything bigger. Simply repeat "I'm sorry, forgive me, I love you, thank you," as many times as you'd like or you feel you need to cleanse that entire energetic interaction.

Now, I invite you to take some time to reflect on today's practice. You may want to write about how you felt about this unresolved energy both before and after trying Ho'oponopono.

When you repeat the words "Forgive me," you can think of this as, "Forgive my part in this," or "Forgive me for everything in a general sense." Again, it does not downplay any event or situation you endured, instead this statement allows you to reclaim your power.

When you repeat the words, "I love you," you can think of this as, "I love the air, ground, my body, my inner child, the sun, the moon, the sky..." or it can serve as a reminder that love is the greatest medicine of all.

When you repeat the words, "Thank you," you can think of this as a "Thank you to the Universe," "Thank you for my body," "Thank you for my loved ones who help me heal, and show me wisdom," or "Thank you for everything." It works to just think of the things you feel grateful for.

Now bring to the surface of your mind something unresolved that you'd like to release, forgive, or reclaim your power over. This may include an experience you feel embarrassed about, a time when you feel you could have done better, or an encounter that you are critical of yourself for. It could also be an unresolved wound between yourself and others or a lingering anger you harbor toward someone else. Remember, this practice is all about clearing old energies and reconciling the energy within ourselves.

For example, I may choose to focus on releasing the resentment I experienced over a falling-out I had with an old friend.

Now that you have decided what you'd like to release, simply imagine this thing, experience, memory, or person in front of you. I recommend bringing this energy about 3-5 feet in front of you unless there was any trauma involved, then you may choose to keep this energy at least 10 feet (or farther) away from you in your visualization.

Simply repeat the following statements out loud or in your mind:

"I'm sorry, forgive me, I love you, thank you"

Continue doing this for at least 5 minutes. You can experiment with your personal Ho'oponopono practice and see what works best for you for the length of time. Once you know how long it takes for you to feel a sense of release, I recommend setting a timer on your phone to keep track of the time so you can focus your attention on the practice while assuring you are spending an adequate amount of time on the exercise.

Before you get angry with me for suggesting you forgive some of the people who have SERIOUSLY wronged you in your life, let me explain the power of this practice.

The process is sort of like the process of cleaning your house. You start with the countertops and then you wipe down the floors and each step of the process improves the environment. But, instead of cleaning the physical atmosphere around you, this cleaning is for the soul. It removes all of the absorbed energies that are unresolved.

In fact, the negative memories you are harboring are your only opponents here. Stated more bluntly, Dr. Len said, "When you ARE your memories, it's all bullshit. When you are whole and complete, all is well. You are home."

So, we must get rid of these negative energies that keep us angry and resentful and that act as our perpetual opponent.

This cleaning process requires repeating the following four short phrases:

I'M SORRY

FORGIVE ME

I LOVE YOU

THANK YOU

When you repeat the words "I'm sorry," you can think of this as, "I'm sorry it had to be this way" or "I'm sorry I've held on to this feeling." It does not mean that you are working to justify the behavior of anyone who harmed or mistreated you. Instead, this statement helps you to release any need to hold onto the memory of the experience in your body.

THIS IS A POWERFUL PRACTICE.

Ho'oponopono, an ancient Hawaiian practice of forgiveness, has since been updated by Dr. Ihaleakala Hew Len. His version of Ho'oponopono is known more specifically as Self Identity Through Ho'oponopono (SITH) and it is the version of this healing work that I personally practice.

Dr. Len is famous for healing a ward of criminally insane patients at Hawaii State Hospital. I've had the pleasure of learning this practice directly from Dr. Len. When asked how he helped these patients heal he replied, "I just kept cleaning." When I heard this I thought, *Huh, what does he mean?* I soon learned that he didn't mean he was cleaning the floors.

It turned out that he never, in fact, sat down to do any traditional therapy with these patients. He healed the patients by healing himself. "I kept working on healing me," said Dr. Len.

So, what's this "cleaning" all about?

Cleaning, in this case, refers to conflict resolution.

To define what Ho'oponopono means, the parts of the word break down as follows:

Ho'o= to make

pono= right

The double use of 'pono' emphasizes the need 'to be right with both yourself and others.'

I was looking back on my course notes and I remembered that Dr. Len said, "When you become right with others, you become right with yourself."

Our bodies often harbor anger and resentment internally in our physical tissues. Everything that surfaces in your life can be cleared, cleaned, and changed forever through forgiveness.

DAY SEVENTEEN

HO'OPONOPONO

"It's one of the greatest gifts you can give yourself, to forgive. Forgive everybody."

-Maya Angelou

Now that you chose the main limiting belief, simply tap on your thymus gland and repeat out loud 5-7 times:

" I RELEASE THIS BELIEF THAT _____."

In my example I would say, "I release this belief that (I have to be perfect)".

To assess whether this thymus gland healing exercise worked, take a deep breath in and out. Notice if you feel any less emotional charge when you think of that past memory. If not, try tapping for a few more rounds.

Reflection

What else was happening in your life during the time of this specific memory? (For example: I was upset with my Dad, I was in a rocky relationship, I was in high school honors classes and I was going back and forth between my parent's houses because they were divorced).

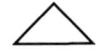

▽

Now, try to answer at least one of the following questions:

WHAT BELIEFS DID YOU HAVE ABOUT YOURSELF?
WHAT BELIEFS DID YOU HAVE ABOUT LIFE IN GENERAL?
WHAT BELIEFS DID YOU HAVE AROUND YOUR BODY?
WHAT BELIEFS DID YOU HAVE ABOUT OTHERS?
WHAT BELIEFS DID YOU HAVE ABOUT MONEY?
WHAT BELIEFS DID YOU HAVE ABOUT HEALTH?

(For example: I always believed that I had to be perfect. So perfect, that even though I was really qualified, I felt paralysis setting in when I was completing my college applications because I was afraid that I might not get into a good college).

Now, pull out one main limiting belief from your answer.
(An example of a limiting belief I pulled from my statement above is 'I have to be perfect.')

Next, ask yourself, what is the primary emotion behind these symptoms? For example: *"When I think about my knee pain I feel frustrated and stuck."* You can work on all the symptoms one by one or you can just choose to work on one for today.

▽

Now, ask yourself what events from your past come up when you think about this emotion? For example: *"When I think about feeling frustrated and stuck, I think about the time I was grounded for not submitting my college applications."* (true story!)

▽

Remember when we discussed tapping on Day 8? We're going to expand on that practice today.

This time you'll be working with your thymus gland.

When I first found out about the thymus gland I thought, *how can I live with an autoimmune disease and not know about this gland*? If you're just hearing about this, don't worry, I'll catch you up!

Your thymus gland is the master gland of your body's immune system. It is located under the hard part of your upper chest, behind your breastbone.

Dr. John Diamond, author and founder of *Life-Energy Analysis* explains that the thymus gland serves as a link between the mind and body.

The thymus gland is also responsible for immune function, and more specifically, it produces T lymphocytes, or T-cells. T-cells are white blood cells that protect the body against foreign invaders (such as bacteria or viruses).

Before we tap on the thymus gland, I encourage you to ask yourself the following questions. This process will help you to discover precisely what your body needs to release today.

First, take a moment to list out all of the main physical symptoms you are currently experiencing in your life (examples include: knee pain, headaches, asthma, eczema, heart palpitations, acne, etc).

DAY SIXTEEN

TAP, TAP, TAP

"When we accept ourselves as we are, we aren't "settling" or "keeping the problem in place." We're showing love and compassion for ourselves- for our feelings, our situation, and our history."

-Nick Ortner

notes:

THE MOST IMPORTANT PIECE OF
ADVICE I CAN GIVE YOU IS:

PRACTICE, PRACTICE, PRACTICE!!

Sometimes instead of general guidance, you may want to ask a specific question. Here are some examples:

- I am looking for guidance on my relationship.
- How is the energy of the past affecting this current situation?
- I would like to receive guidance on my career path.
- Divine Universe, please reveal what I need to know about making this decision.
- What is one way I can support my body today?

You can say all of these things out loud, or just hold the intention in your mind.

Example of a spread:

As you pull each card, you'll want to lay them out in a specific pattern so that each card represents a certain aspect of your answer. This is called a 'spread.' In this example, you will pull seven cards to create the spread. As you pull the cards, call to mind a specific challenge you'd like to work through or a question you have, then lay the cards out in the pattern listed below, keeping them face down:

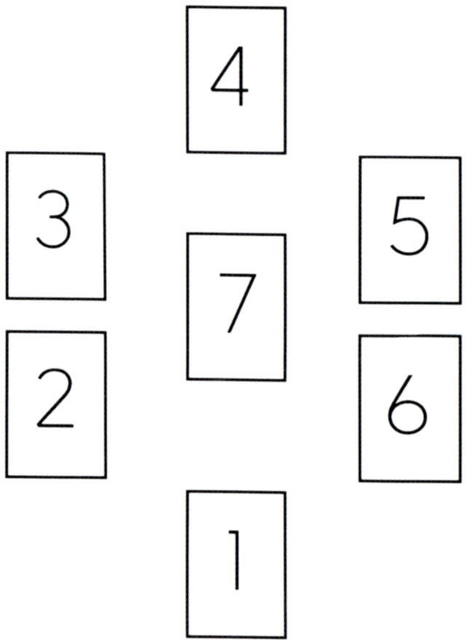

ONCE YOUR CARDS ARE ALL PULLED AND LAID OUT IN THE SPREAD, FLIP THEM OVER ONE AT A TIME AND TAKE IN THEIR INDIVIDUAL MEANINGS ONE BY ONE. HERE IS HOW TO INTERPRET THEM:

Card 1: Represents the present feelings, emotions, and environment
Card 2: Emotions that are currently surfacing or are trying to surface
Card 3: Beliefs that will support you during this time
Card 4: The unconscious, which represents what is hidden
Card 5: Your hopes and dreams
Card 6: The outcome of this situation
Card 7: The heart of what's going on and significance of it

YOU MAY WANT TO WRITE OUT THE THINGS THAT COME UP FOR YOU ON THE NEXT PAGE.

How to pull cards:

Again, there is no Universal Law here, so I encourage you to do what feels best and most natural for you.

I personally shuffle the deck by placing it in my right hand and shuffling it with my left. Then, I let my left fingers grab a place on the deck that feels right, and I pull that card. Instead of pulling from the middle of the deck, you can also pull from the top, or even the bottom.

Another way to pull a card is to spread the whole deck out in front of you in a straight line or in an arc, then hover your hands over the cards, and pick the one you are most called to.

If you don't like shuffling, one more common way of pulling a card involves continuing to cut the deck in half until it feels like it's time to stop.

Note: When a card falls out of the deck as you are shuffling, this is known as a jumping card, and it has special meaning. It's said that jumping cards are *shouts* from the Universe, trying to get your attention, so pay attention to these cards!

What to ask when beginning a reading:

As I said, there are no hard rules on how to do a reading or how to ask for direction or insights. But to align my energy, this is what I choose to say before I pull cards or ask questions of my deck:

Divine Universe, please help me clear my energy and allow me to be an open channel so this message can come through today. I am asking all of my guides, angels, and spirits to support me in discovering this message. May only the messages of the highest good channel through today.

Then, I'll ask my question. Oftentimes, I am just asking for general guidance.

If that were the case I would say something like this:

Please show me what I need to know or understand today.

When you first get your deck:

It's important to note that none of what I am sharing about how to use tarot and oracle cards is set in stone as a Universal Law. Instead these are simply my suggestions based on both what I've learned and what I've been taught during my own trainings.

Once you have your deck in front of you, I suggest that you get to know the cards before beginning to use them. Also, since oftentimes the cards are a little stuck together from the printing process, this gives you a good opportunity to peel them apart.

I recommend going through each card, one by one, and looking at the imagery. Notice if the visuals on the card mean anything to you, or if anything jumps out. When I was learning to use oracle cards, I was also encouraged to journal about each card and write down my own interpretation of it. However, this is optional, the most important part is to look at each card and make sure the deck shuffles well and moves fluidly.

Then, since it's likely your deck has picked up and carried the energy of the creator, the artist, the manufacturer, the postman, or store owner, I suggest you cleanse your deck.

There are many ways to cleanse your deck, but my favorites are:

1. LIGHT YOUR SAGE BUNDLE AND AS IT EMITS CLEANSING SMOKE, WAVE IT GENTLY OVER YOUR DECK.

2. PICK UP THE ENTIRE THE STACK OF CARDS AND GIVE THEM A FIRM KNOCK. YOU CAN DO THIS SEVERAL TIMES, LIKE YOU ARE KNOCKING ON A DOOR.

3. SET YOUR DECK OUT UNDER THE LIGHT OF THE FULL MOON. FOR EVEN MORE INTENSITY, SURROUND YOUR DECK WITH CLEAR QUARTZ CRYSTALS WHILE IT BATHES IN THE MOONLIGHT.

YOU CAN CLEANSE THE DECK WHEN YOU FIRST RECEIVE IT AND AGAIN ANYTIME YOU FEEL CALLED. I ALWAYS CLEANSE MY DECK WHEN IT STARTS TO FEEL STICKY, WHEN SOMEONE ELSE TOUCHES MY CARDS, AND WHEN IT'S BEEN A WHILE SINCE THEY'VE BEEN CLEANSED.

THE TAROT DECK- This is a classic type of oracle card. Each deck contains 78 cards, which are divided between major and minor arcana. Similar to playing cards, there are four different suits, but in tarot cards these suits include Wands, Cups, Swords, and Pentacles. Expert tarot readers have studied and defined the meaning behind each card, based on Universal archetypes. There is therefore less room for your own interpretation and a more definitive meaning within each card. However, though they all use the same basic structure, there are many different styles of tarot decks that feature different imagery.

HERE ARE SOME ORACLE CARD DECK SUGGESTIONS YOU CAN EXPLORE:

EARTH MAGIC
BY STEVEN D. FARMER

GODDESS GUIDANCE
BY DOREEN VIRTUE, PHD

WORK YOUR LIGHT
BY REBECCA CAMPBELL

CRYSTAL READING CARDS: THE HEALING ORACLE
BY RACHELLE CHARMAN

My best advice is to purchase the deck that you feel most called to. If possible, look at the imagery, hold the deck in your hand, or even muscle test like we learned in Day 14 to help you discover your preferences about which one you'd like to work with.

Nowadays, my brother's spirit shows up all the time. He helps guide each of us in the family as we travel along our individual paths and his death is what inspired me to do this work. Losing Jordan forced my soul to crack open — which initially felt like the worst thing that could possibly happen. Yet, I've come to realize that my crumbling offered me an opportunity to rebuild myself and recreate my life and my belief systems (similar to how an illness can help us to reform our lives and reevaluate our paths).

These days I find myself relying on a deep connection to my intuition and trusting the Universe, which you may choose to call many different names.

One of my favorite ways to connect to Universal energy as well as my guides, spirits, and angels, is through the use of oracle cards.

Oracle cards are based on Pythagorean Numerology, which teaches that each number and image vibrates in a very precise, mathematical manner.

To use oracle cards, you simply use your intuition to pull the card you are most drawn to.

Today, I'm going to be giving you some practical tools to get started using an oracle deck of your choice.

Oracle vs. Tarot:

THE ORACLE DECK- These types of cards are very uniquely creative, and they can represent whatever the creator of the deck wants them to convey. Some decks include affirmation cards, moon cards, and goddess cards. The creator picks how many cards they want to include in their deck and the kind of imagery they will use. Most oracle decks come with a companion booklet that describes what each card means, though the reader can also interpret them in their own way. In my opinion, oracle decks are more accessible because they are more open to individual interpretation.

DAY FIFTEEN

INTRO TO CARDS

"The cards give you images and symbols to focus your vague intentions and transform them into action. Your will is the magic. In other words, you are the magic. If you can create something in your heart and then act on it to make it happen, that is magic. Very simple, very straightforward—no witches, no spells, and no broomsticks."

-Theresa Cheung

We went to the funeral home the next day to make memorial service arrangements and later that afternoon we were able to visit Jordan's body.

Seeing and touching his cold hand brought up so many mixed emotions. The disbelief dissolved as I could now see my brother was no longer breathing. The pain deepened as truth set in and then something else happened: I wondered, with a deep curiosity, where my brother's soul had traveled to. His lifeless body now seemed like only an empty vessel. His spirit was no longer residing there.

So, what happens to our soul after death? The idea that he had just gone off into the dark, silent nothingness was a concept that I could not grasp.

Thankfully, in the weeks, months, and years to come he'd help show me that our souls do, in fact, live on.

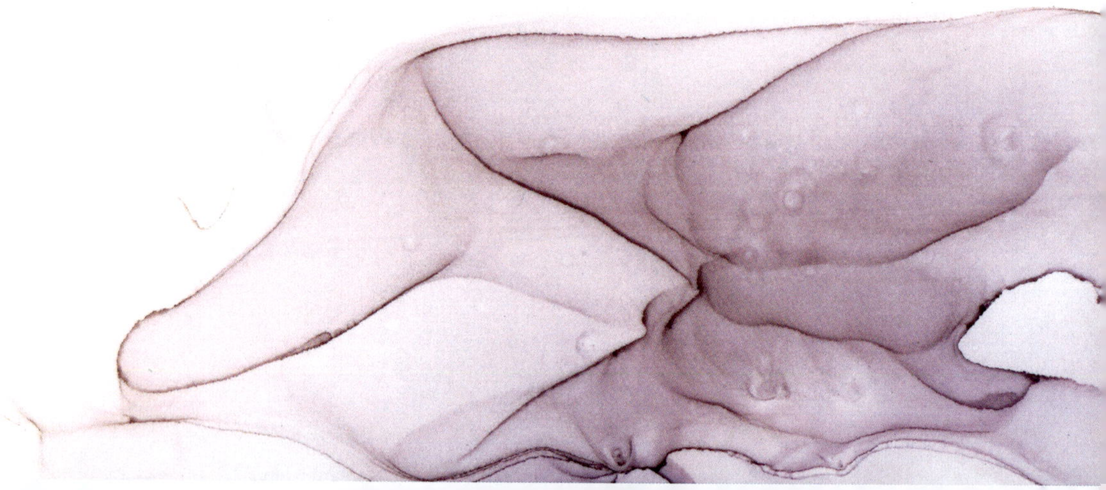

Jordan was my brother, and I had just seen him the Tuesday before when he had come down to Chicago from Michigan to visit a friend. We met for dinner at Blaze Pizza on Belmont Ave and we sat next to the open windows that cozied up to the sidewalk as people walked by. We didn't have too much time to catch up, I was going to a therapy appointment and he was going to a concert with a friend after dinner.

But, while we were together we chatted, we shared the things that were going on in our lives at that current moment. Everything seemed normal, simple, every day. He walked me to the building across the street where I had my appointment and we exchanged a giant hug, said "I love you," and then waved goodbye.

I remember thinking, "He's going to dance his ass off tonight." Jordan loved to dance.

But back to the afternoon I learned about Jordan's death, I was in the car, defeated by grief. I knew I had to get back home to Michigan as soon as possible. I was already the last person in my family to know because I had been preoccupied with the yoga event and I was the farthest away. Everyone was already gathering at my Mom's house, where it had all happened. My Dad said Jordan's body would be gone by the time I got there. He told me Jordan didn't leave a suicide note.

I panicked. My mind couldn't reconcile this unexplainable loss. Because I believe that the soul occupies the body for a time before departing, I felt a strong need to talk to him. I called my Mom and asked her to put the phone next to Jordan's ear.

She wasn't allowed to get that close to him, so the coroner held the phone up to my brother's dead body. I don't remember exactly what I said, but I remember thinking and saying something like, "I hope you can hear me. I hope your soul hasn't traveled too far outside your physical body yet. I need you know I love you. I'm so proud of the human you were. I love you so, so, so much. I hope you are at peace."

And then I heard my Mom's voice again. It was tragic to live with the thought that I would never see Jordan again.

I sat through eight hours of traffic before finally making it home to Michigan.

No one was okay, but everyone was trying to be okay.

The days that followed were heavy and heart breaking.

Welcome to Week 3!

On Sunday June 28, 2015 I was volunteering at an outdoor yoga event in Chicago. The studio I worked at decided to partner with the organizers of the event to provide hands-on assistance to all the participants while they were practicing. So, I spent two hours immersed in guiding and assisting the movement of these yogis.

My boyfriend met me there and after class we walked around the vendor's tents and soaked up the beautiful morning views of the Chicago lakefront.

Then, out of nowhere, I was overcome with a sharp pain in my stomach. This was the kind of pain that made me want to double over. The pain was so intense, I couldn't stand up straight and my boyfriend had to carry me to the car. When I got in, I shut the door and looked at my phone for the first time in hours. I had missed 13 calls, all from different family members.

I decided to call my Dad back first.

The phone rang and my Dad picked up quickly.

"Sarah, Jordan's dead."

I could only mutter out, "What? No!"

"He killed himself, honey."

My eyes welled up with tears and then poured out like sobbing sheets of rain. I pounded my fists against the window and yelled "no, no, no, no, no, no," in disbelief.

Anger swarmed around me and it felt like my heart disintegrated. I was torn. Defeated. Broken. I surrendered to a very deep, deep pain.

I kept asking questions even though I knew my Dad didn't have any answers.

Disbelief and the desire to make logical sense of this insurmountable loss took over. There must have been a reason. There must have been more to the situation than we could see.

Below I've supplied you with a space where you can write out the questions and statements you'd like to use in muscle testing:

STEP 4.

NOW YOU GET TO PLAY! YOU CAN ASK YOUR OWN YES OR NO QUESTIONS OR SAY STATEMENTS TO DETERMINE IF THEY ARE TRUE OR FALSE. BE AS CLEAR AND CONCISE WITH YOUR WORDING AS POSSIBLE WHEN ASKING THESE QUESTIONS. RELAX INTO THE PROCESS AND DON'T FORCE THE ANSWERS TO ARRIVE. TRY NOT TO SHOOT YOUR QUESTIONS OUT IN RAPID FIRE, INSTEAD TAKE A DEEP BREATH IN BETWEEN QUESTIONS SO THAT YOU TAKE TIME TO ALLOW YOUR BODY TO RESET. YOUR BODY WILL KNOW WHEN IT'S TIME TO QUIT FOR THE DAY.

*ANOTHER IMPORTANT THING TO KNOW ABOUT MUSCLE TESTING IS THAT THESE TESTS CANNOT PREDICT THE FUTURE. (SORRY!)

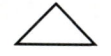

▽

HERE ARE SOME EXAMPLES OF QUESTIONS YOU CAN ASK AND STATEMENTS YOU CAN USE:

_____ CREATES INFLAMMATION IN MY BODY.
(INSERT AN ACTION, ACTIVITY, OR FOOD)

_____ CHAKRA IS OVERACTIVE (OR UNDER
(INSERT THE CHAKRA IN QUESTION)   ACTIVE).

THE ROOT OF THE TENSION IN MY LEFT SHOULDER IS
_____
(INSERT WHAT YOU THINK IT COULD BE)

IS THIS INFLAMMATION IN MY (AREA OF BODY) CAUSED BY AN
EMOTIONAL ROOT? PHYSICAL ROOT?

IS THERE A SPECIFIC EXPERIENCE FROM THE PAST CREATING
THIS _____?
(INSERT A SYMPTOM)

IS THERE A SPECIFIC ORGAN IN MY BODY HOLDING ON TO
THIS _____?
(INSERT AN EMOTION)

IF YOU GET A YES TO THE PREVIOUS QUESTION, THEN YOU
COULD FOLLOW IT UP BY ASKING:
IS IT MY _____?
(INSERT AN ORGAN, LIKE YOUR LIVER, FOR EXAMPLE)

STEP 1.

STAND WITH YOUR FEET AT HIP WIDTH APART. RELAX YOUR ARMS AND LEGS TO GET THEM NICE AND LOOSE, YOU CAN EVEN GIVE THEM A LITTLE SHAKE.

STEP 2.

TAKE ONE HAND (DOESN'T MATTER WHICH HAND) AND TAP YOUR THYMUS GLAND 5-10 TIMES. THE THYMUS GLAND IS UNDER THE HARD PLATE IN THE CENTER OF YOUR CHEST. TAPPING THIS GLAND HELPS YOU CLEAR YOUR ENERGY, SO YOU CAN ACT AS A MORE NEUTRAL VESSEL WHILE PERFORMING THE MUSCLE TEST.

STEP 3.

TO SEE IF YOUR BODY IS TESTABLE, SAY SOMETHING YOU KNOW TO BE TRUE. FOR EXAMPLE, MY NAME IS _____ (INSERT YOUR REAL NAME). TYPICALLY, A YES OR A TRUE ANSWER WILL CAUSE YOUR BODY TO MOVE FORWARD, LIKE SOMEONE IS GENTLY PUSHING YOU. PLEASE NOTE THAT ALTHOUGH THIS RESPONSE IS COMMON, EVERY PERSON'S BODY REACTS SLIGHTLY DIFFERENTLY. YOU MAY ALSO FEEL YOURSELF MOVING FORWARD AND SLIGHTLY TO THE RIGHT, FOR EXAMPLE. NEXT, SAY SOMETHING YOU KNOW TO BE FALSE, FOR EXAMPLE, MY NAME IS _____ (INSERT ANYONE ELSE'S NAME BUT YOUR OWN). NOTICE WHAT YOUR BODY DOES THIS TIME. TYPICALLY, A NO OR FALSE STATEMENT CAUSES YOU TO MOVE BACKWARD, LIKE SOMEONE PUSHED YOU BACK A LITTLE BIT.

Note: If you find that you do not get a clear true or false, you can try the following steps to remedy this: 1) clear your energy again 2) come back to the muscle test at another time and try it again 3) make sure you've dropped any preconceived notions about this activity and perform the test again with an open mind or 4) research the finger or arm muscle test to see other ways to perform muscle tests.

exploring your own super powers and experiencing your own version of what it means to embody your inner Wonder Woman!

So, what is muscle testing?

The technique is also referred to as Applied Kinesiology and it allows us to tap into the programming within our subconscious mind. After all, most experts state that the constructs of our minds are only 10% conscious and 90% subconscious. So, what if you could tap into the vast subconscious and unlock all the programming stored there?

The subconscious mind is the autopilot that guides you through much of your day. It directs you as you navigate your car from home to work, it helps you to walk while also talking, and it brings the fork up to your mouth without you having to look or think about it.

Since your subconscious controls around 90% of your daily life and behaviors, when you begin accessing this part of your mind you discover answers that lead you to witnessing the freaking AMAZING potential you have within to heal.

You can't always access the best possible answers when you use your logical mind as the primary detective, guiding everything you do. We think our logical minds know best, but let's reconsider for a moment. If you continue operating based only on what you currently know, you inevitably leave out a ton of possibilities.

What our conscious minds may not know is that we, as humans, have this electrical field surrounding us. The studies that revealed these electrical fields are very cool, check out *Heart Math Institute* for more research.

These electrical fields are sensitive to your thoughts and when you make a statement that is true, that energy will continue to flow through them. Conversely, when you make a statement that is false, the energy will temporarily short circuit.

To illustrate how this works, I will explain how our energy system responds when we perform the standing muscle test, which is just one of many ways to perform a muscle test.

Muscle test

When I first heard about muscle testing, I was on a family vacation. I found myself reading all about how this practice worked, and I thought, *there's no way this will really work for me,* but I decided to try it anyway.

I went into the bedroom I was staying in, I shut the door, and closed the blinds. I even made sure no one was peeking in at me. Then the thought, "Why are you even trying this, Sarah? What the heck are you doing right now?" crossed my mind.

I was tempted to chicken-out, but at the time my cystic acne was making me feel miserable and I was desperately seeking a solution.

I felt divinely guided to test it out even though fear was pushing me the other way. Instead of allowing fear to stop me, I leaned in even closer to the fear. I got quiet and put my trust in the Universe, and then, the magic happened.

My body, or more specifically my subconscious, began speaking to me.

HOLY SHIT!

This. is. Cool.

I basically felt like Wonder Woman!

It was MAGICAL.

Some of the messages I received from my body during that first practice were:

I was sensitive to eggs.
I learned what other foods I was eating that were causing inflammation.
I discovered the root of my eye inflammation.

Today, I'm going to teach you how muscle testing works so you can start

DAY FOURTEEN

HOW TO MUSCLE TEST

"In conventional medicine you diagnose and treat an illness. In energy medicine, you assess where the energy needs attention and correct the energy disturbances."

-Donna Eden

Laughter

THE BENEFITS OF LAUGHTER HAVE BEEN FREQUENTLY STUDIED AND THERE ARE NOW MANY HEALTHY REASONS TO BRING MORE LAUGHTER INTO YOUR LIFE. IT HAS ALSO BEEN SHOWN TO STIMULATE THE VAGUS NERVE, SO LAUGH AWAY!

(SOURCE: HTTPS://WWW.NCBI.NLM.NIH.GOV/PUBMED/12959437)

Cold Temperature

YOU CAN ATTUNE YOUR BODY TO COLDER TEMPERATURES BY TRYING VARIOUS FORMS OF CRYOTHERAPY LIKE JUMPING INTO THE ICE TUB AT YOUR LOCAL GYM OR TAKING A WALK OUTSIDE IN THE COLD. EVEN SOMETHING SIMPLE LIKE TURNING ON THE COLD WATER WHEN YOU SHOWER OR CREATING YOUR OWN COLD BATH TUB CAN STIMULATE YOUR VAGUS NERVE. THE ACT OF STARTING YOUR DAY OFF WITH A COLD-WATER PLUNGE, WHICH WAS MADE FAMOUS THROUGH THE WIM HOF METHOD, HELPS LOWER STRESS MARKERS IN YOUR BODY. I PERSONALLY TRIED THIS IN SHORT BURSTS, STARTING WITH THE CHALLENGE OF 15 SECONDS OF COLD WATER AT THE END OF MY SHOWER AND I'VE WORKED MY WAY UP TO 1 MINUTE BY ADDING 15 MORE SECONDS EACH TIME.

(SOURCE: HTTPS://WWW.NCBI.NLM.NIH.GOV/PUBMED/18785356)

Breath work

Simply taking in a deep belly breath can actually signal to your body that everything is safe and it is okay to relax. This deep breath signals your parasympathetic nervous system, therefore helping to improve vagal tone. You can find many guided breath work exercises for free on YouTube. I personally like the 4-part box breathing and alternate nostril breathing the best.

Coffee Enemas

Enemas serve to activate the vagus nerve and they are one of my favorite tools because of the numerous health benefits they provide. The actual act of holding the liquid in is what activates the nerve. I typically aim for 10-15 minutes, but while working towards that goal you can just hold it for as long as you can. There are also compounds within (organic) coffee that stimulate your nerve receptors and activate the vagus nerve as well. To learn how to do an at home coffee enema listen to Episode 12 of my podcast, Healing Uncensored. Or you can make an appointment for a colonic at a local med spa.

Gargle

The vagus nerve is activated when the back of the throat is contracted. So, try gargling a sip of water. Ideally, just like with gagging, you want to continue only until your eyes start to water, then you know you have activated the vagus nerve.

BECAUSE IT IS SO IMPORTANT TO BEGIN UNDERSTANDING OUR VAGUS NERVE AND

HOW TO CARE FOR IT, HERE ARE 8 WAYS TO INCREASE YOUR VAGAL TONE:

Apply Essential Oils

RUB 1-2 DROPS OF FRANKINCENSE OIL BEHIND EACH EAR. THIS IS THE LOCATION OF YOUR MASTOID BONE, WHICH IS WHERE THE VAGUS NERVE TRAVELS DOWN FROM YOUR BRAIN. FRANKINCENSE HELPS OPEN THINGS UP TO SUPPORT LYMPHATIC DRAINAGE. OTHER SOOTHING AND CALMING OILS LIKE ROMAN CHAMOMILE, VETIVER, AND CLARY SAGE ARE ALSO HELPFUL WHEN APPLIED THE SAME WAY BECAUSE THEY HELP SIGNAL YOUR PARASYMPATHETIC NERVOUS SYSTEM TO TURN ON.

Sing

RESEARCH SHOWS THAT SINGING HAS A SOOTHING EFFECT ON YOUR BODY. WHETHER YOU SING IN THE CAR, IN THE SHOWER, WITH YOUR BEST FRIENDS, OR EVEN ON STAGE, SINGING AND CHANTING ARE THERAPEUTIC FOR YOUR VAGUS NERVE. THE LOUDER YOU SING, THE MORE YOU ACTIVATE YOUR VAGUS NERVE AND THE MORE YOU ELEVATE YOUR VAGAL TONE.
(SOURCE: HTTPS://WWW.NCBI.NLM.NIH.GOV/PMC/ARTICLES/PMC3705176/)

Gag

USING A TONGUE DEPRESSOR, GENTLY PUSH DOWN ON THE BACK OF YOUR TONGUE. DO THIS JUST UNTIL YOUR EYES START TO WATER. THIS IS AN EXERCISE THAT PROVIDES STRENGTH TRAINING FOR YOUR VAGUS NERVE, HELPING YOU TO IMPROVE IT'S TONE.

*NOTE: IF YOU HAVE A MEDICAL HISTORY OF EATING DISORDERS, THIS IS NOT THE BEST METHOD FOR YOU.

Vagus Nerve

We're taking a turn on this healing highway today and getting off at the Vegas exit!

Okay, maybe not THAT Vegas! Instead we're going to discuss your vagus nerve. Yes, yes, this workbook is all about the emotional side of healing, but I can't help but insert a little bit of my inner biology nerd into this process. Plus, learning how to stimulate your vagus nerve could be life changing for some of you on both a physical AND emotional level!

So, what IS the vagus nerve?

The vagus nerve is known as the "wandering nerve" (vagus is Latin for 'wandering') because it has multiple branches that are rooted to two stems in the cerebellum and brainstem. These branches touch almost every organ in your body, therefore this nerve is a master controller of your body. The vagus nerve releases acetylcholine which is like your body's self-administered Xanax (only much safer). It helps calm your body down and it naturally reduces inflammation.

The way the vagus nerve is operating can be measured by vagal tone. Healthy vagal tone indicates your body can effectively enter parasympathetic mode, allowing your heart rate to slow down and your blood pressure to decrease during times of stress. High vagal tone is associated with overall health, wellbeing, and homeostasis. Whereas, low vagal tone is accompanied by depression, inflammation, heart attacks, and loneliness.

When you have a toxic vagus nerve (also referred to as lack of motility) it can affect all the downstream functions in the body, especially the digestive system. This can lead to malabsorption issues and leaky gut.

Are you starting to see why I wanted to include this 'trip to Vegas' in the book?

DAY THIRTEEN

VEGAS BABY

"One of the most neglected things that I think most practitioners don't understand, whether they're conventional or alternative, is that there's this brain-to-gut axis."

-Datis Kharrazian

Here's a little example:

▽

DEAR FEAR,

I KNOW YOU ARE TRYING TO KEEP ME SAFE, BUT I'M OKAY, REALLY. YOU ARE KEEPING ME IN A STATE OF FIGHT OR FLIGHT OVER THINGS THAT ARE NO LONGER HERE TO HARM ME, AND I SO DESPERATELY WANT TO RELAX. FEAR, I NEED YOU TO FUCK OFF. I CHOOSE A LOVING STATE. I TURN TO LOVE. I BREATHE IN LOVE. AND YOU KEEP GETTING IN THE WAY. SO SERIOUSLY... YOU CAN LEAVE NOW!

LOVE, SARAH

I like to follow all of this healing work up with a dance party. There is something magical that happens when we move our body to a rhythm or beat. It elevates our vibration and brings us into coherence. We move from the low vibration of fear to the higher vibration of LOVE.

So, when you are ready I invite you to turn on a song you love, close your eyes, and dance away rest of the fear!

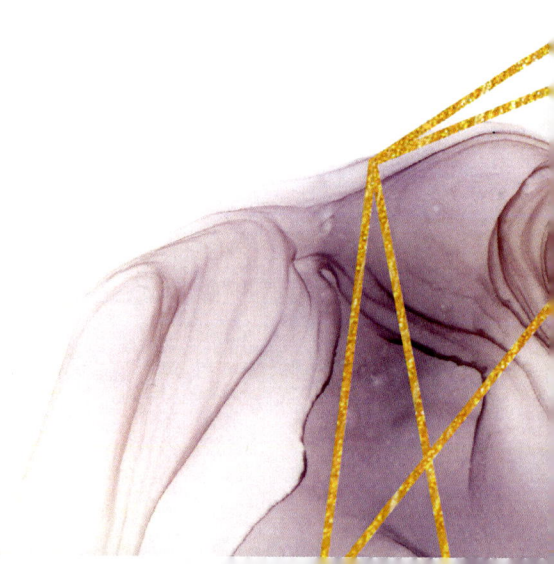

3. WRITE ABOUT IT AND WRITE TO IT - CONTINUED.

Now go back and read what you wrote and notice WHERE you felt this fear inside your body as well.

I felt the fear of _____ in my_____.

EXAMPLE:

I FELT THE FEAR OF THIS MAN IN MY CHEST.

4. RELEASE FEAR'S CONTROL OVER YOU. TURN TO LOVE.

Next, I encourage you to treat yourself gently, especially if you have experienced trauma in the past and these recent triggers have caused you to feel that same sense of fear. Close your eyes and imagine sending healing thoughts and energy to your deepest fears. You can do this by simply visualizing a golden sparkly light circling around and encompassing the things that create fear and wishing those things the best.

Then, bring your hands to your heart... and scoop your power back in.

Feel your heartbeat. Feel the love that lives inside you.

I also find it helpful to write a letter to the fear.

3. WRITE ABOUT IT AND WRITE TO IT.

Next, I encourage you to allow yourself to write about this fear freely and intuitively. When you do this, you allow yourself to access your stream of consciousness, versus writing what you think "should" or "shouldn't" feel. After you write out what you are afraid of, take each item and write out WHY you are feeling afraid of this thing...

I feel afraid of _____ BECAUSE _____.

EXAMPLE:

I FEEL AFRAID OF THIS MAN BECAUSE HE HAS HURT ME IN THE PAST AND I DON'T FEEL SAFE WHEN HE IS AROUND.

YOUR TURN:

I feel afraid of . . . because . . .

I feel afraid of. . .

EXAMPLES:

I feel afraid of this man coming back to hurt me.
I feel afraid of letting people down.
I feel afraid of not being perfect.
I feel afraid of losing someone.
I feel afraid of hurting myself.
I feel afraid of messing up.
I feel afraid of dying.

What do YOU feel afraid of? Take some to write down the fears you thought of above and write them out in as much detail as you'd like.

I feel afraid of. . .

My boyfriend came out of the bedroom and asked what was wrong because he could see I was having a panic attack. I couldn't explain. I muttered out... "Nicole Kidman's husband is abusive on the TV show." He looked at me EXTRA confused. (I don't blame him.)

I recognize now that I experienced a trigger. That trigger brought up an old emotion from a past experience. And the fear came back in full force.

After re-experiencing all of this fear, I found ways to reconcile it and I want to share the following activity with you. It is one way that you can cope when something triggers fear in you.

1. ACKNOWLEDGE IT.

Say, "Hi fear! I see you there. I see you trying to keep me on high alert for a reason."

Then, realize that not all fear is bad, sometimes fear is an indication of excitement, passion, or strong feelings towards something. It's also one way our bodies are continually trying to keep us safe.

2. GIVE IT A NAME. WHAT ARE YOU AFRAID OF?

Close your eyes. Put your hands on your belly. Ask yourself: "What am I afraid of? What is the deeper root here?" I encourage you to try not to overthink it.

The other day I found myself triggered by something I saw on a TV show that caused me to spiral into fear and panic.

I was watching the show *Big Little Lies* on HBO and if you haven't watched the show, it features an abusive husband who scares the living shit out of his wife. She's terrified of him.

Being an empath, I cry all the time while I'm watching TV shows. I also feel happiness when I see joyful things occurring and I feel fear when I see violence. (Note: This is why it is so important to develop strong BOUNDARIES for yourself, so you can differentiate what pain or joy is actually yours and what your simply picking up from a TV show!)

On this particular day when I was triggered by the show, not only did I pick up on the fear from the actors (who were obviously just acting), but I was also transported back to a personal experience. The old emotions affiliated with this experience reminded me of a memory when someone scared the living shit out of ME.

I felt like I had lost control. I was transported back to 2016 when I was threatened in my own bed, under my own light blue sheets. Feeling violated. Feeling terrified. Powerless. Numb, and full of fear.

For 2 weeks after this frightening encounter I barely left the house. For 2 weeks I took at least one hot bath per day. For 2 weeks I anxiously waited for test results and lab work. For 2 weeks I felt like another human had taken away every ounce of power I ever had.

After those 2 weeks passed, I called my energy healer for an emergency appointment. She told me I was going to be okay and she encouraged me to take back my power. She recommended that I send love and angels to the man who violated me because it was better than the alternative of continuing to give him power through my anger and fear. So, I sent him those angels and I reclaimed my power.

I also forgave him. (But that's for your day 17 lesson...)

So there I was, a year or so later, watching a TV show that catapulted me into a panic attack before I could even really process what was going on. Though my mind did not make obvious connections to the pains of the past, my body remembered the fear and I felt as if the event were happening all over again.

DAY TWELVE

FUCK FEAR

"Our deepest fear is not that we are inadequate. Our deepest fear is that we are powerful beyond measure."

-Marianne Williamson

STEP SEVEN: What have the negative consequences been?

It has affected my health. I've lost sleep over it. I've put others first constantly. It has stressed me out. It has ended in hurt feelings.

STEP EIGHT: Is this belief that "I'm responsible for everyone" ultimately true?

No

STEP NINE: What would someone who loves you say to you if you shared this belief?

They would say… Sarah, you are a great sister and daughter. You will still be a great sister and daughter even if you don't fix everyone else's problems. You need to take care of yourself first and then you can support others more effectively.

STEP TEN: Tap and release.

I RELEASE THIS BELIEF THAT I AM RESPONSIBLE FOR EVERYONE.
I RELEASE THIS BELIEF THAT I AM RESPONSIBLE FOR EVERYONE.
I RELEASE THIS BELIEF THAT I AM RESPONSIBLE FOR EVERYONE.

STEP ELEVEN: Install a new, supportive belief.

I AM ONLY RESPONSIBLE FOR MYSELF.
I AM ONLY RESPONSIBLE FOR MYSELF.
I AM ONLY RESPONSIBLE FOR MYSELF.

TO MAKE THIS EVEN EASIER TO UNDERSTAND, I WILL SHARE AN EXAMPLE OF HOW I WORKED THROUGH ONE OF MY OWN LIMITING BELIEFS BELOW.

STEP ONE: If possible, identify your belief.

I wasn't able to pinpoint my belief right away, so I proceeded to step two.

STEP TWO: What is the story you tell?

I often heard myself saying that family issues stressed me out. That I had to be there for everyone all the time, no matter what, no excuses. Family comes first. If someone had a problem, I needed to help fix it.

STEP THREE: Pull out the limiting belief(s).

I am responsible for everyone.
I should put myself last.
I have to fix other people's problems.

STEP FOUR: Pick one belief to work through today.

I am responsible for everyone.

STEP FIVE: When do you first remember this belief?

Around age 12-13 when my parents got divorced. My Dad moved out of the house and we were splitting time between Mom's house and Dad's new house.

STEP SIX: How has this belief served me or kept me safe?

It made me feel like I had control over something in my life. It made me feel like I could keep my family safe.

10.

Hopefully by now you've realized that this limiting belief is not ultimately true, and you have come to see the origins of the belief and how it now no longer serves you. To affirm that you have chosen to let go of this belief, fill in the blank below. Repeat this statement to yourself 3-5 times as you tap your fingers on your chest (around your thymus gland).

I RELEASE THIS BELIEF THAT

_____

_____

You can also imagine yourself releasing the belief energetically. You may visualize it floating away, or burning up, or disconnecting from your body, whichever visual feels strongest for you.

11.

Choose one new supportive or positive belief to install into your subconscious programming. Fill in the blank below. Repeat this statement to yourself 3-5 times as you tap your fingers on your chest, just like you did above.

I INSTALL THIS BELIEF THAT

_____

_____

And so, it is done.

7.

How has this belief, which you once created to serve and protect you, also created negative consequences in your life? What has happened to you up until now or what is happening to you now as a result of this belief?

8.

Is this belief ultimately TRUE?

YES   NO

9.

Imagine telling someone you love, and who loves you very much, about this belief that you have been holding onto. How do you think they would they respond to you? What do you think they would say about it? Spend some time reflecting on this below:

4.

Next, I invite you to pick one limiting belief you want to work through today and list it below:

5.

I encourage you to imagine going back in time until you find the moment when you first developed this belief. At what age do you first remember having this belief? Please feel free to take the time necessary to write about this experience in the box below:

6.

How has this belief served you in the past or how has it kept you safe in the present? This part of the work can be hard to think of because we might just view the negative parts of the limiting belief, but at some point, you created this belief because it helped you or protected you. Spend some time recognizing how this belief once served and protected you in the space below:

1. To begin the process, do you resonate with any of the limiting beliefs listed on the previous page? If not, do you already know some of the beliefs you have? Write them out first.

2. Next, what do you believe about yourself or your circumstances when you think of the story surrounding your chronic illness? How about the beliefs you hold onto about your life in general or about the world as a whole? What are some of the most common things you talk about or that come up in conversation that might be limiting?

3. Now, can you deconstruct what you wrote about above and pick out any beliefs that do not serve you? If you see any that are limiting you, please list them in the box below. This is a big step so please be gentle with yourself when these limiting beliefs become apparent.

A limiting belief constrains us or holds us back in some way. Limiting beliefs can also give us a false sense of safety. By accepting these limiting beliefs as truth, we continue to live in a place of lack. Our beliefs are powerful, and they dictate how we interact with the world, how we view ourselves, and how we behave in our relationship with others.

HERE ARE SOME EXAMPLES OF COMMON LIMITING BELIEFS:

- I lack motivation.

- I'm not worthy of love.

- I don't have time.

- I don't have enough resources.

- It's too late to change.

- I am responsible for everyone.

- I have no clue where to start.

- The world is not a safe place.

- I have to be perfect.

- I don't deserve good health.

Today, I encourage you to try my step-by-step process to release your limiting beliefs.

This is honestly one of the most powerful activities I've done in my healing journey.

Originally, I worked with an energy healer and she helped me identify the limiting beliefs I was holding within me, then she helped me release them energetically. I do recommend working with a coach if you wind up feeling stuck at any point during this experience.

DAY ELEVEN

RELEASE LIMITING BELIEFS

"Remember: We all get what we tolerate. So, stop tolerating excuses within yourself, limiting beliefs of the past, or half-assed or fearful states."

-Tony Robbins

Next, I want you to reach out to the people on your list and tell them what you appreciate about them.

There are no heavy expectations. Just reach out and share your appreciation and LOVE.

You can choose to reach out in the form of a text, a phone call, an email, a Facebook message, or even a handwritten note. It's up to you!

As a part of my own appreciation challenge, I wrote the following email to my Dad.

HI DAD, I JUST WANTED TO SEND YOU A NOTE OF APPRECIATION THIS MORNING. I APPRECIATE YOUR GUIDANCE, YOUR WISDOM, YOUR LOVE, YOUR HUMOR, YOUR ATHLETICISM (PARTIALLY PASSED ON TO ME), YOUR COMPETITIVENESS (ALSO GOT THAT FROM YOU), YOUR SENSITIVE HEART, YOUR DESIRE TO MAKE SURE EVERYONE IS HAPPY, YOUR ABILITY TO EXPRESS YOUR GRIEF FROM LOSING JORDAN (THAT MEANS A LOT TO SEE THAT OTHER PEOPLE ARE JUST AS SAD). YOUR ADVENTUROUS SOUL, YOUR FATHERLY WORRY (MAYBE NOT WHEN I WAS 16), YOUR THOUGHT YOU PUT INTO EVERY WORD YOU SPEAK, YOUR FUN, YOUR LAUGHTER, AND YOUR PASSION FOR A WELL-LIVED LIFE.

I FEEL GRATEFUL TO HAVE YOU AS A FATHER. AND AS A COACH IN THE PAST (I THINK THAT DEFINED A LOT OF WHO I AM TODAY).

I LOVE YOU VERY, VERY MUCH.

WISHING YOU AN AWESOME DAY.

LOVE,

SARAH

Now, consider 5 people you appreciate having in your life.

Write one name in each of the boxes below and then write down a couple reasons why you appreciate them.

PERSON 1

PERSON 2

PERSON 3

PERSON 4

PERSON 5

HERE IS YOUR OPPORTUNITY TO EXPLORE THE THINGS THAT MATTER MOST TO YOU RIGHT NOW:

Today I appreciate...

Example

TODAY I APPRECIATE:

- THE MOUNTAINS
- MY DOG, BELLA
- MONK FRUIT
- MY JOB
- MY INSTANT POT
- MY MEDITATION APP
- MOTHER EARTH
- JASMINE ESSENTIAL OIL

When I think of traditional gratitude messages and practices (not ALWAYS, but sometimes) it feels like I am being asked to write out how lucky I should feel for having _____ (ex: love). When the truth is, I feel I am always worthy of having _____ (ex: love).

So, here's how I've come to change the script!

I use the word APPRECIATE.

AP·PRE·CI·ATE (verb): recognizing the full worth of

WHOA! What a shift! So, when you appreciate yourself, someone else, or something you have you are recognizing it's WORTH, and how WORTHY you are as a human being.

It is also defined as knowing the VALUE of something. You may have heard the word 'appreciate' used in relation to finances. It is used to explain how the value of something GROWS over time.

What you appreciate GROWS.

You invite MORE of what you appreciate into your life.

I'm not suggesting you never write a gratitude list ever again or that you never say the word 'gratitude', but instead I suggest that you just notice the energy behind the word gratitude when you say it. Does it mean that you are simply 'feeling lucky' to have what you have? Or are you conveying 'a deep appreciation?

Now that we've explored the meaning of the words gratitude and appreciation, we're going to try an APPRECIATION challenge today!

Start by writing out some of the things you appreciate (people you care for, experiences that are meaningful, things you enjoy, use all of your senses to explore the things you appreciate).

Let me get brutally honest with you. When I'm having a ROUGH day and someone suggests that I focus on all of the things I should be grateful for, it can feel somewhat cold or insensitive. I know they mean well and I recognize that to some extent this can be good advice, but it can also leave me feeling like I'm either grasping for support, forcing myself to get through things based on someone else's sense of timing, or that my feelings are invalid.

What are your thoughts on this topic? Have you received this type of advice yourself?

It goes kind of like this...

ME: "WHOA AM I HAVING A CRAZY DAY. MY EMAIL SERVER WAS DOWN FOR MAINTENANCE ALL DAY. THEN THE COFFEE SHOP CLOSED FIVE MINUTES BEFORE I COULD GET THERE. AT LUNCH, I SPILLED KETCHUP ALL OVER MY WHITE PANTS. AND THEN I HIT EVERY RED LIGHT ON THE WAY HOME."

SALLY: "JUST THINK OF ALL YOU HAVE TO BE GRATEFUL FOR."

ME: "YEAH, YOU'RE RIGHT. I'M WHINING. THERE ARE SO MANY PEOPLE WHO HAVE BIGGER PROBLEMS THAN MINE."

SALLY: "RIGHT. SO, THINK OF HOW LUCKY YOU ARE."

ME: **IN MY MIND I'M THINKING** "UGHHHHH...I GET THAT, BUT THAT MAKES ME FEEL LIKE MY EMOTIONS ARE NOT VALID AND LIKE I'M NOT WORTHY OF THE GOOD THINGS I DO HAVE GOING FOR ME IN MY LIFE." **BUT INSTEAD, I SAY OUT LOUD** "YEAH... I'M REALLY LUCKY."

I often find myself writing gratitude lists, and after a while I start to feel like since I've just acknowledged that I have food on my table and a roof over my head, I'm not "allowed" to feel frustrated about anything. I have money in my bank account, but do I even deserve it? I having an amazing fiancé, does that make me lucky? I don't think so. I think I'm worthy and deserving of all those things. I'm not 'lucky' to have an amazing fiancé, I am an energetic match for him. And I am amazing too!

Gratitude is NOT a bad thing. I just like to practice it in a different way.

DAY TEN

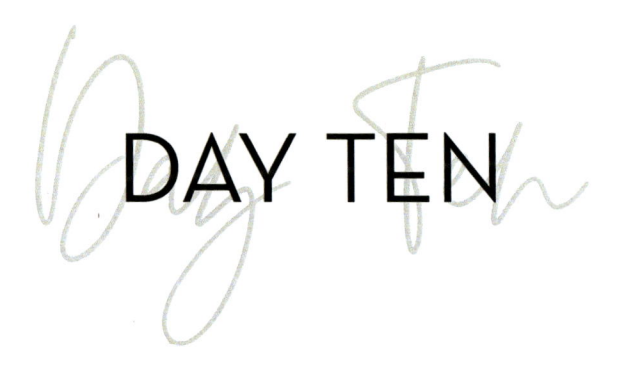

APPRECIATION CHALLENGE

"The roots of all goodness lie in the soil of appreciation for goodness."

-Dalai Lama

Healing practice:

TO BEGIN EXPERIENCING THE HEALING BENEFITS OF CRYSTALS, PICK UP YOUR FAVORITE STONES FROM EACH COLOR CATEGORY (THESE CAN BE FOUND EITHER ONLINE OR AT YOUR LOCAL CRYSTAL SHOP). THEN, FIND A COMFORTABLE PLACE TO LAY DOWN AND PLACE ONE OF THE CRYSTALS ON EACH OF THE CORRESPONDING CHAKRAS. REFER TO DAY TWO FOR A VISUAL REPRESENTATION OF WHERE EACH OF THE CHAKRAS ARE IN YOUR BODY. SO, FOR EXAMPLE, YOUR GREEN CRYSTAL WILL BE PLACED ON YOUR HEART CHAKRA, WHICH IS NEAR THE CENTER OF YOUR CHEST. THEN, TURN ON YOUR FAVORITE MUSIC AND SIMPLY LAY QUIET OR LISTEN TO YOUR FAVORITE GUIDED MEDITATION WHILE LETTING THE CRYSTALS DO THEIR WORK. REST THERE FOR ABOUT 10-20 MINUTES AND NOTE WHETHER OR NOT YOU FEEL A SENSE OF HEALING AFTER YOU HAVE TAKEN THIS TIME TO ALLOW THE CRYSTALS TO DO THEIR VIBRATIONAL MAGIC. THERE IS ONLY ONE RULE: PLACE YOUR ROOT CHAKRA STONE ON YOUR BODY FIRST, AND REMOVE IT LAST BECAUSE IT HELPS YOU STAY GROUNDED THROUGHOUT THE ENTIRE PROCESS!

red

RED CRYSTALS ARE ASSOCIATED WITH YOUR ROOT CHAKRA. THEY HELP YOU CULTIVATE GROUNDING, STABILIZATION, REJUVENATION, CENTERING, ANCHORING AND WARMING YOUR PHYSICAL BODY, STIMULATING YOUR CIRCULATION AND GETTING YOURSELF OUT OF SURVIVAL MODE.

orange

ORANGE CRYSTALS ARE ASSOCIATED WITH YOUR SACRAL CHAKRA. THEY HELP WITH CULTIVATING CREATIVITY, COURAGE, CONNECTIONS TO YOUR FEMININE ENERGY, FORMING NEW IDEAS, EXPERIENCING SENSUALITY AS WELL AS YOUR SEXUAL NATURE AND YOUR GODDESS ENERGY.

yellow

YELLOW CRYSTALS ARE ASSOCIATED WITH YOUR SOLAR PLEXUS CHAKRA. THEY HELP WITH CULTIVATING SELF-WORTH, SELF-CONFIDENCE, TAKING ACTION, LESSENING INFLAMMATION AND ANXIETY, IMPROVING DIGESTION AND SKIN HEALTH, ENHANCING EXCITEMENT FOR LIFE AND PROVIDING EMPATH PROTECTION.

green

GREEN CRYSTALS ARE ASSOCIATED WITH YOUR HEART CHAKRA. THEY HELP WITH OPENING AND HEALING YOUR HEART, DEVELOPING ENERGETIC BOUNDARIES, EMBRACING FORGIVENESS, COMPASSION AND EMPATHY, REDUCING INFLAMMATION, IMPROVING THE HEALTH OF THE HEART, IMMUNE SYSTEM, LUNGS, AND NERVOUS SYSTEM, AS WELL AS RETAINING A CONNECTION TO MOTHER EARTH.

blue

BLUE CRYSTALS ARE ASSOCIATED WITH YOUR THROAT CHAKRA. THEY HELP YOU FEEL EMPOWERED TO SPEAK YOUR TRUTH, EXPRESS YOURSELF, AND TAKE BACK YOUR POWER, THEY IMPROVE THYROID HEALTH AND SWALLOWING, AND PROVIDE YOU WITH AN OPPORTUNITY TO EXPERIENCE PEACE AND ACCEPTANCE.

purple

PURPLE CRYSTALS ARE ASSOCIATED WITH YOUR THIRD EYE CHAKRA. THEY HELP WITH CONNECTING TO YOUR INTUITION (ALSO KNOWN AS THE CLAIR SENSES), IMPROVING YOUR ABILITY TO TRUST YOURSELF AND TO BETTER LISTEN TO OTHERS. THEY CAN LESSEN MIGRAINES, AWAKEN YOUR SPIRITUAL SELF, HELP YOU TO CONNECT TO YOUR HIGHER SELF FOR PURPOSES OF TRANSFORMATION, AND DEEPEN MEDITATION.

white

WHITE CRYSTALS ARE ASSOCIATED WITH THE CROWN CHAKRA. THEY HELP YOU WITH FINDING YOUR PURPOSE AND YOUR PLACE IN THE WORLD, CULTIVATING SPIRITUAL BELIEFS, MORALS AND VALUES, RETAINING BALANCE AND A SENSE OF BELONGING, RELEASING THE NEED FOR PERFECTION, AND EXPANDING YOUR CONNECTION TO YOUR SOURCE AND THE DIVINE.

Let's get two things straight:

1. Crystals are not a religion.

2. Crystals are not too "woo-woo" to work.

If you want the deeper details and more scientific explanations beyond what I'm going to teach you today, go pick up the book *Vibrational Medicine* by Richard Gerber and you'll have plenty to study!

On the most basic level, a crystal is a natural mineral form created from the Earth.

Some crystals are sold in their natural state, while others are cut into different shapes (like hearts, pyramids, etc.) by lapidary artists, to give off the energy of that shape. They each also possess a natural color.

Those colors are light emissions in various frequencies that are visible to our human eyes. But, our human eyeballs can see only a teeny tiny part of the electromagnetic spectrum. The colors (light frequencies) arrange themselves in order based on decreasing vibrational wavelengths. So, red is the longest wavelength and this is affiliated with the lowest frequency of your seven main chakras. Violet is the shortest wavelength and it correlates with the highest frequency of your seven main chakras.

Each color has a specific frequency, just like your chakras. Crystals also vibrate and oscillate based on their color.

One reason crystals are so amazing for chakra healing is that crystals are always going to retain a higher amplitude frequency because their molecular structure retains a more stable frequency. Did I lose you there? ;)

To put it another way, crystals have a very precise atomic structure. That's what makes a crystal a crystal. Their molecular blueprints contain a precise geometric pattern. As humans, we do contain some crystalline parts, but we are not as geometrically perfect as a crystal. So, because crystals maintain their geometric perfection, they maintain their specific frequency, and we can use that affiliated frequency to attune our subtle energy body, which is the energy field around our physical body.

Let's dive into what some of these colors represent!

DAY NINE

CRYSTAL HEALING

"If you want to find the secrets to the Universe, think in terms of energy, frequency, and vibration."

-Nikola Tesla

Now let's do a positive round.

INNER EYE- I choose to be open to the possibility that I can let go of this stress

OUTER EYE- What if I started putting myself first?

UNDER EYE- Maybe I don't have to worry so much...

UNDER NOSE- Maybe I don't have to spend so much time being stressed

CHIN- I choose to release this stress

CHEST- I choose to release the tension in my body

UNDER ARM- I choose to let it all go

TOP OF HEAD- I don't have to be stressed out anymore

YOU CAN LISTEN TO A GUIDED TAPPING SESSION ON STRESS HERE: THEUNCENSOREDEMPATH.COM/21DAYSOFHEALING

6. ONCE YOU ARE DONE TAPPING, TAKE A DEEP BREATH AND RATE THE INTENSITY OF THE STRESSOR YOU LISTED ABOVE ONCE AGAIN. IF YOU RATE THE LEVEL OF INTENSITY OF THE STRESSOR ABOVE A 5 I SUGGEST YOU LISTEN AND FOLLOW ALONG A SECOND OR EVEN A THIRD TIME UNTIL IT COMES OUT TO RATING BELOW 5.

| 1 | 2 | 3 | 4 | 5 | 6 | 7 | 8 | 9 | 10 |

let it out

INNER EYE- All of this stress
OUTER EYE- It feels like too much
UNDER EYE- It will never go away
UNDER NOSE- Nothing ever works
CHIN- All of these symptoms
CHEST- They add to my stress
UNDER ARM- Will I ever NOT feel broken?
TOP OF HEAD- So many doctors...

INNER EYE- So much time spent trying to heal
OUTER EYE- And all of this stress
UNDER EYE- It feels so heavy in my body
UNDER NOSE- There is so much I feel like I have to do
CHIN- And never enough time
CHEST- I feel so stressed
UNDER ARM- I worry so much
TOP OF HEAD- And it feels like the world is closing in
on me

INNER EYE- All of these symptoms
OUTER EYE- So many questions unanswered
UNDER EYE- It doesn't seem fair
UNDER NOSE- Why me?
CHIN- Why do I have to have all of this stress?
CHEST- All of this stress and worrying
UNDER ARM- How do I release it?
TOP OF HEAD- How can I feel free?

HERE ARE THE BASICS OF HOW YOU CAN START TAPPING TO TRANSFORM YOUR LIFE:

1. CONSIDER WHAT YOUR BIGGEST STRESSOR IS RIGHT NOW. WRITE IT BELOW:

_____

2. RATE THE INTENSITY OF THIS STRESSOR ON A SCALE OF 0-10, 10 BEING THE MOST INTENSE.

1	2	3	4	5	6	7	8	9	10

3. GET ACQUAINTED WITH THE 9 MAIN TAPPING POINTS.

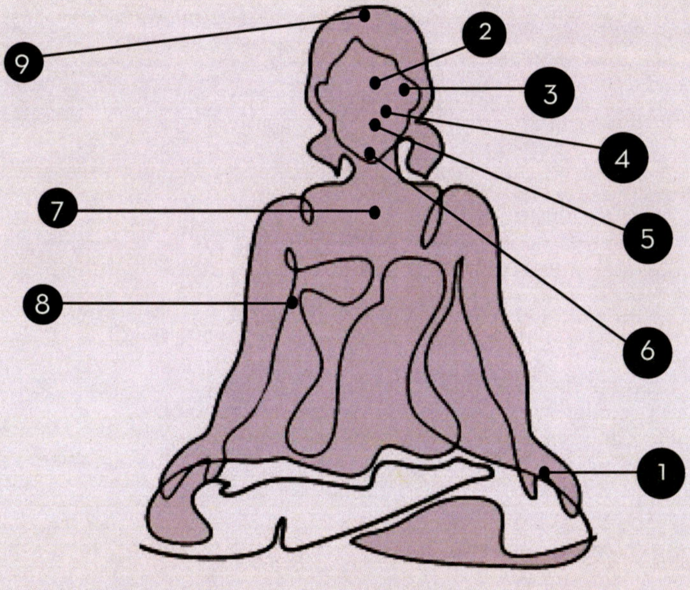

4. START TO TAP ON THE KARATE CHOP POINT OF YOUR HAND. IN THIS CASE, WHICH HAND YOU USE DOESN'T MATTER. WHILE TAPPING, REPEAT THE FOLLOWING STATEMENT 3 TIMES.

EVEN THOUGH I AM EXPERIENCING THIS _____ (INSERT MAIN STRESSOR), I DEEPLY ACCEPT AND LOVE MYSELF.

5. NOW WE'LL TAP ON THE REST OF THE ENDPOINTS TOGETHER.

In a study published in the *Journal of Nervous and Mental Disease* that discusses the effectiveness of tapping, researchers compared the differences in our physiological responses when engaged in either conventional talk therapy, tapping, or no treatment at all. The tapping group decreased cortisol levels (your stress hormone) by an average of 24 percent, whereas the groups that experienced talk therapy or no treatment, saw no significant change in cortisol levels. SO COOL, right?

When your body is in a constant state of stress it can lead to adrenal fatigue which has a snowball effect that impacts various processes in the body. That is why I'm excited to help you experience tapping to decrease the effects of stress and reduce cortisol levels in your own body today!

Plus, tapping is not only amazing for reducing stress levels, it also helps you shift your mindset around illness. Instead of living with the 'poor me' mentality, we can become our own greatest healers. Tapping helps rewire your brain, it rewrites your limiting beliefs, and it can help you send love to your illness.

It's time to stop fighting this constant battle with stress and illness! It's time to stop avoiding the truth about your own health concerns and to stop saying you're "fine" when you know you would like to feel better. It's time to use these tools to transform your life.

Part of what I love about the emotional freedom technique (aka tapping or EFT) is that you aren't expected to pretend like everything is okay while you are using the technique. You aren't expected to cover up your real-life emotions with flowers and butterflies. Instead, the process encourages you to invite some of your very real feelings into your conscious mind. Then, through tapping, you begin to rewire your thoughts.

So, if you're new to tapping you're probably wondering what the heck tapping even is, right?

Don't worry, I'm going to teach you how it works and then we're going to begin tapping together today.

Tapping is a combination of ancient Chinese acupressure and modern-day psychology. It intertwines eastern and western medicine. This technique was originally developed by Roger Callahan in the 1980s and it was modified by Gary Craig a few years later. Today, thousands of practitioners use it, from psychiatrists to coaches. I learned from Nick Ortner who is one of the most well known teachers today.

Tapping quite literally means tapping your fingers directly on the endpoints of your energy meridians, an action which serves to reprogram the brain.

It might sound a little "woo-woo" to some of you, but I assure you, it's not.

Your stress responses begin in your brain and more specifically, in your amygdala. Your amygdala is an almond shaped part of your midbrain and limbic system. It's the source of your emotions and it is also the place where our brain forms and stores negative experiences for survival purposes.

The amygdala signals the brain to turn on your fight or flight response. To explain how this works, let's use an example. Say something caused you stress at age five, like falling into the deep end of the pool, causing you to develop a fear of deep water, which is stored in the amygdala part of your brain. Well, whenever you are around deep water thereafter, your brain triggers a similar physiological stress response in your body.

The AMAZING thing about tapping is that it turns off this stress alarm. When you tap on the body's energy meridian endpoints, it sends a calming response throughout the body which reprograms the amygdala, the part of your brain that determines whether something is a threat or not.

DAY EIGHT

TAPPING

"Trying to be 'perfect' is all about living in fear. Fear of what they'll think. Fear of what you'll think about yourself. Fear of being judged, or wrong. The greatest gift you can give yourself today is to let go, even just a little bit, of this need or desire to be perfect."

-Nick Ortner

I still have to catch myself when anxiety peaks and I want to seek control. I find myself walking towards the bathroom mirror to revert back to my old behaviors. I have to tell myself "WAIT! You know WHY you are doing this, now let's choose a different behavior that reflects self-love instead."

The new behaviors I have chosen are actually an array of things that help me to feel content, calm, or find greater states of peace and well-being. Sometimes I meditate until the anxiety simmers. Sometimes I smell a feel-good essential oil. Sometimes I dance. Sometimes I tune into a podcast. Sometimes I turn on the water for a salt bath. Sometimes I just look at myself in the mirror and say, "I love you."

All the while I remind myself that I am worth the time and attention it takes to create this alternate pathway in my neural programming and I tell myself that my well-being matters, I matter.

Slowly, my thoughts changed as I started confronting the root of my anxiety. As I committed to change, I gradually shifted towards self-love. I began regularly telling myself I didn't always have to be in control. I reminded myself I was safe. I reunited my physical body and my energy body. I realigned. I decided to love myself... including my imperfections.

love IS THE GREATEST MEDICINE OF ALL.

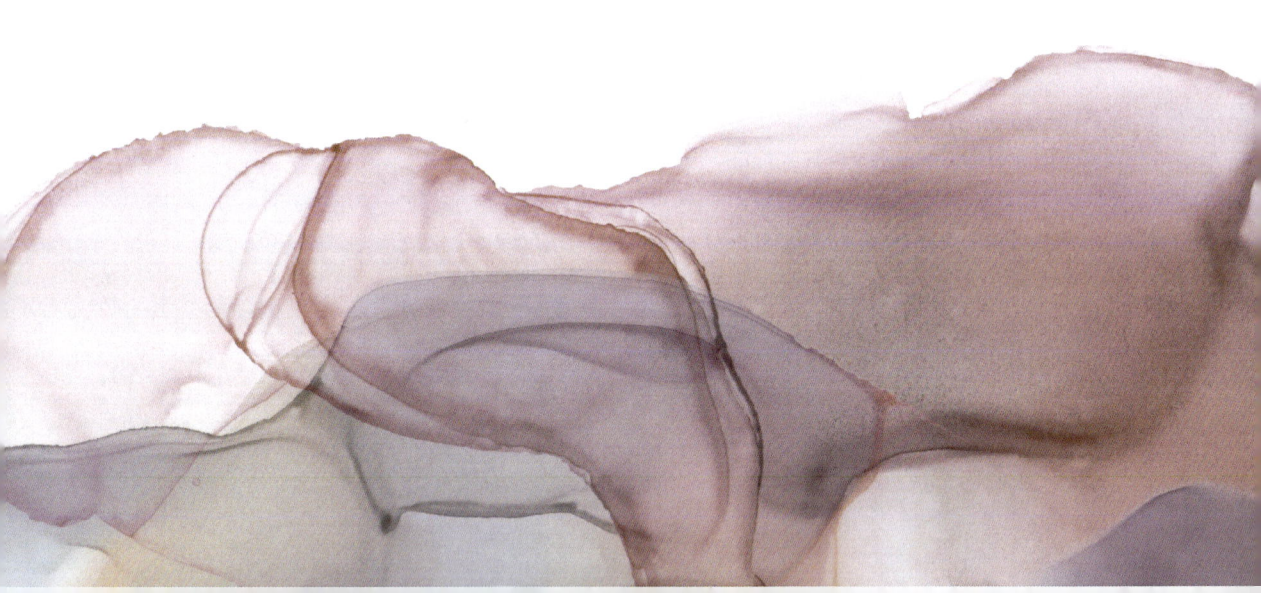

Yet, I never thought I was picking because of my emotions or an addiction to control. I thought I was picking to fix my imperfections and manage my skin conditions. I convinced myself of this for several YEARS.

I can tell you firsthand, the mind is a powerful, powerful thing.

I thought to myself "why me? It's so unfair that MY skin looks this way." And I proceeded to try to remedy the situation, which felt empowering for a while until I realized... I was actually harming myself.

One of the greatest things I've come to understand through the process of healing addiction and chronic illness is the power of our thoughts.

Dr. Bruce Lipton, PhD wrote, "Thoughts can heal you physically because thoughts can change the chemistry of the culture medium and the culture medium, blood, is what feeds and organizes the behavior of the cells."

Your thoughts are such an integral part of healing. At some point, I realized that there was no topical cream, oil, or face mask that was going to heal my skin if my issues were rooted in emotional distress. It was a deep epiphany for me to recognize that there was no pill to "fix" me. I started to see that the healing that I needed to embark upon was an internal job.

I found the most integral steps to healing my mind and changing my behaviors include having enough awareness of the issue to take a different action, and the ability to repetitively practice new behaviors.

I told myself dozens of times, "Sarah, don't pick, you'll regret it later."

But, that never stopped me.

What eventually did help me was consistently trying a new action or behavior in order to address the emotional roots of this addiction.

EMOTIONAL ROOT OF MY BEHAVIOR = ANXIETY
THE NEW ACTION OR BEHAVIOR = SELF-LOVE

I craved control over something (okay, everything) in a world where we have very little real control over anything.

I couldn't control anyone in my family, whether it was their ability to listen, their mental health, or their choices. But, it wasn't just my family, I couldn't control ANY person on this planet.

I also couldn't control stop lights and stop signs, the weather, the number of emails I was getting at my old job, the cost of groceries, the fact that I was allergic to gluten, the vitiligo on my skin, or the fact that there are only 24 hours in a day.

But, alas, I could control my actions.

This addiction to controlling things manifested as anxiety which needed to be released in some way. For me, it manifested into a condition known as excoriation (aka skin picking or dermatillomania).

People who are afflicted with this condition can cause themselves bleeding, sores, and scars. It's characterized by repeatedly scratching or trying to remove things you see as imperfections on the skin (which is a condition comparable to obsessive compulsive disorder or OCD).

Maybe you know someone who constantly picks at their cuticles or fingernails. Or maybe they got a bad scrape or cut and it simply won't heal because they won't stop reopening it. These are some examples of excoriation. But, for me it primarily manifested as picking at my chest.

To release all of the anxiety surrounding a need for control, I fell into the addiction of picking.

It felt liberating. I sensed I had found something that I had control over and a way to release these anxious feelings. Finally, I was winning!

Until the picking was over. Then I felt worse. I felt sad. I felt shameful. I felt embarrassed.

Picking at my skin was my attempt to control the skin conditions I was experiencing (which included vitiligo, melasma, and cystic acne). It was a (false) attempt to feel powerful. When I picked, it provided me with 30 minutes of sweet, sweet endorphins and then left me with a shitty shame hangover afterwards.

Welcome to Week 2!

What are some of the worst habits you've developed? Have anxious, fearful, or stressful feelings ever made you a person you didn't recognize or someone you didn't like?

This has happened to me, but it took me a long time to share publicly, because I was still healing from it, and frankly, mortified to share it.

I used to feel like a stranger in my body. It seemed like my physical body and my energetic body were detached. I felt the stress of everyone else's issues weighing on top of my own concerns. I also found that I was consistently striving for perfection in everything I did. I felt I needed to have perfect teeth, a perfectly made bed, perfectly applied makeup, a perfect home, and even perfect coloring skills in my freaking adult coloring books (I didn't dare color outside the lines). Perfect. Perfect. Perfect.

YUCK.

At some point, the standards I held myself accountable to, which included the stress of extending care to my family, the stress of maintaining a loving relationship with my partner, the stress of juggling the responsibilities involved in my previous career, the stress of looking a certain way, and the physiologically stress on my body from illness all became way too much for me to handle.

Yet, throughout my life I was taught that it was not appropriate to express negative emotions. So, instead of having any sort of outward explosion or melt down, I kept it all in. It was too scary and too much to handle everything that was going on within, but I didn't have a healthy outlet that would allow me to let things go, and I thought I would be judged if I did.

So, I kept holding in all the stress and anxiety. It is hard to find the words to describe how I felt during this time, but I would say it was a process of continually folding inward on myself. Truly, it was a form of self-sabotage. When you are a recovering perfectionist, let's face it, you still have a lingering fear of what people might think of you if you were to express your hidden emotions or screw up in some way.

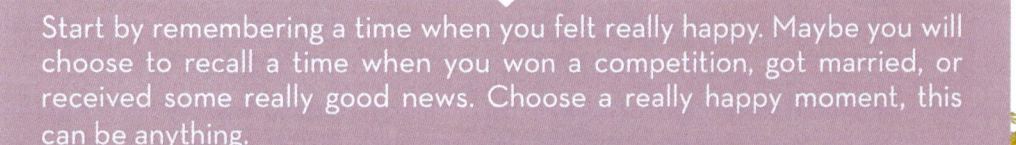

To help you really understand this process, let's move through an example.

Start by remembering a time when you felt really happy. Maybe you will choose to recall a time when you won a competition, got married, or received some really good news. Choose a really happy moment, this can be anything.

In your head, play out the story of what happened and what things led up to that happy moment. Be vivid, specific, and remember how you felt when that feeling finally arrived. Picture all the aspects of that happy moment in your head, and recall the sensation in your body.

Then, at the height of re-experiencing all the sensations that came together to form your happy feeling, bring your left thumb and ring finger together. Immediately release your thumb and ring finger as the happy memory begins to fade.

Then bring that moment back to your heart, body, and mind. Again, bring your left thumb and ring finger together at the peak of your happiness. Repeat as many times as you'd like. Each time imagine that happiness multiplying.

You have now laid your anchor.

You can test the anchor by bringing your left thumb and ring finger together to see what emotions it evokes.

MY FAVORITE ANCHORS ARE ESSENTIAL OILS.

I use Citrus Bliss to anchor happiness.

I use Balance to anchor feeling grounded.

I use Clary Sage to anchor releasing.

Learn more about these blends and essential oils here:
theuncensoredempath.com/oils

How to install an anchor:

1. Decide on an emotion or feeling you want to anchor. (Examples might include: motivation, joy, hopefulness)

2. Decide which anchor you will attach to this emotion or feeling. (Examples might include: smelling Siberian fir essential oil as an olfactory anchor OR a black bird as a visual anchor)

3. Recall a time when you had a strong experience with the desired emotion or feeling that you chose in step one. Visualize it and feel the intensity of this positive experience moving through you.

4. At the height of this feeling, use your visual, auditory, kinesthetic, or olfactory anchor. (Example: Smell the Siberian fir oil or look at the image of a black bird)

5. As the intensity of the desired feeling begins to fade away, release the anchor and focus your attention on something else. You can think of this as clearing the screen.

6. Repeat the process of deeply experiencing the desired emotion or feeling it at least one more time and again bring in the anchor at the peak of the emotion, then remove the anchor right away when the feeling or emotion fades.

7. Next, you can test the anchor to see if the feeling or emotion was successfully implemented. Use just your anchor (like the smell of the oil or the image of the black bird) and see what emotion comes up for you, is it the one you just implemented? Then it was a success!

8. Any time you want to feel the positive emotion you just installed, use your anchor.

programmed to bring you a deep sense of hope, despite the apparent challenges. When you use this tool, you are able to access the resources of hope and trust.

It's almost like living in a choose-your-own-adventure book ;) Which page will you turn to next?

Today, I'm going to teach you how to create different types of anchors and how to use them.

Let's start by looking at the four types of anchors that you can use:

TYPE OF ANCHOR	EXAMPLES
VISUAL	Specific visual symbols that mean something personal to you, like a whale or other animal, a person you may or may not directly know, an object like a flower, pyramid shaped crystal, or a landscape such as a mountain range or sun rise.
AUDITORY	Sounds that you can say to yourself internally (ex: affirmations or poems you read) or external sounds (ex: a song you love to listen to).
KINESTHETIC	Simple actions you can perform like bringing your hand to your heart, pressing your thumb and pointer finger together, or pulling gently on your earlobe.
OLFACTORY	Surrounding yourself with a specific smell that is pleasant to you, like an essential oil, a food, or a perfume.

Anchoring

Whenever I smell Abercrombie & Fitch cologne, I'm transported back to 8th grade when I was with my first boyfriend. It feels like I'm 14 again, sitting on the couch with him at his parent's house, nervously holding hands and watching TV.

When I see an image or symbol of a whale, whether it's on a bumper sticker, lamp, or printed as a pattern on a blanket, I'm reminded of my brother, Jordan, who tattooed a whale on his arm when he was 16.

When I hear the song "White Flag" by Dido, I envision myself sitting in the backseat of my Dad's Dodge Durango alongside my siblings and grandparents. It's Christmas Eve and we're all sharing a powerful moment together while driving around the neighborhood looking at Christmas lights. The song is turned up loud and we're all belting out the lyrics. It's an anthem for my Grandma who survived breast cancer.

There is a set of guiding principles used in behavioral therapy, called Neuro-Linguistic Programming (NLP), that include the process of 'anchoring.' When you learn how to use this process, you can associate an internal response with an external trigger so that you can easily access the response at any time.

Let me give you an example of how NLP can be helpful for people who are healing chronic illness:

Let's say you are having a downright crappy day. It feels like everything is going wrong. You're running late for your eye doctor appointment. Your kid peed his pants or the dog wet on the floor. You look in the mirror and you see that the eczema on your face is flaring up again. You're constipated and nothing seems to relieve the discomfort. Life feels hard today.

Although you may not have experienced these exact circumstances, I'm sure you've all had similar days in the context of your own lives. We've all had days when things just didn't go our way and we've felt overwhelmed and discouraged. Yet, ultimately you are always in control of how you react to these stressors.

So, when you walk back inside your house at the end of the day, you have a choice. You can throw a pity party and throw your arms up to the sky and say, "I give up on today!" Or you can grab your anchoring tool that has been

DAY SEVEN

ANCHORING

"I am present within myself. I can center myself with the ease of my breath. I feel grounded, confident, worthy, & whole."

-Mala Collective

How can you celebrate your uniqueness even more? Spend time thinking of ways that you can allow your unique qualities to proudly shine through and share them below:

To further release the suffering that results from comparison, I invite you to listen to this meditation to release comparison:
theuncensoredempath.com/21daysofhealing

We are all so beautifully unique. Our physical makeup is unlike ANY other person who ever existed, and that's pretty frickin' amazing. We have unique genes, microbiomes, environmental surroundings, and many more special traits and qualities. This is part of the reason that some things that work for your best friend may not always work for you.

Now, I encourage you to start graciously appreciating some of the very special qualities that you possess. What makes you unique? Please share some of your most special qualities and traits below:

$\triangledown$

I am unique

Instead, let's begin focusing on the very special individual skills that define who you are. What are you especially good at? Feel free to use the area below to share some of the things that you feel you do especially well:

I am awesome at

Have you ever experienced a comparison hangover?

I describe comparison hangovers as the feeling you get after scrolling through Instagram and comparing yourself to the perfectly tanned, thin, cutely dressed (or barely dressed) social media influencers. It's also that feeling you might get after seeing other health coaches post about their high income month or talking to an old high school friend on the phone whose life seems perfectly polished.

I've experienced my own fair share of comparison hangovers throughout the years, and I've found that engaging in comparison sometimes induces paralysis. Instead of feeling inspired by someone else's success, their perfect body, or gorgeous house, I just end up feeling like I want to binge on Netflix and wear my sweat pants.

This is an especially rampant compulsion within the autoimmune healing world. I've seen boatloads of women desperately asking why things like the autoimmune paleo protocol (AIP diet), haven't worked for them after they've seen one of their celiac friends lose 20 pounds in 1 month on this plan. They wonder, "why haven't I seen the same results?"

So, how do you avoid debilitating comparison? Don't worry, you don't have to delete social media forever (although I do highly recommend an occasional leave-of-absence for "spiritual maintenance").

Instead, we are better served when we can confront our truths.

First truth: You are too hard on yourself. Know that when it comes down to it, you are your own harshest critic. It's time we all realize that our biggest strength is our ability to express and embrace our authentic selves. If you try impersonating or copying someone else (this applies to everything, from clothing choices to nutrition plans), it's not always going to work out for you. You can't authentically embody someone else's life and no one else can embody you better than you can. So, you must begin by knowing and believing that your greatest gift is your uniqueness!

It's time to stop comparing ourselves and our life paths to the paths of others, and tap into our own strengths instead.

REPEAT AFTER ME: I WILL NOT COMPARE MYSELF TO STRANGERS ON THE INTERNET.

DROP COMPARISON

"Your story is so unique and so different, it's not worthy of comparison."

—Unknown

Day Six

Crystals

YOU'RE GOING TO LEARN MUCH MORE ABOUT CRYSTALS IN A COMING LESSON, BUT I WANT TO SHARE INFORMATION ABOUT THE PROTECTIVE QUALITIES OF SOME OF MY FAVORITE CRYSTALS WITH YOU TODAY.

RED JASPER AND BLACK TOURMALINE ARE BEAUTIFUL ROOT CHAKRA/GROUNDING STONES THAT CAN BE PLACED AT THE BASE OF YOUR FEET OR SACRUM DURING MEDITATION.

PURPLE JADE PURIFIES AND CLEANSES YOUR AURA BY HELPING YOU GET RID OF NEGATIVE ENERGY, AND CONNECTING YOU TO EARTH ENERGY. I SUGGEST PUTTING PURPLE JADE IN YOUR EPSOM SALT BATH.

MAGNETITE IS THE STONE THAT OFFERS PSYCHIC PROTECTION. IT HELPS GROUND YOUR ROOT CHAKRA AND BALANCES YOUR ENERGY. TO STAY PROTECTED, I SUGGEST CARRYING THIS CRYSTAL AROUND WITH YOU IN YOUR BRA OR POCKET.

Laughter

THIS PRACTICE WILL LIKELY FEEL AWKWARD AT FIRST, BUT I ENCOURAGE YOU TO TRY MAKING YOURSELF LAUGH. START WITH A SIMPLE "HA, HA, HA," AND YOU'LL ALREADY FEEL SO SILLY TRYING THIS FIRST STEP THAT IT WILL CATAPULT YOU INTO AUTHENTIC LAUGHTER. ANOTHER OPTION TO PROMPT LAUGHTER IS TO WATCH A FUNNY VIDEO. LAUGHTER IS A GREAT WAY TO RID YOURSELF OF NEGATIVE PATTERNS AND IT IS ALSO A GREAT AVENUE TO RELEASE NEGATIVE ENERGY.

Honor your human-ness

GRAB AN ICE CUBE AND HOLD IT IN ONE OF YOUR HANDS. THIS WILL IMMEDIATELY SNAP YOU OUT OF AN ANXIOUS STATE AND RETURN YOU BACK INTO AN AWARENESS OF YOUR PHYSICAL BODY. ONCE YOU'VE CALMED YOUR ENERGY DOWN, TAKE A MOMENT TO LOOK AT EACH OF YOUR FINGERS. NOTICE THE UNIQUE AND INDIVIDUALIZED PATTERNS ON YOUR FINGERPRINTS AND REMEMBER HOW ALIVE YOU ARE TODAY. THEN TRY AND CONNECT WITH SOMEONE TODAY TO FURTHER AFFIRM YOUR PHYSICAL PRESENCE. YOU MIGHT CHOOSE TO CONNECT IN AN INTIMATE WAY BY HUGGING YOUR PARTNER OR CALLING A FRIEND, OR YOU MIGHT SIMPLY CHOOSE TO LOOK A STRANGER IN THE EYES. FEEL YOUR HUMANNESS.

BELOW ARE SOME OTHER ENERGY PROTECTION TOOLS YOU MAY WISH TO TRY AS WELL:

Visualization

CLOSE YOUR EYES AND IMAGINE YOU ARE SURROUNDED BY A SEMI-PERMEABLE SHELL. ENVISION THAT THIS BUBBLE OF GOLDEN LIGHT POSSESSES GUARDIAN GATEKEEPERS WHO ALLOW YOUR BUBBLE TO RELEASE ANYTHING THAT NO LONGER SERVES YOU WHILE ONLY ALLOWING IN ANYTHING THAT IS MEANT FOR YOUR HIGHEST GOOD. KNOW THAT ANY NEGATIVE ENERGIES THAT ATTEMPT TO REACH YOU WILL BOUNCE OFF, AND ARE THEREFORE TURNED AWAY. FOR THE BEST EFFECTS THROUGHOUT THE DAY, VISUALIZE THIS BUBBLE AROUND YOU EVERY MORNING.

Meditation

FOR THOSE OF YOU WHO ARE ENERGY SENSITIVE, I HIGHLY RECOMMEND CREATING A REGULAR NIGHTLY MEDITATION PRACTICE. MEDITATION HELPS YOU CLEAR YOUR MIND BEFORE YOU SLEEP. IT HELPS RELEASE NEGATIVE ATTACHMENTS, IT ALLOWS YOU TO DE-STRESS, AND IT PROMPTS A QUIETING OF THE MIND SO YOU CAN DECIPHER WHICH ENERGY IS ACTUALLY YOURS, VERSUS THE ENERGY YOU'VE PICKED UP FROM YOUR SURROUNDINGS. TO BEGIN A MEDITATION PRACTICE OR TO ENHANCE YOUR CURRENT PRACTICE, FEEL FREE TO LISTEN TO SOME OF MY FREE MEDITATIONS HERE: AUTOIMMUNETRIBE.COM/21DAYSOFHEALING.

Chanting

THIS PRACTICE HELPS GROUND AND PROTECT YOUR ENERGY. WHEN I LISTEN TO OR SING CHANTS, WHETHER IN ENGLISH OR SANSKRIT, I LET THE VIBRATION OF THE MUSIC PENETRATE MY ENERGY BODY, WHICH HELPS TURN ON MY PARASYMPATHETIC NERVOUS SYSTEM (THIS IS ALSO KNOWN AS THE REST AND DIGEST MODE).

I will not allow

I will allow

To start learning how to protect your energy, try reading the invocation below out loud:

I CALL IN MY GUIDES, ANCESTORS, ANGELS, SPIRIT ANIMALS, THE HEALING SPIRITS, THE DIVINE, THE FELLOW EMPATHS, AND THE WISE ONES.

I CALL IN THE UNIVERSE, PLEASE SURROUND ME IN A SACRED CONTAINER OF PROTECTION. I ASK THAT THIS CONTAINER PREVENT ANY NEGATIVE ENERGIES FROM REACHING ME WHILE ALLOWING IN THAT WHICH IS HEALING AND PROTECTIVE.

I ASK YOU TO HELP KEEP ME SAFE FROM ANY INTRUDING ENERGIES AND TO CLEANSE MY AURA OF ATTACHMENTS. I AM SO GRATEFUL FOR YOUR LOVE AND PROTECTION.

and so it is.

Part of learning to protect your energy involves creating strong, soulful boundaries.

On the next page, you'll find boxes you can use to start establishing your own self-honoring boundaries. I invite you to spend some time filling out the first column with the actions you will not tolerate. For example, you might write, "I will not allow people to expect or demand that I show up for every invitation extended to me, especially when they invite me to a place that is not my scene."

In the second column, I invite you to create some permission slips that affirm your right to protect your energy. For example, "I allow myself to say 'no' to attending family gatherings when I feel the need to protect my energy."

DO YOU WANT TO LEARN MORE ABOUT THE TRAITS OF EMPATHS THAT YOU MIGHT POSSESS?

TAKE MY EXPANDED EMPATH QUIZ BY VISITING THIS LINK:

theuncensoredempath.com/21daysofhealing

Let's be clear, being an empath is NOT a bad thing, nor is it a curse to be an empath. I see it as a truly beautiful thing. However, it is super important for empaths to learn to protect themselves so that their susceptibility to outside energy does not leave them feeling chronically drained.

For me the life of an empath looks like this: I often ask people to turn down the volume on the TV (seriously, why does it have to be so loud?!), I perform daily rituals to protect my energy, I tend to take a lot of salt baths to detox the energy I pick up from others, I find myself saying 'no' to invitations when people want to go places that are really crowded, and I found that I needed to significantly reduce my alcohol consumption to reduce anxiety (as of now, I don't drink alcohol at all).

When you easily pick up on or absorb energy from people around you, it may feel overwhelming, and may induce fear or panic in you, but it doesn't have to.

I'm here to tell you that it is okay to feel this way. You are safe. You are so loved. You are unconditionally protected by the Universe. The energy you feel is not evil or bad, it is just energy that is hungry for a student. Energy will always be present, forever surrounding us. It's up to us to decide how to respond to it. We can act as a sponge, soaking up these external energies, or we can choose to transmute these energies.

Today we're focusing on protecting our energy and becoming a better transmuter. We will also witness how this energy can teach us about the incredible power we have to heal ourselves and how to harness this energy for transformation.

Have you ever

Have you ever experienced panic or anxiety attacks? Have you ever gotten overwhelmed in a crowded place? Have you ever felt claustrophobic, even when you weren't crammed into a small space, such as when the music around you was loud or people were talking loudly at the table next to you? Do you ever get weird vibes from certain people and feel like you need to back away from them? Have you ever felt a sense of compassion and sensitivity toward the suffering and pain of other people?

These are just some of the ways you may experience the world as an empath. An empath is someone who can pick up on or absorb the energy, emotions, or physical sensations of other people. Empaths are highly sensitive beings. My guess is that many of you will resonate with the traits of an empath. After having worked with hundreds of clients, I have found that almost every woman in my community identifies as an empath.

Here is a quick quiz for you to take which will help you to determine how strong of an empath you are. Circle the statements that are true for you below.

I CAN'T WATCH THE NEWS.

I CRY DURING SAD MOVIES AND TV SHOWS.

I AM THE GO-TO PERSON FOR PEOPLE TO VENT TO.

I CAN ONLY RECHARGE WHEN I HAVE ALONE TIME.

I AM ALWAYS HELPING OTHERS.

I AM SPIRITUALLY INCLINED.

I GET OVERWHELMED IN CROWDS.

I KNOW WHEN PEOPLE ARE LYING.

I LOVE BEING OUTSIDE IN NATURE.

I LOVE ANIMALS.

I AM CREATIVE.

If you circled 6 or more of these items, you are likely an empath.

DAY FIVE

PROTECT YOUR ENERGY

"Now is the time to take back your energy, your power, and your peace."

-Debbie Ford

Reactions & Reflections

This morning after my shower, I did this exercise. I started by scanning my body. I looked at the wrinkles on my stomach, the tattoos on body, and my wisps of hair. Then I found the courage to look myself right in the eyes, and as I did, I deepened my breath and counted to 30.

It felt so emotional. It also felt like an energetic shift, almost like I just finished a workout. My blood started flowing fast, I could feel my heart beat in my chest, and instead of seeing all the things I would want to change about my body, I just observed my body and said "thank you, I love you."

When you do this exercise, your body will tell you what it needs, and as long as you are open to listening, this mirror work can be very healing.

Today, my body told me it just needed acceptance.

Here's what I want you to do to courageously boost your self-love:

TURN ON SOME MUSIC YOU LOVE.

TAKE AN AMAZING BATH OR SHOWER, FEEL THE WARM WATER ON YOUR BODY.

WHEN YOU GET OUT OF THE BATH OR SHOWER AND GENTLY TOWEL OFF, LOVINGLY NURTURE YOUR SKIN WITH SOME HYDRATING LOTIONS OR BODY OILS.

STAND IN FRONT OF THE MIRROR (FULL LENGTH PREFERRED).

SET YOUR PHONE TIMER FOR 30 SECONDS TO START.

GAZE AT YOURSELF FOR A FULL 30 SECONDS, TRY NOT TO DIVERT YOUR ATTENTION AWAY.

SIMPLY NOTICE WHAT EMOTIONS COME UP (FEAR, SADNESS, JOY, APPRECIATION, SURPRISE, GRIEF, ETC). GENTLY ALLOW THEM TO APPEAR.

ACKNOWLEDGE YOUR COURAGE FOR TRYING THIS EXERCISE.

TAKE THE TIME YOU NEED TO PROCESS THE EXPERIENCE AND ONCE YOU ARE COZY AND SETTLED, WRITE YOUR REACTIONS DOWN ON THE NEXT PAGE.

NEXT TIME YOU BATHE, TRY THIS PROCESS AGAIN, BUT INCREASE BY 10 SECONDS.

Naked + Afraid

Have you heard of that Discovery Channel show, *Naked and Afraid*? It's a reality show in which two people are challenged to venture into the world's harshest environments, and they must survive for 21 days — completely naked, with just a map and a machete. Okay, I have never actually watched a whole episode, but based on the title, it's clear that nudity is associated with fear in our culture. My question is, do the two need to be affiliated? Does nakedness have to be terrifying?

Sure, being naked can feel vulnerable. I still remember a time in kindergarten when a boy walked in on me in the bathroom and I was mortified that he saw my "privates."

Yet, this vulnerability is kind of silly when you think about it. We all have these similar bodies, we all have nipples, we all have belly buttons, we all have butt cheeks. Yet, not only do we cover up for the sake of securing ourselves from the

world, we may also cover up to hide from ourselves. Now, I know there are laws about indecent exposure, so I'm also not suggesting you go streaking in all your self-love glory (however, I've done this and it was extremely liberating).

Instead, I'm challenging you to see yourself naked.

Stay with me here... I'm not proposing that you strip down to your birthday suit and get dropped off in the wilderness with a stranger.

I know... it's vulnerable.

But, when did you last really look at yourself? When is the last time you really saw yourself? When is the last time you held eye contact with yourself in the mirror? When is the last time you stood in front of the mirror naked for a bit, instead of putting your clothes on right away?

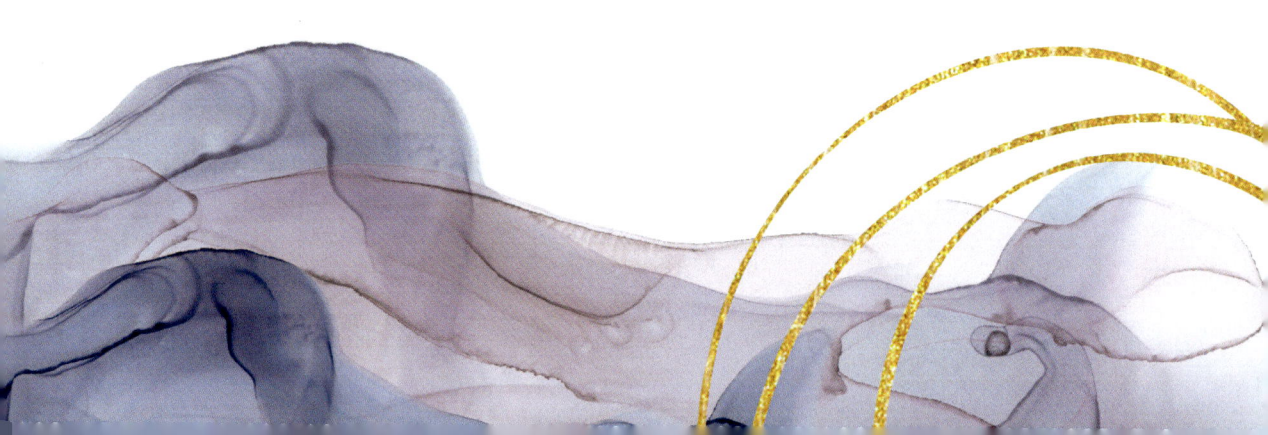

DAY FOUR

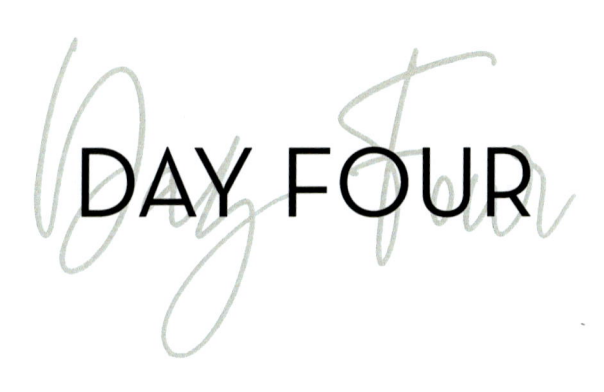

MIRROR WORK

"Like all explorers, we are drawn to discover what's out there without knowing yet, if we have the courage to face it."

-Pema Chodron

Here are some of my favorite self-love affirmations. I encourage you to add your own favorites to the list too.

LOVE IS MY BIRTHRIGHT.

I AM A MANIFESTATION OF LOVE.

I CHOOSE TO STOP APOLOGIZING FOR BEING ME.

I LOVE THE WOMAN THAT I AM.

I ACCEPT MYSELF UNCONDITIONALLY.

I CHOOSE TO LOVE MYSELF.

I AM SAFE. I AM SUPPORTED. I AM PROTECTED.

I AM POWERFUL BEYOND MY WILDEST DREAMS.

I RELEASE THE NEED TO JUDGE MYSELF AND MY BODY.

I LET LOVE IN.

I DEEPLY ACCEPT AND APPROVE OF MYSELF.

I AM EXACTLY WHERE I NEED TO BE.

Now try writing some for yourself!

Close your eyes for a moment and imagine yourself as healthy, whole, abundant, thriving, energized, and completely full of love. What other words come to mind that you want to embody?

Really use your visualization powers and practice seeing yourself as those things.

Hold your hands to your heart.

I invite you to say the following statement out loud:

MAY I ALL RAISE MY CONSCIOUSNESS, MATCH MY VIBRATION TO THAT OF SELF-LOVE, AND ALLOW THESE AFFIRMATIONS TO ENTER MY LIFE IN THE EASIEST AND MOST ALIGNED WAYS. MAY I ALLOW THIS SELF-LOVE JOURNEY TO BE FLOWING AND FUN.

And so, it is.

▽

DESCRIBE A CHALLENGE THAT YOU FACED WHICH YOU TURNED INTO A LESSON.

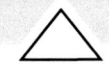

▽

WHAT ARE YOU INCREDIBLY GRATEFUL FOR?

▽

IF YOU COULD LEARN ABOUT ANYTHING, WHAT WOULD IT BE?

▽

WHAT ARE YOU MOST PROUD OF?

▽

WHAT TOPICS, SKILLS, OR EXPERIENCES DO YOU KNOW A LOT ABOUT?

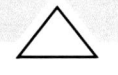

▽

ARE THERE THINGS THAT YOU USED TO BELIEVE IN THAT YOU DON'T
BELIEVE IN ANYMORE? IF SO, WHAT ARE THEY? WHAT SHIFTED?

For today's action step, I invite you to complete the following self-love reflection questions and create some of your own self-love affirmations.

▽

WHAT DO YOU KNOW TO BE TRUE ABOUT YOURSELF?

▽

WHAT ARE 3 THINGS YOU ARE GOOD AT?

Now that you've read my story, I encourage you to spend some time thinking of your own self-love story. Looking back, do you recognize moments when you began to doubt yourself, or when you habitually put yourself last? What are your beliefs about slowing down and showing yourself love? What messages did you learn from your family or your ancestral lineage?

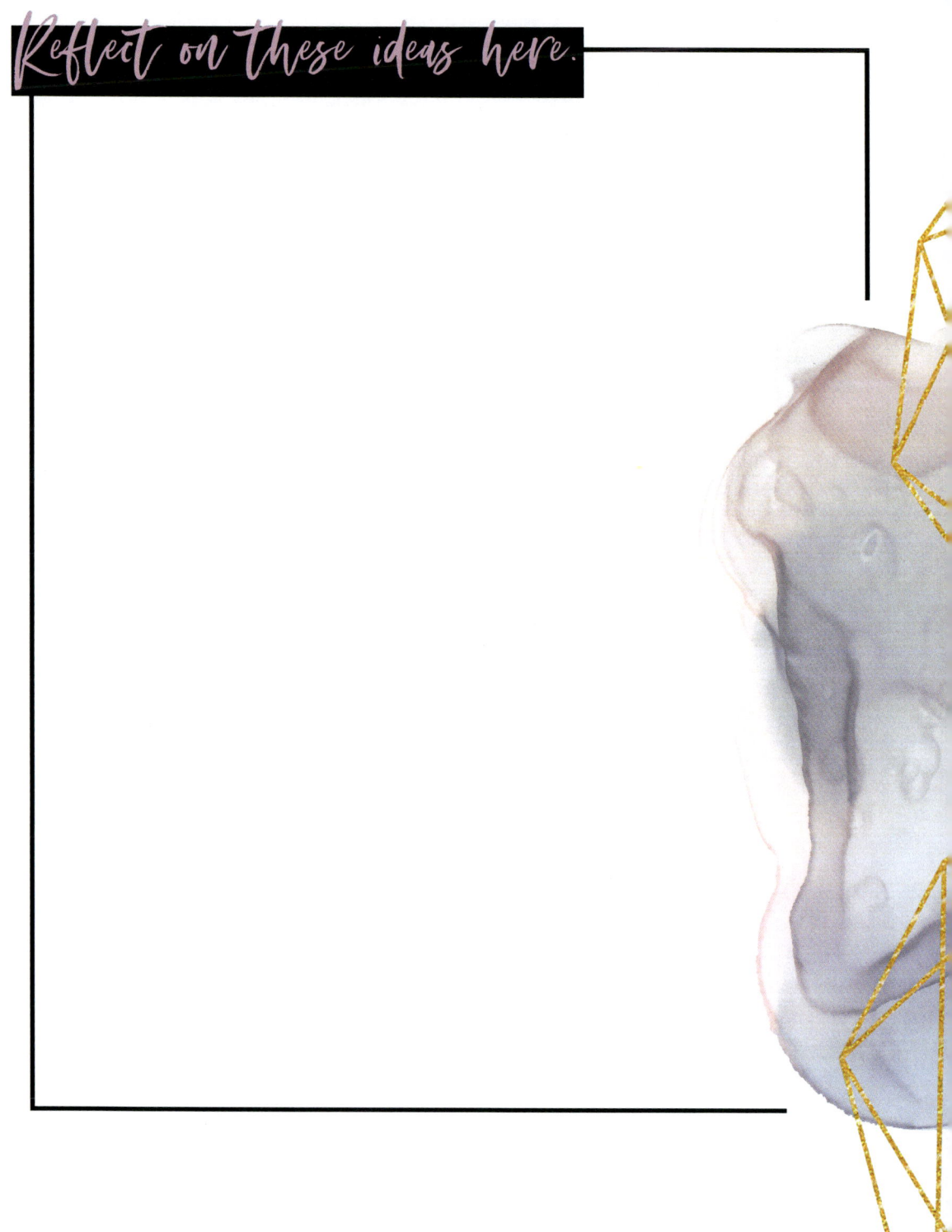

Reflect on these ideas here.

Here's part of mine.

I used to self-sabotage. I constantly picked at the imperfections on my skin. I also drank more alcohol than I knew I should. I put self-care at the bottom of my to-do list. I conformed to the people around me in order to feel liked. But, none of this made me happy. None of this filled me up inside.

I remember one moment when I was in college and I was walking around campus with an ex-boyfriend. The air was crisp and we sat on a ledge by the tennis courts and all I could think about was everything that was WRONG about me and my life. I could only see how misaligned, lost, and stuck I felt. It was frustrating. I wanted to fall off the ledge to get rid of all my pain. I told him how much I hated this feeling inside me, the feeling that I was lost, crawling out of my skin, and totally unclear about how to change.

I realized that for a long time I thought self-love was selfish. Now, I know that this was a limiting belief.

I also believed that I always had to keep going, going, going, whether I was doing homework, or maintaining a clean home, I felt I had to constantly be working or else I wasn't worthy of success, love, or happiness.

The idea of slowing down and taking care of myself didn't occur to me. In my mind I saw self-care as a sign of weakness. And I didn't want to be weak. I wanted to be a warrior. I wanted to be strong.

I didn't see how a person could slow down and remain strong at the same time. But now I know that when you slow down, you are much, much stronger than when you are living in a state of constant chaos.

When I took the time to reflect on my family lineage, I saw a long line of women who'd put themselves last. I never thought it was wrong for them to behave in this way, I just thought that was how it was supposed to be. I figured, if these women put themselves last, I should too.

This pattern lasted for many years, until I was shown a different path by some powerful spiritual teachers who taught me a new way of creating a healthy relationship with myself.

I learned that to have a positive and loving relationship with yourself is the most important relationship of all.

At some point, all this people pleasing becomes exhausting, don't you think?

It's time we started putting ourselves first again. It's time to listen to our bodies, to honor every scar and stretch mark for the stories they tell. It's time to own our imperfections and to begin radically loving ourselves.

Love is the greatest medicine of all. I believe that when we hone in on loving ourselves, we take the first step in healing our illnesses.

This will take courage, but let's let love heal us and invite love in.

How would you rate your level of self-love on a scale 1-10?

1	2	3	4	5	6	7	8	9	10

*1 = totally lacking, self-hatred   10= I'm a freaking goddess, I love myself

If just reading the phrase, "I'm a freaking goddess," made you feel uncomfortable, then I challenge you to say it out loud three times.

I'M A FREAKING GODDESS.
I'M A FREAKING GODDESS.
I'M A FREAKING GODDESS.

I believe the discomfort surrounding self-love also comes from the society we grew up in.

Did adults in your life ever tell you that you were strong, smart, and/or beautiful?
Did your mother show you that she loved herself?
Did you grow up thinking that it was selfish to take care of yourself or do kind things for yourself?

Each of us have stories that we've created around self-love. Next, we will begin looking at our individual self-love stories.

My dad's message immediately transported me to when I was 9-years-old. That 9-year-old version of me didn't give a shit about wearing makeup. She didn't care that her teeth were all sorts of crooked. She didn't obsess over what people thought of her. Her priorities involved spending as many hours as possible playing outside, staying up past my bedtime at sleepovers, and making the biggest cannonball splash at Grandma's pool.

For me, everything started changing in 5th grade, shortly after the car sing-alongs with my Dad. A boy made fun of me for my buck teeth, and I started to keep my lips closed more to hide my teeth. Then all the other girls in school started wearing bras and shaving their legs. Since I wasn't allowed to, I became self-conscious about my hairy armpits and how my little nipples poked through my shirt. During that same year, AOL Instant Messenger was created. My girlfriends and I would chat online together and join chat rooms (without our parents' knowledge). I remember one of my friends chatting with older boys, and she started teaching me how to say the things that the boys wanted to hear, which were totally inappropriate for an 11 year old.

At that point, life became more about pleasing other people and less about loving myself.

In the coming years, I spent a LOT of time people pleasing. I wore clothes based on what other people thought was cool, rather than wearing what made me feel beautiful or comfortable. I also began wearing way too much eyeliner. (I've got pictures to prove it.) Looking back, I see now that I lost touch with what I really wanted. When someone asked me what I wanted, it became hard for me to answer. Instead, I said what I thought they wanted me to say.

▽

Self reflection:

WHEN WAS THE FIRST TIME YOU STARTED BEING CRITICAL TOWARDS YOURSELF?

Self Love. It's that mystifying concept that you hear people talk about, but you may not be completely grasping. You may want to experience self-love, but might not know how to achieve it. Or, you may feel self-love sometimes, but desire to experience it more. Brené Brown writes, "practicing self-love means learning how to trust ourselves, to treat ourselves with respect, and be kind and affectionate towards ourselves."

To me, self-love is the scariest AND the most liberating thing you can practice. Self-love involves confronting yourself head on, looking at yourself in the mirror, saying, "I LOVE YOU," and genuinely believing it.

When we practice self-love we own our story, accept our imperfections, take care of ourselves, put ourselves first, say NO without feeling guilty, uphold strong soulful boundaries, invest in deep self-awareness, seek what our soul truly craves, know how to tell ourselves "it's okay," accept and forgive our mistakes, allow ourselves to be vulnerable, build strong values, know ourselves better than anyone else, and allow our needs be met instead of burying them. Self-love is brave. Self-love is a necessary part of healing.

What does self-love mean to you?

Love is our birthright. We're born with it. So, what went wrong that caused us to stop loving ourselves?

While I was writing this my Dad sent me a text. It said... "Do you remember when we would go on road trips and create our own songs? Can't think of all the words, but went like this... just riding along, singing our song, on a beautiful sunny day, yeah, man!"

DAY THREE

THE ART OF SELF LOVE

"A massive and essential part of self-love is forgiveness and acceptance. So while you're making an effort and striving to be the best person you can be, at the same time you need to recognize your own humanity. Try not to hold yourself to impeccable standards, and just do the best you can right now."

-Gala Darling

Now, after learning about the chakras, let's reflect on the areas you intuitively feel are most balanced and those that are out of balance. Take some time to write down what you learned below.

Notes

Now, I encourage you to listen to the chakra balancing meditation at
theuncensoredempath.com/21daysofhealing

4TH CHAKRA: HEART	5TH CHAKRA: THROAT	6TH CHAKRA: THIRD EYE	7TH CHAKRA: CROWN
Heart	Throat	Between Eyebrows	Top of head
Lungs, Circulation, Heart, Arms, Hands, Immune System	Throat, Jaw, Neck, Thyroid	Eyes, Ears, Nose, Pineal Gland	Skull, Skin, Pituitary Gland, Nervous System
Air	Sound	Light	Thought
Green	Blue	Indigo	Violet/White
Malachite, Aventurine, Green Calcite, Rose Quartz	Sodalite, Blue Lace Agate, Lapis	Amethyst, Labradorite, Third Eye Agate	Quartz, Selenite
Forgive, Bergamot, Lavender	Basil, Peppermint, Breathe	Serenity, Balance, Peace	Frankincense, Purify, Lavender
To love, Self Love, Love of others, Connection to nature, Forgiveness	To speak, communication, Self Expression, Stores fear or love, Truth center	To see, Intuition, Self Reflection, Inspiration, Dream State, Wisdom, Intellect	Clarity, Peace, Connection to the Divine, Healing on all levels, Connection to the higher self
Feeling unloved or unworthy of love, Indecisiveness, Afraid to forgive	Unable to express self, Trouble speaking up or clearly, Easily peer pressured	Extremely sensitive, Fear of success, Dizziness, Headaches	Loss of joy and creativity, Feeling isolated, Disconnected, Scattered thoughts
Manic Depressive, Tight or tense	Constantly talking, Rude, Arrogant, Trying to force, Strong opinions of others	Ego, Self Righteous, All knowing, Condescending	Migraines, Frustration, Anger, Spiritual Obsession
Empath with boundaries, Love of the world, Compassionate, Balanced Emotions	Artistic, Creative, Speaks clearly and truthfully	Love over fear, Clear vision, Clear understanding of self, In tune with inner guidance	Open to receiving life's messages, Clear thoughts, Peace in the world, Balance

ASSOCIATED WITH:	1ST CHAKRA: ROOT	2ND CHAKRA: SACRAL	3RD CHAKRA: SOLAR PLEXUS
LOCATION	Base of the spine	Below the navel	Above the navel
BODY PARTS	Knees, Hips, Spine, Feet	Ovaries, Reproductive Organs, Bladder, Womb, Lower Back	Stomach, Gallbladder, Digestion, Nervous System
ELEMENT	Earth	Water	Fire
COLOR	Red and sometimes black	Orange	Yellow
CRYSTALS	Smoky Quartz, Black Tourmaline, Red Jasper	Carnelian, Aragonite	Citrine, Tiger's Eye
OIL	Vetiver, Balance	Clary Sage, Ylang Ylang, Passion	Cheer, Ginger, DigestZen, Motivate
MEANING	To be here, Survival, Basic needs, Protection, Groundedness	To feel, Creativity, Passion, Sexuality, Relationships, Creation	To act, Power, Drive, Inner Fire, Energy, Happiness
SIGNS IT IS UNDER ACTIVE	Feelings of insecurity, Financial stress, Feeling unsafe, Head in the clouds	Resentful, Shy with feelings, Guilt around sex, Hides emotions, Lacking creativity	Low Self Esteem, Self Conscious, Insecure, Low Energy
SIGNS IT IS OVERACTIVE	Big Ego, Materialistic, Selfish	Aggressive, volatile emotions, Manipulative in relationships	Workaholic, Always wants to be the authority
SIGNS OF BALANCE	Grounded, Understands how to manifest abundance into life	Room to explore your creative nature, In touch with your feelings as well as others	Strong Boundaries, Personal Power, Self Esteem

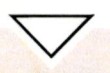

THE MAIN CHAKRA SYSTEM CONSISTS OF THE FOLLOWING SEVEN ENERGY CENTERS.
ALTHOUGH WE ACTUALLY HAVE MANY MORE THAN SEVEN CHAKRAS.

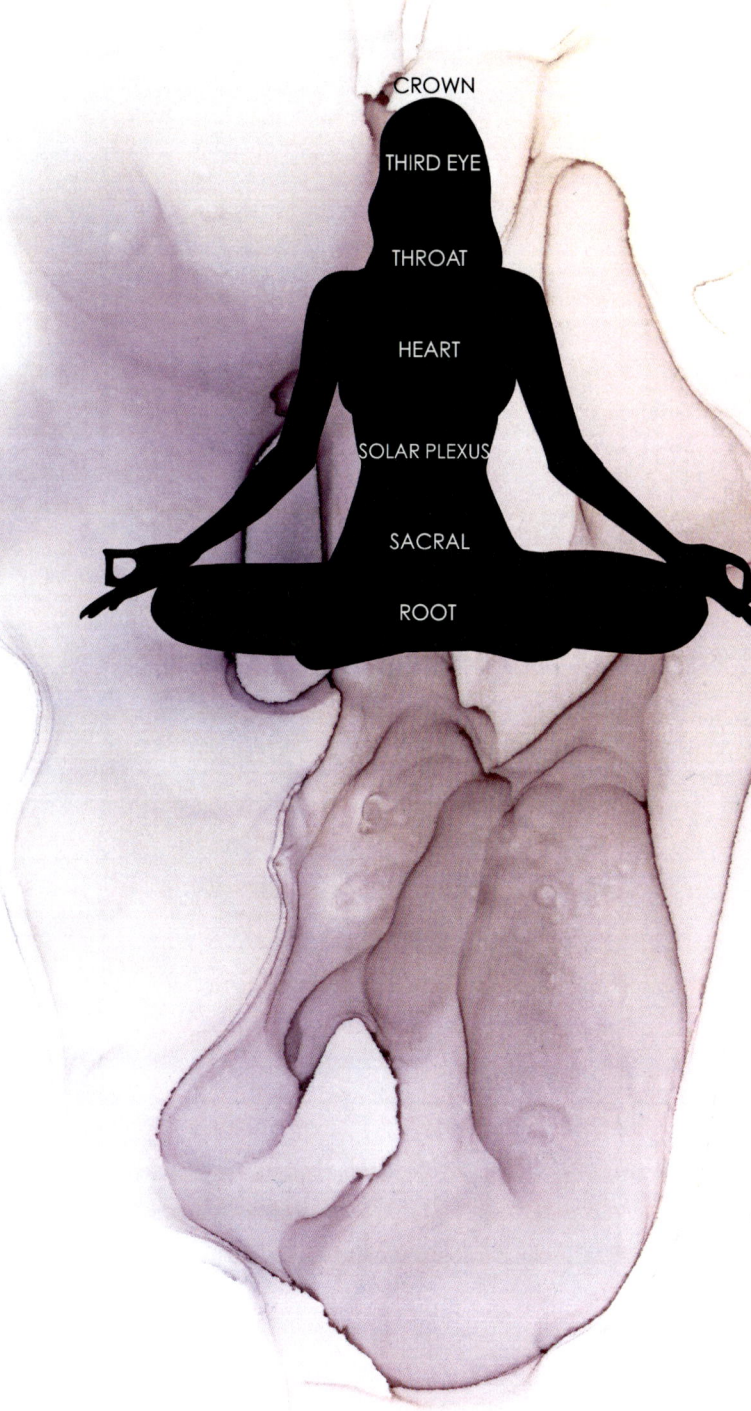

CROWN

THIRD EYE

THROAT

HEART

SOLAR PLEXUS

SACRAL

ROOT

When you experience an imbalance in one of your chakras, you will often feel it reflected in your physical body as well.

For example, if your throat chakra is under-active, your shoulders might feel tight, you may have a sore throat, or you might even experience issues with the thyroid. Similarly, if your root chakra is under-active, you may experience knee pain, changes in sex drive, or depressive thoughts.

Just as your mind influences your emotions, your chakras influence your physical being.

Today, you're going to learn more about each of the main chakra centers, then I'll guide you through a chakra balancing meditation.

Chakras

Chakra is a Sanskrit word meaning 'wheel' or 'disc', and it is the point of intersection where the mind and body meet. There are seven main chakras, or energy centers, within the human body which comprise our physical life force or prana. As chakras spin, they generating the shape and behavior of our physical bodies. They are therefore a vital part of our healing. Yet, humans are not the only ones who have these types of energetic bodies, so do flowers, insects, and even grains of sand. In fact, it is said that the entire Universe is composed of spinning wheels of energy.

Stay with me on this. I understand that in the world we live in, it is sometimes challenging to discuss chakras and other forms of energy medicine because these topics are sometimes labeled "woo-woo." I'm here to make a bold declaration: That's a bunch of BS.

The quickest, easiest way to dispel skeptics is to let them feel their own chakras.

Try it for yourself! Extend your arms out in front of you so that they are parallel to the ground. Turn the palm of one hand toward the sky and one toward the ground. Open (stretch out your fingers) and close (in a fist) your hands quickly about 20 times. Then switch directions so the opposite palms are now facing up and down. Open and close your hands quickly another 20 times, for a total of 40 times. Then stop and keep your hands open. You should feel them start tingling right away. To intensify the experience, turn your palms to face each other and hold them out in front of you. Keep them about 6 inches apart from each other and see what happens. Notice if you feel anything. I love playing with this sensation by moving my hands around, as if I were molding an imaginary ball between them. You'll feel how the energy shifts and changes as you move your hands.

Now that you've experienced your palm chakras you may have a better understanding of how all chakras exist within your subtle energy body (which includes many layers of energy that exist just outside of your physical body).

If you'd like to see images of a subtle energy body, look up "Kirlian photography." Using this photography method, the subtle energy body is actually visible as an electromagnetic force field surrounding the body.

DAY TWO

THE WHEELS OF LIFE

"Chakras generate the shape and behavior of the physical body."

-Anodea Judith

NOW, TAKE ALL THE DESIRES YOU MAPPED OUT AND PUT THEM INTO ONE BIG VISION PARAGRAPH BELOW.

Believe this statement as if it is already true.

Consider writing this paragraph out on a separate piece of paper so you can set it out or keep it somewhere that you can view often, like on the front of your refrigerator or as a picture you keep on your phone.

Be open to it happening in ALL possible ways. Let go of the how.

Create a timeline

When you create a timeline, you get to decide how quickly you want to see this vision come to life. Do you want it to be completed within:

1 week? 21 days? 6 months?

Write out your vision as if it is already happening, in the present tense. Below are some examples.

I GO ON A DATE WITH MY PARTNER ONCE A WEEK.

I MEDITATE 3 TIMES A WEEK.

I MOVE MY BODY IN A SOULFUL WAY THAT FEELS GOOD 4 TIMES A WEEK.

I INVEST IN A TRAINING OR WORKSHOP FOR MYSELF ONCE A MONTH.

Here is one of my old visions I'd like to share with you as an example. I set this vision for 2 months into the future at the time I wrote it.

I am a lifelong student. I complete one online course every 2 months. I am a certified Ho'oponopono practitioner. My partner and I have amazing sex at least once per week. Our chakras are aligned, allowing us to openly communicate and support each other's dreams. I see him and I see love. My circle of soul sisters has expanded to include 3 new spiritual babes that are local. I always have someone to talk to about all the things I love and am passionate about. I am making regular $10K months. Money supports me, but does not control me. I am constantly manifesting more abundance into my life. My debt is entirely paid off. I wake up feeling inspired and energized every day of the week. My business is fun, work doesn't have to be hard. I release the hustle, I let my heart guide me. I'm free of intestinal parasites! My estrogen and testosterone levels have normalized. Even better, now that the parasites are gone, I no longer feel anxious nor do I get anxiety attacks. This is a huge milestone for me and I am celebrating by taking a weekend trip up into the mountains. I begin each day with 30 minutes of morning rituals that nourish my mind and body. I pull myself an oracle card every day for guidance. My spiritual mentor continues to help me strengthen my intuition and I easily invest in her ongoing programs. Life supports me in every way.

quick tip

Use numbers when you can to help make your list more specific. For example: "I desire to lose 10 pounds," is much more clear than "I want to lose weight."

"I desire to have one date night per week with my partner," is much more clear than "I want to spend more time with my partner."

Creativity	Joy	Home Environment
Career	Spirituality	Health
Finances	Relationships	Education

NEXT, I WANT YOU TO CONSIDER EACH OF THESE ASPECTS OF YOUR LIFE AND WRITE WHAT YOU DESIRE WITHIN EACH CATEGORY. TRY TO BE AS SPECIFIC AS POSSIBLE!

THE UNIVERSE RESPONDS TO CLARITY. SPEND SOME TIME WRITING OUT A DETAILED DESCRIPTION OF WHAT YOU MOST DESIRE HERE.

It is so energetically powerful for you to have arrived here in the pursuit of healing. It is powerful that you followed your intuition and picked up this workbook.

You may feel confused or unsure of what will transpire over these next 21 days, but I am here to assure you that you are here for your soul's purpose.

Breathe in and focus on the thing you most desire from this experience. Feel it as if it is already true. See it in front of you. Smell it in the air around you. Hear the sounds it creates. Touch it. Believe it is already yours, because it is.

There are no limits to what you can create and transform over these 21 days.

AND SO IT IS.

So, to avoid aimlessly wandering, today you're going to set your specific goals for this program and create a vision for your future. Then you're going to practice manifesting it right away.

First, to prepare yourself for this life changing experience, I invite you to ground yourself by trying a short meditation. You can record yourself reading this meditation and then play it back or you can listen to it here:

THEUNCENSOREDEMPATH.COM/21DAYSOFHEALING

Close your eyes and take several moments to notice your breath. Witness the length of your inhales and the length of your exhales.

I ask that you allow these words to touch every part of your body. I ask you to feel the vibration and meaning behind the words so that they become a part of who you are.

Know how powerful it is that you chose to be here for these 21 days of healing. Acknowledge that it was no mistake for you to embark on this special healing journey. Believe that you will find meaningful healing messages during this 3 week journey.

Be open to this message:

you are the co-creator of your life.
You get to create the meaning and purpose of your life as you desire.

The first time someone taught me how to set goals, I thought... this is too simple, why am I even learning this? I figured it just involved brainstorming what I wanted to achieve and writing it out as a goal. Then I was done! Right?

Sure, this method works if you want to set goals just for the hell of it. But let's be honest, how often have you set and kept goals that you only made for the hell of it, like New Year's resolutions? Or the fitness goals that you wrote down and/or told someone about but never followed through with?

One time I set a goal to stick with a 5-day detox. I found a nutrition plan that seemed simple enough, but I didn't prepare AT ALL and it was a total flop. After day one of trying to follow the nutrition plan, I realized I was missing some ingredients and well, that was the end of the detox.

So, how do you fully commit to your goals? How do you set a vision that manifests into your reality? How do you make sure you follow through? How do you keep working towards your goal when you come across stumbling blocks?

I have found that when I use the power of the Law of Attraction to set my goals and visions, they quickly manifest into my life. In the simplest of terms, the Law of Attraction means that "like attracts like." It states, "you are a creator; you create with your every thought."

Here's what I learned about creating a vision with some *oomph* behind it (rather than for the hell of it).

When you get clear about what you want, the Universe shows up for you. When you truly know what you want, you can have it. When you envision how you want to feel, a seed of that truth gets planted in the Universe. When you manifest what you want, you live in your truth. Yet, without a vision, you might feel lost, stuck, confused, and like you are wandering around aimlessly. You feel me? Without a goal, it won't be clear how to move forward or what next steps to take.

DAY ONE

LIVE IN THE VORTEX

"Hold the vision. Trust the process."

-Unknown

If all your symptoms were gone, how would your life change and what would you do differently?

_____

_____

_____

_____

_____

_____

On a scale of 1-10, how committed are you to completing the lessons in this workbook? How do you plan to stay accountable?

_____

_____

_____

_____

_____

_____

_____

_____

_____

Note:

WHILE THERE ARE NO MATERIALS REQUIRED FOR THIS PROGRAM, I DO HIGHLY RECOMMEND A SET OF CHAKRA CRYSTALS, A STARTER SET OF ESSENTIAL OILS, AN ORACLE CARD DECK, AND A SMUDGE STICK.

IN ORDER TO PREPARE YOURSELF FOR THE NEXT 21 DAYS, LET'S EXPLORE YOUR ANSWERS TO THE *following questions*

Where and when are you planning to sit down and complete each day's exercise? I suggest you choose a sacred, safe space where you will soak up these materials. Preferably somewhere quiet and in the presence of things that set the stage for healing such as crystals, sage, flowers, candles, salt lamps, a meditation pillow, or a comfy corner. Write it down and commit to it!

_____

_____

_____

What is it that you want to heal? What brought you here?

_____

_____

_____

_____

How do you want to feel in 21 days?

_____

_____

_____

_____

Since I lacked understanding and the doctors didn't give me anything to reduce the pain, I just forged ahead.

There I was, 13 years old, stressed the fuck out, with zero tools and no support.

I came to realize later that, in that moment, my journey with chronic illness really began.

MY STORY IS LONG AND COMPLICATED, NOT UNLIKE YOURS, I'M SURE. AS WE PROGRESS THROUGHOUT THIS 21-DAY EXPERIENCE, I'LL BE REVEALING MORE PIECES OF MY HEALTH PUZZLE TO HELP YOU SEE THAT EVEN WHEN YOU HIT THE BIG OBSTACLES, HEALING IS POSSIBLE.

"PEACE IS NOT THE ABSENCE OF CHAOS OR CONFLICT, BUT RATHER FINDING YOURSELF IN THE MIDST OF THAT CHAOS AND REMAINING CALM IN YOUR HEART."

• UNKNOWN •

On that day, I made a decision that would impact my life and my health for many years to come.

I decided that I would become the grounding force for my three younger siblings who were just eleven, eight, and five years old at the time. The 13-year-old version of me felt it was the only choice I had (I would learn later in life that it was not).

And so my journey began. I took on many roles from that point forward. I stepped in and adapted to whatever anyone wanted or needed me to be. I served as a messenger between Mom and Dad. I provided a shoulder for my little sister Anna to lean on. I coached soccer for my little brother, Joe. I was the voice that stood up for my little brother, Jordan. I was the dinner chef at my Dad's house. I ran the school caravan at my Mom's house. I supported my Mom as her sounding board. I became a great soccer player and straight-A student to please my Dad. I tried to be a cool sister by taking Anna to the mall. I tried to be a role model for my brother Joe, and a secret keeper for my brother, Jordan.

Within a year I developed unrelenting, and sometimes debilitating, stomach pains. It wasn't the kind of pain one might anticipate after eating something bad nor did it have anything to do with my bowel movements. It was the kind of pain that struck from out of nowhere and made my belly expand to the point that it felt like it was going to explode. It was the kind of pain that would make me curl over and succumb to it. It would also randomly appear in the middle of soccer practice or in the middle of the night. But, the worst thing about the pain was that nothing made it go away. There was no quick fix.

My Mom decided to take me to the doctor for some tests after these stomach "attacks" kept occurring. After having an electroencephalography (EEG) which monitors and records the activity of the brain, I was diagnosed with stomach migraines.

Often migraines, which are induced by stress in children, present themselves in the stomach instead of the head.

I lacked enough self-awareness or mindfulness at the time to understand what stress even meant. I felt the pressure to complete my homework, to score goals, to have a lot friends, and to get straight A's, but this new kind of 'emotional' stress didn't make any sense to me. I didn't even fully comprehend when stress was present and I certainly didn't know how to cope with it.

I'm a 30-year-old woman stuck in an 80-year-old woman's body. A few years ago, I had a session with an energy healer who told me she saw in me, an old woman with long gray hair. She saw this image of an old woman who was missing an eye and sitting cross-legged, hunched over with palms forward, as if she was going to send out healing light from her hands. This image really stuck with me.

I'm not saying I feel like I'm 80 years old all the time. But, I am saying that I relate to the image of an 80-year-old healer because living with chronic illness has humbled me, strengthened me, and brought wisdom into my life. And it continues to teach me every damn day.

Chronic illness has also slowed me down in ways that were healing, causing me to focus my attention on strengthening my soul and move away from the party lifestyle I used to live.

MY PHYSICAL HEALING STORY BEGAN IN THE *seventh grade*.

My parents got divorced that year and it came as a shock to me. When my Mom and Dad asked us to sit down in the family room for a "family talk," I assumed that the four of us kids were about to be scolded for being too rambunctious, too messy, or misbehaving. I anticipated a boring lecture about how we needed to behave better or clean our rooms.

Boy, was I wrong! The "family talk," turned into a "divorce talk," and we learned that Dad was going to move out and that we would be splitting our time between our parent's houses.

I think there's something to be said about how unaware we were. At the time, we had no idea how unhappy or angry our parents were with each other. To me, it meant they covered it up damn well.

Hello beautiful, soul!

Welcome to 21 Days of Healing! Congratulations on saying "YES" to your own personal healing transformation. You showed up even though, as humans, we tend to resist change. You have committed to something new and different that will allow you to help heal yourself.

I'm already so proud of you for investing in yourself and I can't wait to get this healing party started!

Let me start by saying that this is not going to be a conventional healing path.

Don't expect:

Grades on your assignments

Perfection

Instructions on what supplements to take

A one-size-fits-all anything

Do expect:

A lot of love

Some challenges

To heal the past

An abundance of tools

Deep transformation

NOW LET ME TELL YOU A LITTLE BIT *about myself*

Table of Contents

Introduction 09

Day 1: Live In The Vortex 15

Day 2: The Wheels Of Life 23

Day 3: The Art Of Self Love 29

Day 4: Mirror Work 41

Day 5: Protect Your Energy 45

Day 6: Drop Comparison 52

Day 7: Anchoring 57

Day 8: Tapping 66

Day 9: Crystal Healing 72

Day 10: Appreciation Challenge 76

Day 11: Release Limiting Beliefs 82

Day 12: Fuck Fear 90

Day 13: Vegas Baby 97

Day 14: How To Muscle Test 102

Day 15: Intro To Cards 1111

Day 16: Tap, Tap, Tap 118

Day 17: Ho'oponopono 123

Day 18: Discover Wisdom 128

Day 19: BYOT 133

Day 20: Generational Wisdom 141

Day 21: Moving Forward 145

Closing 151

DEDICATION

To everyone struggling with invisible illness and chronic symptoms... you are not alone and healing is *possible*.

Copyright © 2019 Autoimmune Tribe LLC

21 Days Of Healing™

All rights reserved. This book, or parts thereof, may not be reproduced in any form, scanned, or distributed in any printed or electronic form without written permission from the author.

ISBN: 9781096328698

Edited by: Maria Weeks
Proofreading by: Krysta Voskowsky
Headshot by: Meg K Fink Photography
Content Design and Layout: Jacqueline Joseph
Cover design: Jacqueline Joseph

Please direct all inquiries to the author: sarah@theuncensoredempath.com

www.theuncensoredempath.com

Disclaimer: This book is for information purposes only. The author of this book does not dispense medical advice or prescribe the use of any technique as a form of treatment for physical, emotional, or medical problems without the advice of a physician, either directly or indirectly. The intent of the author is only to offer information of a general nature to help you with your well-being. It is not intended to provide specific guidance for particular circumstances. Readers should obtain professional and/or medical advice where appropriate before making any such decisions. To the maximum extent permitted by law, the author disclaims all responsibility and liability to any person arising directly or indirectly from any person taking or not taking action based on the information in this publication.

21 DAYS OF
healing

A SELF-GUIDED WORKBOOK TO HELP YOU NAVIGATE CHRONIC ILLNESS, RELEASE EMOTIONAL INFLAMMATION, AND FIND THE MEDICINE WOMAN WITHIN.

BY SARAH SMALL